# Mastering Java Full Stack Development

# Mastering Java Full Stack Development

## From Spring Boot to ReactJS

Usharani Bhimavarapu

Department of Computer Science and Engineering,
Koneru Lakshmaiah Education Foundation, Vaddeswaram,
Andhra Pradesh, India

ELSEVIER

MK
MORGAN KAUFMANN PUBLISHERS
AN IMPRINT OF ELSEVIER

Morgan Kaufmann is an imprint of Elsevier
50 Hampshire Street, 5th Floor, Cambridge, MA 02139, United States



For accessibility purposes, images in electronic versions of this book are accompanied by alt text descriptions independently provided by Elsevier, generated with the aid of AI. For more information, see https://www.elsevier.com/about/accessibility or Radarweg 29, 1043 NX Amsterdam, Netherlands.

Books and Journals published by Elsevier comply with applicable product safety requirements. For any product safety concerns or queries, please contact our authorised representative, Elsevier B.V., at productsafety@elsevier.com.

Publisher's note: Elsevier takes a neutral position with respect to territorial disputes or jurisdictional claims in its published content, including in maps and institutional affiliations.



**Notices**
Knowledge and best practice in this field are constantly changing. As new research and experience broaden our understanding, changes in research methods, professional practices, or medical treatment may become necessary.

Practitioners and researchers must always rely on their own experience and knowledge in evaluating and using any information, methods, compounds, or experiments described herein. In using such information or methods they should be mindful of their own safety and the safety of others, including parties for whom they have a professional responsibility.

To the fullest extent of the law, neither the Publisher nor the authors, contributors, or editors, assume any liability for any injury and/or damage to persons or property as a matter of products liability, negligence or otherwise, or from any use or operation of any methods, products, instructions, or ideas contained in the material herein.

ISBN: 978-0-443-51683-2

For Information on all Morgan Kaufmann publications
visit our website at https://www.elsevier.com/books-and-journals

*Publisher:* Mara Conner
*Acquisitions Editor:* Chris Katsaropoulos
*Editorial Project Manager:* Ruchi Bhargava
*Production Project Manager:* Abirami Amarnath
*Cover Designer:* Bakyalakshmi S



Typeset by MPS Limited, Chennai, India

# Contents

# 1

# Introduction to enterprise application development

## 1.1 Application of enterprise development

Enterprise application development is an action that involves the creation of robust, creative, and robust computer applications that are supposed to meet the demands of either a business unit or an organization. These are typically integrated, and large-scale applications that are applied to support business functions that are complex, like customer relationship management (CRM), supply chain management (SCM), enterprise resource planning (ERP), and human resource management systems (HRMS).

Programming Requirement: Enterprise Application Development:

1. Business Process Automation: Auto-increases and automates repetitive tasks and leads to productivity and efficiency.
2. Data Integration: Offers the free flow of information across different departments or systems to streamline the decision-making process.
3. Scalability: Supports different business growth without affecting its performance.
4. Customization: Adapts applications to the requirements of the organizations.
5. Security: Protects the important business data against computer attacks.
6. Competitive Advantage: Enhances the efficiency of operation and raises the degree of customer contentment and competitive setting.

Enterprise Applications Features:

1. Scalability: Is able to accommodate a sizable amount of users and transactions.
2. Interoperability: Can be easily related to other systems and platforms.
3. Data Management: Offers cloud-based centralized data storage, data retrieval, and data analytics.
4. User Roles and Permissions: Provides access control using role-based access control.
5. Customization: Adaptable to meet definite business requirements.
6. Multiplatform Support: It can be used on various devices with different operating systems.
7. Reliability: Provides stability in performance and minimum downtime.

Enterprise Applications Characteristics:

1. Complexity: It is frequently constructed to accommodate several work processes, user profiles, and departments.
2. Performance-Based: Fast and reliable.
3. Data-Driven: It is formulated to process, analyze, and visualize large volumes of data.

**Mastering Java Full Stack Development. DOI: https://doi.org/10.1016/B978-0-443-51683-2.00015-1**

4. Safe: Deploys advanced security controls such as encryption, access control, and regulatory compliance.
5. Long Lifecycle: Long-life development and frequent updates.

Enterprise Applications:

1. Efficiency: Makes work processes lean and more productive.
2. Collaboration: Enhances communication and coordination between departments.
3. Live Data: Updates on data to be used in decision-making.
4. Cost Savings: Lowers manual labor and operational costs.
5. Optimized Customer Experience: Customer satisfaction and service delivery.
6. Regulatory Compliance: Assures that the standards of the industry and legal requirements are met.

Enterprise Applications Advantages.

1. Customer Relationship Management: CRM can be used to manage customer relationships, such as Salesforce or Zoho CRM.
2. Enterprise Resource Planning: ERP systems such as SAP, Oracle, or Microsoft Dynamics.
3. HR Management Systems: Software such as Workday or BambooHR to handle HR data and payroll.
4. Supply Chain Management: SCM applications such as SAP SCM or Kinaxis.
5. Financial Management: Applications to be used to deal with accounting, budgeting, and financial planning.
6. E-Commerce Systems: Magento or Shopify Plus.
7. Working Tools: Team communication and file sharing services such as Microsoft Teams or Slack.

In contemporary programming, enterprise application development plays a crucial role since it makes technology respond to the business requirements to ensure the organization keeps its pace in an already dynamic digital environment.

## 1.2 Enterprise application development usage

Enterprise application development is implemented in numerous industries and sectors to meet complex business requirements, streamline the operations, and/or provide efficiency. The major ones are the following spheres of its use:

1. Business Operations Management:
   A system that is centralized and shuts down beyond the hours when business operations are permissible.
   Customer Relationship Management (CRM):
   Utilize customer information, sales cycles, and marketing efforts with applications through Salesforce or Zoho CRM.

Another software solution that might assist is the ERP software.
It integrated the main business processes, for example, finance, supply chain, and human resources (e.g., SAP, Oracle ERP).

2. Human Resource Management Systems (HRMS):
   HR represents the processes by which an organization functions and handles employee tasks.
   Oversee payroll, information on the employees, and hiring activities (e.g., Workday, BambooHR).
3. Banking and Finance:
   - Core Banking Systems: Process customer accounts, transactions, and financial services (e.g., Finacle, TCS BaNCS).
     Financial Analytics Robots and Reporting: Come up with insights on budgeting, forecasting, and performance.
     Risk Management: Risk management includes both the process and practices that are viewed as involving risk aversion, acknowledgment of the risk, and estimation of risk and cost, along with methods to reduce the likelihood of future occurrence.
     Track and address risks and provide regulation compliance.
4. E-Commerce and Retail:
   Inventory Management Systems:
   - Within e-commerce transactions, the inventory management systems enable companies to trace the flow of goods in order to reduce counterfeit products (Diaz, 2013).
   - Monitor the supply chains and stock levels
   - Online Shopping Platforms:
     Operate big-box e-commerce sites (e.g., Shopify Plus, Magento).
   - Individualized Marketing Campaigns:
     Promote and recommend it with data-driven applications.
5. Gaming Industry:
   - Multiplayer Game Servers:
     Administer online multiplayer with platforms such as Photon and PlayFab.
   - Cloud Gaming Platforms: Play games in the cloud via demand infrastructure (e.g., NVIDIA GeForce NOW, Google Stadia).
     Analytics and Player Engagement: The analytics functions will recognize the core players and will offer feedback to the team as well as the coaches regarding their performance and history of games.
     Employ analytics to enhance game development and retention of players.
6. Healthcare
   The availability of electronic health records (EHR) will enable nurses to store and retrieve data regarding patients.
   - Telemedicine Platforms: Make virtual consultations and remote patient monitoring a possibility (e.g., Teladoc Health).
     The Hospice at Walmart's management system is called Hospital Management System (HMS):
     Combine such processes as billing, inventory, and patient care.

7. Education
   Learning Management Systems (LMS): Provide and coordinate online courses, quizzes, and tests (e.g., Moodle, Blackboard).
   Clearly, the future of education will fundamentally depend on technology, and this system must be demonstrated to be a user-friendly advancement in the technological domain.
   - Student Information Systems (SIS):
     Administrate student records, course enrollments, and grades.
   - Virtual Classrooms: Establish interactive learning platforms (i.e., Microsoft Teams, Zoom for Education).
8. Producing and Supply Chain:
   - Supply Chain Management (SCM): Streamline logistics, inventory, and procurement (e.g., Kinaxis, SAP SCM).
     Product lifecycle management (PLM) includes a product lifecycle management software, a philosophy, and a process
     Manage the complete product lifecycle, that is, design through production.
9. Government and Public Services:
   - e-Governance Platforms:
     Administer citizen functions such as filing taxes, licensing, and voting.
     Janibal et al. (2007), together with Hagli and Kahn (1987), discovered that implementing extensive emergency management was one of the solutions to flood control effects.
   - Disaster Management Systems:
     Using the discoveries made by Janibal et al. (2007), along with Hagli and Kahn (1987), it was found that the solution to the effect of floods was the implementation of extensive emergency management.
     Marshal resources and efforts in times of emergency.
     The software can be applied to perform law enforcement activities, such as analyzing crime scenes and the individuals who are questioned.
10. Media and Entertainment:
    Corporate portals allow an organization to provide information to various stakeholders like customers, colleagues, and suppliers, among others.
    Content Management Systems (CMS): Design and maintain web materials (e.g., WordPress, Drupal).
    - Streaming Platforms:
      Operate large-scale video and music streaming (e.g., Netflix and Spotify).
    - Digital Rights Management: Prevent illegal viewing of copyrighted materials.
11. Smart Cities and Internet of Things (IoT)
    - Infrastructure Management:
      Operate the utilities such as electricity, water, and transportation.
    - IoT Platforms: Connect and invoke smart devices and sensors in real time (e.g., AWS IoT, Azure IoT Hub).

**12.** Logistics and Transportation.
- Fleet Management Systems:
  Monitor and trace the use of vehicles.
  **1.** RTA 124: Route Optimization Applications: Route optimization seeks to arrange application routes in a manner that is optimal over both short and long distances.

Enhance efficiency of delivery with real-time information (e.g., FedEx routing systems).
Warehouse Management Systems:
Oversee storage, packing, and shipping.

**13.** Energy and Utilities:
- Smart Grids:
  Energy distribution and consumption management.
- Predictive Maintenance: Predict and preclude equipment failures with IoT and analytics.

Enterprise application development is diverse and plays a crucial role in the quest to do away with the challenges of modern businesses. It can be utilized in those locations where scalability, security, and integrated systems are required.

## 1.3 Why enterprise application development

Businesses and organizations need business enterprise application development to support the complex process, enhance efficiency, and satisfy customer needs as they keep changing. The following are the main reasons why one should use enterprise application development:

**1.** Scalability with Increasing Requirement:
Why: With the growth of business, there is a requirement for a system that can address the growing number of users, data, and transactions without affecting the performance of the system.
- Advantage: Enterprise applications are to be scaled with the organization in a smooth manner.

**2.** Systems and Data Integration:
Why: Companies tend to use numerous tools and platforms. The failure to integrate brings about data silos and inefficiencies.
- Advantage: Enterprise applications are deployed to integrate various departments (HR, finance, sales) and systems, allowing the free flow of data and communication.

**3.** Automation and Efficiency:
Why: Keypad processes are time-consuming, prone to error, and inefficient.
- Advantage: Enterprise applications eliminate repetitive business processes, like the payroll process, inventory processes, and order tracking, enhancing accuracy and consuming less time.

**4.** Enhanced Security:
Why: Businesses deal with sensitive data (e.g., financial, customer, and operational).
- Advantage: Enterprise programs have upper security levels, such as role-based access, and encryption, as well as adherence to data protection laws.

**5.** Unique Business Customization:

Why: The industry might be challenged or may apply to workflows, which might not be resolved by generic solutions.

- Advantage: Enterprise applications would be configured to suit a particular need of an organization.

**6.** Real-Time Intrigue and Decision-Making:

Why: Businesses require proper and timely data in order to make informed decisions.

- Advantage: Enterprise applications will have real-time operations and customer behavior dashboards and analytics.

**7.** Long-Term Cost Efficiency:

Why: Although low-quality tools would seem to save in the short run, this will translate into increased costs by raising inefficiencies and low scalability.

• Advantage: Although the cost of the investment of the enterprise applications may be higher at the beginning of the venture, it saves money in the long term.

The following are the restrictions that enterprise application development has conquered.

**1.** Poor Intersystems Integration:
- Limitations: Disconnected systems cause inefficiency and inconsistencies in data.
- Conquer: Enterprise applications bring data and processes together on a system, but they are a single source of truth.

**2.** Inefficient Processes:
- Limitations: Manual processes are very slow and can also be error-prone.
- Overcome: Processes such as invoicing, payroll, and supply chain processes can be automated, improving efficiency and accuracy.

**3.** Limited Scalability:
- Little to no scalability: Traditional systems cannot process a large amount of data or users.
- More: Enterprise applications are developed to expand easily with the increasing business demands.

**4.** Poor Data Security:
- Limitations: Legacy systems are usually not based on modern security protocols.
- Conquered: Enterprise applications are supported with new security options such as encryption, multifactor authentication, and compliance (e.g., GDPR and HIPAA).

**5.** Lack of Real-Time Insights:
- Limitations: Static reports lose time in the decision-making process.
- Conquered: Enterprise applications have real-time reporting and analytics.

**6.** Expense of Legacy Systems of High Maintenance:
- Limitations: The old systems have to be repaired and updated frequently, which makes the system expensive in the long run.
- Combated: The new enterprise application systems are built to last and are updated and serviced regularly.

7. Limited Collaboration:
   - Restriction: Inequalities in systems will fight teamwork and communication.
   - Overcome: Enterprise applications bring business operations together, which helps to collaborate more across departments and locations.
8. Poor User Experience:
   - Limitations: The interfaces and functionalities of legacy systems are usually not current.
   - Overcome: Enterprise applications are built using modern, convenient interfaces and workflows that are tailored.

Enterprise application development is a solution to the weaknesses of the traditional systems, thus making sure that the businesses run efficiently, securely, and flexibly in the competitive environment. It offers creativity in the lapses of scalability, integration, and innovation and is essential to the current organizations.

## 1.4 Different versions/generations of enterprise application development

The application development is varied among different versions/generations of enterprise application development.

Enterprise application development has been redefined by major changes in the technological advancements, modes of architecture, and methodology. The following is a review of the various versions or generations of enterprise application development:

1. Mainframe Applications (first generation: 1950s–1970s) were developed during this period of time.
   - Key Features:
     - Mainframe system computing.
     - Payroll, accounting, and inventory batch processing.
     - Very specific applications, written in COBOL and Fortran languages.
   - Limitations:
     - Costs of high-priced hardware and development.
     - Minimization of user interaction and real-time capabilities.
2. Client-Server Applications (Second Generation: 1980s–1990s):
   - Key Features:
     - Decentralized design that has the client (user interface) and server (data, logic) division.
     - Written in such technologies as C++, Visual Basic, and early versions of Java.
     - Examples: Older ERP systems (SAP R/2), database-oriented applications.
       The mainframe has drawbacks such as low scalability and slowness when compared to an enhanced scale and faster performance of the new platform.
     - Improved interaction and performance.
     - Docs and reports could be shared and accessed by multiple users.

- Limitations:
  - Limited scalability.
  - Reliant upon local network infrastructure.

3. Web-Based Applications (Third Generation: Late 1990s–2000s):
   - Key Features:
     - Pioneered in the use of technologies such as HTML, Java, JavaScript, PHP, and ASP.NET to build it on the internet.
     - Provides web browser access all over the world.
     - Centralized data in servers that have easy-to-use web interfaces.
       Result: Better than client-server.
     - Available at any place.
     - Less robustness of client machines required.
   - Limitations:
     - Issues of security of data and reliability of the internet in preimplementation phases.
4. Cloud-Based Applications (Fourth Generation: 2000s–2010s):
   - Key Features:
     - On cloud services such as AWS, Azure, or Google Cloud.
     - Offered either as Software as a Service (SaaS), Platform as a Service (PaaS), or Infrastructure as a Service (IaaS).
     - Sustained microservices architecture of scalable applications, which are modular.
     - Salesforce, Google Workspace, SAP S/4HANA.
   - Improvements over Web-Based:
     - High availability and scalability.
     - Pay-as-you-go models offer cost savings.
   - Limitations:
     - Reliance on cloud companies.
     - Data sovereignty and vendor lock-in.
5. Mobile and API-Powered Applications (Fifth Generation: 2010s–Present):
   - Key Features:
     - Mobile-first and responsive-oriented designs.
     - Dependent greatly on APIs to service other systems and services.
     - Live processing using technologies such as REST and GraphQL.
     - Slack, Microsoft Teams, and mobile ERP/CRM applications are examples.
   - Advancements over Cloud-Based:
     - Better user experience supported by mobile access.
     - Better connection to the outside world and third-party applications.
   - Limitations:
     - Heightened complexity to handle APIs as well as cross-platform compatibility.
6. Low-Code/No-Code Platforms (Sixth Generation: 2015s–Present):
   - Key Features:
     - Apps such as Mendix, OutSystems, and PowerApps enable developers to create an application without a lot of knowledge on how to do it.

    - Drag-and-drop interfaces and ready-made modules to develop it more quickly.
    - Focussed on citizen developers and business users.
  - Advantages Better than API-Driven:
    - Reduced time-to-market of applications.
    - Less reliance on the specialized developers.
  - Limitations:
    - Lack of customization and complex application flexibility.

7. Applications Driven by Artificial Intelligence (Emerging: 2020s–Present):
   - Key Features:
     - Mechanical automation and artificial intelligence (AI) and machine learning (ML).
     - The chatbots and virtual assistants are run on natural language processing (NLP).
     - Decision-making and personalization of predictive analytics.
     - Examples: AI-powered CRM, recommendation system, and smart ERP tools.
   - Improvements over Low-Code:
     - Improved decision-making and automation of processes.
     - Greater individualization and customization.
   - Limitations:
     - An AI/ML model development and integration may be quite complex.
8. Next Generation Edge Computing and Quantum Use:
   - Key Features:
     - Edge Computing: Distributed processing: Move data to a location nearer to the source (e.g., IoT device) as a means of reducing latency and enhancing performance.
     - Quantum Computing: Tackle true optimization tasks in the field of logistics, cryptography, and resource management.
   - Potential Improvements:
     - Decisions in real time on scale.
     - Industry-revolutionary capability, such as finances, healthcare, and supply chain.
   - Challenges:
     - New technology that is not extensively available and is expensive.

## 1.5 What is the programming language we would use to do an enterprise application development?

Some of the programming languages best applied in the development of enterprise applications include requirements of scalability, performance, integration capability, and platform compatibility, among others, depending on the needs. The following are some of the most widespread programming languages when it comes to enterprise application development:

1. Java
   - Why Use It?
     - Very popular as enterprise applications because of its platform independence (Write Once, Run Anywhere).

  - Full rich ecosystem comprising Spring, Hibernate, and Java EE.
  - Good when there is a complex business logic and when the business is huge.
- Applications:
  - Banking systems, ERP systems and web applications.
  - ERP systems and financial applications.

**2.** Python
- Why Use It?
  - High productivity and simple syntax.
  - Well-regarded web development platforms, such as Django and Flask.
  - Superior in data analytics, ML and AI integration in business systems.
- Applications:
  - AI-powered enterprise applications, APIs, and backend services.
  - Examples: Analytics systems, automation systems.

**3.** C# (.NET Framework)
- Why Use It?
  - Perfect for making Windows-based enterprise applications.
  - Based on the Microsoft.NET environment, full integration with the Azure cloud services.
  - Offers desktop, web, and mobile application tools.
- Applications:
  - 24 Enterprise desktop, web, CRM.
  - Examples: Microsoft Dynamics, desktop enterprise software.

**4.** JavaScript (and TypeScript)
- Why Use It?
  - Required to develop the frontend aspect using such frameworks as React, Angular, and Vue.js.
  - TypeScript improves the development of enterprise-level applications in scalability and type safety.
  - Full-stack development with Node.js.
- Applications:
  - Web portals, Single Page Applications, dashboards.
  - Examples: Real-time collaboration tools and web apps that are directly facing the clients.

**5.** PHP
- Why Use It?
  - Popular server-side web development.
  - Larger architectures such as Laravel and Symfony simplify enterprise development and increase their security.
  - Affordable to medium-sized and small businesses.
- Applications:
  - Web applications and CMS.
  - Enterprise intranets, e-commerce sites.

6. Ruby
   - Why Use It?
     - Popular with fast growth using the Ruby on Rails platform.
     - Appropriate in case of startups and small businesses that require fast implementation.
   - Applications:
     - LFT Enterprise software and internal applications.
     - Examples: Web applications that are oriented toward rapid development.
7. Kotlin
   - Why Use It?
     - Android development has an official programming language, which replaces Java in use by many programmers.
     - Applied using the construction of mobile applications that are connected with enterprise systems.
   - Applications:
     - Mobile-first enterprise applications.
     - Mobile CRM and workforce management applications.
8. Go (Golang)
   - Why Use It?
     - High performance and scalability, but used to a microservices architecture.
     - Easy to develop and portable to construct cloud-based enterprise applications.
   - Applications:
     - Containerized services, backend, and Cloud applications.
     - Examples: Scalable APIs, enterprise cloud tools.
9. Swift
   - Why Use It?
     - Key to developing iPhone Operating System (iOS) enterprise applications.
     - Provides safe and high-performance mobile applications on Apple services.
   - Applications:
     - Business applications on iOS.
     - Examples: Mobile employee productivity.
10. Structured Query Language (SQL)
   - Why Use It?
     - Basic in controlling and accessing databases in business applications.
     - Collaborates with programming languages to process data storage at the backend.
   - Applications:
     - ERP, CRM, and analytics database management.
     - Examples: Backend of enterprise system, which would need data processing.
11. Rust
   - Why Use It?
     - Memory safety and high performance are known.
     - Appropriate with systems programming and backend enterprise applications.

- Applications:
  - Critical systems that are security sensitive.
  - Examples: Finance or manufacturing real-time systems.

**12.** Scala
- Why Use It?
  - It is compatible with Java and can be used to process big data.
  - Apache Spark is regularly used alongside it.
- Applications:
  - Data analytics, real-time data processing in companies.
  - Examples: Business intelligence applications, big data platforms.

**13.** R
- Why Use It?
  - Special-purpose statistical analysis and visualization.
  - Sometimes employed in the decision-making and forecasting of enterprise applications.
- Applications:
  - Predictive analytics and reporting dashboards.
  - Business analytics tools.
  - Risk management.

    Choosing the Right Language

    The choice of a programming language is based on:

    Type of Application: Web, desktop, mobile, or cloud.
- Scalability Requirement: Languages Java, Go, and Python are very good in dealing with large-scale applications.

  Technology Ecosystem: Compatibility with existing tools (e.g., NET with Windows systems).
- Expertise of Developers: The supply of skilled developers of a given language.

Java, Python, C#, and JavaScript are the dominant languages in the development of enterprise applications because of their strength and scalability and rich ecosystem. Nevertheless, more recently developed and popular languages such as Kotlin, Go, and Rust are becoming popular as modern enterprise requirements.

## 1.6 Java enterprise application development

Java is a programming language that has been widely used in enterprise application development and is so popular. It is the language of business, suitably sized to popularize a business of any size, including minienterprises and Fortune 500s.

Virtues by Java since it is an enterprise development?

**1.** Platform Independence:
- Java has a note of write once, run anywhere (WORA), which allows it to execute on any platform having a Java Virtual Machine (JVM).

2. Scalability:
   - Applicable in small-scale applications, as well as in large-scale, distributed systems.
3. Robust Ecosystem:
   - Development tools such as Spring, Hibernate, and Java EE offer excellent development tools.
4. Security:
   - Inbuilt security systems like encryption, secure socket layer, and secure authentication systems.
5. Community Support:
   - Sizable developer base means constant upgrades, updates, and bug fixing.
6. Integration Capabilities:
   - Java is easily compatible with different databases, APIs, and third-party tools.

Java Enterprise Development Features:

1. Object-Oriented Programming (OOP):
   - Java has OOP concepts, which simplify the development of modular and reusable code for large-scale systems.
2. Rich APIs:
   - Java has an extensive array of APIs on networking, I/O, concurrency, and database connectivity.
3. Multithreading:
   - Can process several user requests at the same time, which is vital to enterprise-level applications.
4. Supporting Distributed Computing:
   - The Remote Method Invocation (RMI) and Enterprise JavaBeans (EJB) support of Java make the construction of distributed systems easier.
5. Frameworks and Libraries:
   - Such frameworks as Spring Boot and Hibernate make developers work faster and easier to set up.
6. Java EE (Jakarta EE):
   - It offers a strong base to build scalable, distributed, and transactional enterprise.
7. Microservices Architecture Support:
   - Java is compatible with microservices systems such as Spring Cloud and Eclipse Microprofile, and so it can support the needs of a modern enterprise.
8. Tooling and Integrated Development Environments (IDEs):
   - Enterprise applications developers can find tools such as IntelliJ IDEA, Eclipse, and NetBeans that have advanced features.

Enterprise Development Java Frameworks:

1. Spring Framework:
   - Web/api/microservice framework based on lightweight.

  - Features: Dependency Injection (DI), Aspect-Oriented Programming (AOP), and Spring Boot to develop faster.
2. Hibernate:
   - DB Object-Relational Mapping framework to simplify database queries.
   - Applications: SQL generation is automated, and the database is portable.
3. Java EE (Jakarta EE):
   - Generalized platform of scalable and safe enterprise applications.
   - Features: JSP, Servlets, EJB, JMS, JPA, and others.
4. Apache Struts:
   - Web application building framework that is based on Model-View-Controller (MVC) architecture.
   - Features: Easy to handle requests and responses.
5. Vaadin:
   - Java rich and interactive web application graphical framework.
   - Characteristics: Server-side coding with inbuilt UI elements.

Favorable Points of Java Enterprise Development:

1. Cross-Platform Compatibility:
   - Applications are interoperable across all operating systems (Windows, Linux, and macOS).
2. Extensive Ecosystem:
   - Libraries, tools, and frameworks are available and decrease the time of development.
3. High Performance:
   - Java has Just-in-Time (JIT) compiler and optimization that improves the performance of run-time.
4. Scalable Applications:
   - Scales well with both large data and traffic.
5. Robust Security:
   - Its deployment in critical applications is acceptable due to features such as the access control, cryptography, and secure communication.
6. Modularity:
   - Java packages and modules facilitate improved reusability and organization of the code.

Java Usage in Enterprise Development:

1. Banking Systems:
   - Transactional systems, account management, and financial data processing use.
   - Examples: Bank applications, such as Barclays and Citibank.
2. Enterprise Resource Planning:
   - Streamlines business operations supply chain, HR, and inventory.
   - Example: SAP solutions based on Java.

3. Customer Relationship Management:
   - Customer interaction management and data analysis tools.
   - Examples: Salesforce integrations.
4. E-commerce Platforms:
   - Online store shopping, scalable, and well-integrated in terms of payment.
   - Examples: Amazon has backend systems such as Flipkart.
5. Big Data and Analytics:
   - Java is also supported by other tools such as Apache Hadoop and Apache Spark to perform data analytics.
   - Example: Data processing programmes.
6. Healthcare Systems:
   - Hospital management systems, patient portals, and telemedicine applications.
7. Mobile Applications:
   - Android applications are mostly written in Java.
8. Gaming:
   - Internet gaming online client support.
   - Multiplayer online games.

Limitations Java Does Away with in Enterprise Development:

1. Cross-Platform Challenges:
   - The JVM of Java gets rid of any reliance on a particular operating system.
2. Scalability Problems with Legacy Systems:
   - Such frameworks as Spring and microservices architecture deal with scalability needs.
3. Complicated Setup Management:
   - Containers such as Spring Boot envision parameters which are automated and hence not complex.
4. Database Dependency:
   - Hibernate is database independent using ORM.
5. Web Application Security Hazards:
   - Security Inbuilt security prevents such vulnerabilities as SQL injection and cross-site scripting.

Java is a powerful language within the enterprise application development since it is reliable, scalable, and has a rich set of tools and frameworks. It is perfect in developing a broad set of enterprise solutions, including web applications to highly scalable distributed systems, and therefore businesses are capable of adjusting to changes in technology.

## 1.7 Spring Framework overview

Eventually, Spring Framework is an effective, lightweight, and generalized framework that aids in the development of enterprise-level applications written on the Java platform. It has a complete infrastructure support, and it can also be easier to do application development because it has tools and features like DI, data access, transaction management, etc. It is very popular to build applications based on web, enterprise, and microservices.

### 1.7.1 Why do we need Spring Framework?

1. Makes Enterprise Development Easier:
   - Spring also simplifies the complexity in enterprise application development through offering ready-made solutions and tools.
2. Dependency Injection:
   - Spring has forced loose coupling of components using DI, and application maintains and extends more easily.
3. Multipurpose Application Development:
   - Spring is compatible with many types of applications, including web applications, REST APIs, and microservices.
4. Minimizes Boilerplate Code:
   - Enabling repetition and abstraction, Spring saves developers of repetitive and low-level code the number of lines they must write.
5. Modularity:
   - The modular nature of Spring enables a developer to use the bare minimum of the framework as opposed to the whole structure.
6. Integration Support:
   - Spring is fully compatible with third-party libraries, databases, and frameworks, such as Hibernate, Apache Kafka, and RabbitMQ.
7. Microservices Architecture:
   - Spring can be one of the main development options with Spring Boot and Spring Cloud because of its strong application to create a microservice-based application.

Significant Characteristics of the Spring Framework:

1. Dependency Injection:
   - Makes object dependencies easier to manage and gives loose components coupling.
2. Aspect-Oriented Programming:
   - Facilitates the separation of cross-cutting concerns (e.g., logging, security, transaction management) in the core business logic.
3. Spring MVC:
   - An apt MVC structure to create web applications.
4. Spring Boot:
   - A subproject of Spring that provides a very easy-to-use application development with embedded servers, automatic configuration, and minimal setups.
5. Spring Data:
   - Makes it easier to interact with databases as it offers an abacus over JPA, MongoDB, Cassandra, and other data sources.

6. Spring Security:
   - Offers authentication, authorization, and secure means of communication tools.
7. Spring Cloud:
   - Provides distributions that can be used to create distributed systems and microservices such as service discovery, load balancing, and configuration management.
8. Transaction Management:
   - Isolates the adventures of processing transactions and offers a standardized programming victimization amid the various transaction APIs.
9. Integration Framework:
   - Spring has support for integration with messaging systems such as JMS, REST, and SOAP APIs.
10. Testing Support:
    - Offers unit and integration test creation tools, including dependency injection to the test environment.

The Features of Spring Framework:

1. Lightweight:
   - Core container and fundamental modules are lightweight and may be deployed in resource-strained environment.
2. Noninvasive:
   - Spring allows developers to not be bound to Spring when they want to make the migration into or away to other frameworks.
3. Open Source:
   - Spring is free and has a high number of people working on making improvements on it.
4. Modular Architecture:
   - It can be composed of numerous modules, which gives developers the option of the types of modules to pick and choose.
5. Integration-Centric:
   - Integrates with different frameworks, databases, and messaging systems.
6. Framework for All Tiers:
   - Favors growth at every level, including the presentation layer (web) to the business layer and data layer.

Benefits of Spring Framework Use:

1. Reduces Development Time:
   - Spring Boot simplifies a great number of setups, and it leaves the developer to concentrate on application code.
2. Enhances Code Quality:
   - DI features ensure maintainable, readable, and testable code.
3. Promotes Microservices Development:
   - Spring Cloud is a solution that offers the microservices architecture and is therefore suitable for contemporary enterprise applications.

4. Rich Ecosystem:
    - Spring is offered with tools at each step of development with a large number of subprojects (e.g., Spring Boot and Spring Security).
5. Enterprise-Ready:
    - Enterprise level, designed to accommodate the challenges level, that is, scalability, security, and integration.
6. Flexibility:
    - It is applicable in many ways; it has individual programs as well as cloud-native applications.
7. Active Community Support:
    - The framework has a big community of developers that supports it, gives tutorials, and also has extensions.
8. Improves Testing:
    - Built-in testing can be used by Spring to render the test cases that a developer needs to write and execute.

Spring Framework is an extremely flexible and ubiquitous framework of enterprise application development. Its use in complex tasks is simplified, and it supports a broad range of types of applications, and has wide integration opportunities where it is favored by developers that intend to develop scalable, safe, and efficient applications in Java.

Limitations that the Spring Framework Overcame:

The Spring Framework was designed to overcome various drawbacks and problems of the traditional Java development as well as earlier-developed frameworks. The major weaknesses that Spring has broken through:

1. Applications Form of Tight Coupling.
   The Traditional Challenge: With normal Java applications, the classes tend to be directly reliant on the rest of the classes, thus being tightly coupled until it becomes difficult to maintain and extend.
    - How Spring Overcomes This:
        - Dependency Injection (DI): Spring DI system encourages loose coupling by that to the point where object dependencies are defined by configuration either via XML or annotations.
2. Enterprise JavaBeans Complexity:
   Classical Problem: The EJB as a traditional enterprise solution was large, heavy, and consumed a lot of boilerplate code.
    - How Spring Overcomes This:
        - Lightweight Framework: Spring offers characteristics that resemble those of EJB, such as transaction management and declarative services, but has much less complex and simpler components.
        - POJO-Based Development: With POJOs, enterprise applications can be developed in plain old Java objects, free of the rigid EJB specifications.

3. Boilerplate Code:
   To solve this: It was common in Java development to require boilerplate code to perform such tasks as logging, database connection, and exception handling.
   - How Spring Overcomes This:
     - Utilities and abstractions (e.g., Spring JDBC, JPA templates) within Spring contain code to perform repetitive tasks; fewer low-level code requirements arise.
     - Example: Facilitates operations of a database with Spring Data JPA.
4. Absence of Application Modularization.
   - Traditional Challenge: Older models and custom Java applications did not support modularity, and it was hard to isolate the concerns and add features at the same time.
   - How Spring Overcomes This:
     - Modular Architecture: Spring is a modular architecture that enables the developers to only need the necessary components without including the whole framework.
5. Lack of Convenience in Setups:
   - Conventional Probability: The configuration of large-scale applications, particularly those based on XML, had been prone to error and time-sensitive.
   - How Spring Overcomes This:
     - Annotation-Based Configurations: Spring also supports annotations (e.g., to annotate a configuration, to annotate a bean, to annotate an autowired object, etc.) to simplify configuration.
     - Spring Boot Auto-Configuration: Spring Boot is further configured and less prone to manual configuration.
6. The Absence of Cross-Cutting Concerns Management:
   Traditional Challenge: Cross-cutting issues such as logging, transaction management, and security demanded redundant code in several modules.
   - How Spring Overcomes This:
     - Aspect-Oriented Programming (AOP): AOP provides Spring with the ability to centralize the cross-cutting concerns and leave the main business logic unpolluted.
7. Scalability Issues:
   - Traditional Challenge: The traditional Java applications that were available were not adapted to work well with large distributed systems in terms of scalability.
   - How Spring Overcomes This:
     - Spring has scalability application tools, including:
       Spring MVC: Scalable web application.
     - Spring Cloud: In microservices and distributed systems.
       DR: Spring Boot: To create production-ready applications in less time.
8. Security Vulnerabilities:
   Traditional Challenge: The need to offer authentication, authorization, and encryption was complicated and mostly needed third-party solutions.
   - How Spring Overcomes This:
     - Spring Security: It offers a powerful platform to administer authentication, authorization, and securing web applications with the least effort.

9. Integration Challenges:
   - Traditional Challenge: Solid State Drive: The integration of third-party tools, APIs, and legacy systems was tedious and had to be customized.
   - How Spring Overcomes This:
     - Integration Framework: Spring is compatible with a wide array of integrations into databases (JDBC, JPA) and messaging systems (JMS, RabbitMQ) as well as web services (REST, SOAP).
10. Testing Challenges:
    Traditional Challenge: There was a trick to all of the traditional applications, particularly those with tight coupling, to test them at the portability level since they were also poorly designed.
    - How Spring Overcomes This:
      - Testing Support: Spring has a wide range of testing tools and mock objects that enable easy unit and integration testing.
11. Slow Development Process:
    Traditional Challenge: Enterprise applications required a lot of time to establish because of a lot of boilerplate code and manual setups.
    - How Spring Overcomes This:
      - Spring Boot provides embedded servers, auto-configuration, and a collection of starter classes to simplify Spring application development.
12. Application Servers of Heavy Weight:
    Traditional Challenge: Previously, the deployment of enterprise applications needed to be done using heavyweight servers such as WebLogic or WebSphere.
    - How Spring Overcomes This:
      - Lightweight servers such as Tomcat or Jetty can support Spring applications.
      - Spring Boot: It has an inbuilt server so that the external server is not required to be setup.

An enterprise Java development that comes on a framework like EJB is revolutionary with Spring Framework showing how mostly it is able to overcome the shortcomings of these traditional approaches and frameworks. It makes development easy, encourages modular development, facilitates testing, and allows scalable, safe, and maintainable applications. It is still a popular option to use to develop modern enterprise and microservices applications with such tools as Spring Boot and Spring Cloud.

## 1.8 What is Hibernate Framework?

Hibernate is a Java Object-Relational Mapping (ORM) framework that is an open-source project. It eases database interaction in that it registers the mapping of Java objects into database tables. Hibernate gives Java developers a framework upon which to operate databases without necessarily writing SQL code directly. It abstracts database interaction and gives automatic mapping between the Java objects and database records.

Requirement of Hibernate Framework:

- Simplification of Database Interaction: Hibernate simplifies the complexities of dealing with databases by providing the database user with an opportunity to deal with Java-based objects rather than developing intricate SQL statements.
- Portability: Hibernate supports a variety of database management systems (DBMS), and so a developer can use different databases with minimum change in code.
- Less Boilerplate Code: It minimizes the size of the writing required by code developers to interface with a database, for example, JDBC-related boilerplate code.

Features of Hibernate:

1. Object-Relational Mapping:
   - Mapping Java classes to database tables is done either through annotations or through XML configuration files. In the database, every object in Java is a row that corresponds to it.
2. Automatic Table Generation:
   - Hibernate is able to create the schema (objects, tables, indexes, etc.) of the database automatically by defined Java objects.
3. Data Query Language:
   - Hibernate is an extraordinarily well-powered Hibernate Query Language (HQL) that is not unlike SQL except that it works with Java objects instead of database tables. HQL is independent of the database and so an application can be applied to any database.
4. Caching:
   - There is the inbuilt support of first-level and second-level caching in Hibernate, which enhances performance by minimizing the number of queries to the database.
5. Lazy Loading:
   - Hibernate has many options of lazy loading where only the correlated data is loaded once the entity is accessed, which is a better way to consume more performance and less memory.
6. Transaction Management:
   - Hibernate is compatible with Java Transaction API (JTA) and offers database transaction management, consisting of Brazilian data consistency and integrity.
7. Cross-Database Compatibility:
   - It can support various databases, including MySQL, PostgreSQL, Oracle, SQL Server among other databases, and there are few changes made to application code.
8. Inheritance Mapping: The implementation supports inheritance mapping.
   - Hibernate also offers various approaches to the mapping of object-oriented programming inheritance relations to relational databases, including Single Table Inheritance, Joined Subclass Inheritance, and Table Per Class Hierarchy.
9. Spring Framework: Very High:
   Integration with Spring Framework: Very high.
   - Hibernate is also interconnected with the Spring Framework with high transaction management skills and accessibility to data.

Characteristics of Hibernate:

- ORM Mapping:
  - Hibernate takes care of the transfiguration of Java objects into database rows, and it does not require a human to type in the data in Java objects and SQL data types.
- Database Independence:
  - Hibernate will not be dependent on the underlying database, and therefore, when you alter the database, you can make very few alterations to the Java script. It renders applications more mobile.
- Automatic Query Generation:
  - May a SQL query can be generated on the fly by Hibernate meaning that there is little need to write SQL.
- Reduced Boilerplate Code:
  - Hibernate has an important effect, namely the reduction of the boilerplate code (setting JDBC connections and releasing resources) in databases.
- Transparent Persistence:
  - Persistence Hibernate has transparent persistence, meaning that objects can be saved, updated, or deleted without necessarily calling on the database operations. Caching: This is used to optimize the performance of popular applications.
  - Hibernate utilizes caching (first-level and second-level) to reduce the number of times a single database query is made, which will maximize performance.

Advantages of Hibernate:

1. The Simplicity and Productivity:
   - Hibernate enables developers to write business logic and less database specifics, which results in a quicker development.
2. Portability:
   - Database independence is offered by Hibernate. Hibernate applications are able to be migrated to alternative database systems with no major modifications to the Java codebase.
3. Reduced Complexity:
   - It manages interactions with the database at an abstract stage and eliminates creating SQL, connection management, and JDBC boilerplate code.
4. Performance:
   - Hibernate has various performance optimization features such as caching, lazy loading, and batching, among other features that can be used to optimize the performance of database queries and minimize the amount of round trips back to the database.
5. Automatic Data Mapping:
   - Hibernate is able to map Java items to records in the database automatically, thereby saving time and minimizing the time errors may occur during manual flourishing of the database.

6. Flexible Querying:
   - Hibernate offers a variety of querying mechanisms, such as HQL, Criteria API, and native SQL, allowing for flexible and efficient queries.
7. Maintains Data Integrity:
   - Hibernate supports automatic transaction management, which helps in maintaining data consistency and integrity across operations.
8. Integration with Other Frameworks:
   - Hibernate works seamlessly with various Java frameworks, such as Spring, Java EE, and JSF, providing a unified approach to application development.
9. Versioning and Change Tracking:
   - Hibernate provides built-in support for optimistic locking and versioning, ensuring that data consistency is maintained during concurrent access and updates.

## Bibliography

Alur, D., Crupi, J., & Malks, D. (2003). *Core J2EE patterns.* Prentice Hall.

Fowler, M. (2012). *Patterns of enterprise application architecture.* Addison-Wesley.

Hibernate. (2024). Hibernate ORM Documentation. https://hibernate.org/orm/documentation/.

IBM. (2024). Enterprise Application Development. https://www.ibm.com/topics/enterprise-application-development.

Microsoft. (2024). Enterprise Applications. https://learn.microsoft.com.

Oracle. (2024). Java EE Documentation. https://docs.oracle.com/javaee/.

Pressman, R. S. (2005). *Software engineering: A practitioner's approach.* Palgrave Macmillan.

Red Hat. (2024). Enterprise Applications Overview. https://www.redhat.com.

Sommerville, I. (2021). *Yazılım mühendisliği: Software engineering.* Nobel Akademik Yayıncılık.

VMware. (2024). Spring Framework Documentation. https://docs.spring.io/spring-framework/docs/current/reference/html/.

# 2

# Setting up the development environment

## 2.1 Development environment for enterprise application development

An enterprise application development landscape is usually where there is an assembly of tools, technologies, frameworks, and platforms to help in fulfilling the whole software development cycle.

1. **Hardware requirements**
   - Workstations and servers: Development and test machines of high performance.
   - Cloud infrastructure: To be able to scale and work remotely (e.g., AWS, Azure, Google Cloud).
2. **Operating systems**
   - **Windows**: Widely used for .NET-based enterprise development.
   - **Linux**: Preferred for open-source stack (e.g., Java-based development).
   - **macOS**: Common for mobile (iOS) enterprise app development.
3. **Integrated development environments (IDEs)**
   - IntelliJ IDEA: Java and Kotlin-based applications, as well as Spring.
   - Eclipse: Java EE and enterprise open source IDE.
   - Visual studio: .NET-based development.
   - VS code: Multilanguage IDE that is lightweight and extensible (JavaScript, Python, and Go).
4. **Programming languages**
   - Java: Enterprise applications (Spring, Hibernate).
   - C#: popular in.NET applications.
   - Python: AI/ML integration.
   - JavaScript/TypeScript: JavaScript is used to develop front-end and full-stack applications (React, Angular, Node.js.).
5. **Frameworks**
   - **Backend**:
   - **Spring Framework**: For enterprise-grade Java applications.
   - **ASP.NET Core**: For .NET applications.
   - **Django**: Python-based web framework.
   - **Frontend**:
   - **Angular**: For single-page applications.

Mastering Java Full Stack Development. DOI: https://doi.org/10.1016/B978-0-443-51683-2.00003-5

- **React.js**: For component-based UI development.
- **Vue.js**: Lightweight front-end framework.
- **Microservices**:
- **Spring Boot**: For Java microservices.
- **Micronaut**: Lightweight Java framework.
- **Quarkus**: Optimized for Kubernetes environments.

6. **Database management systems (DBMS)**
   - **Relational databases**: MySQL, PostgreSQL, Oracle DB, Microsoft SQL Server.
   - **NoSQL databases**: MongoDB, Cassandra, Redis, DynamoDB.
7. **Development methodologies**
   - **Agile**: Iterative and collaborative development.
   - **DevOps**: Continuous integration and deployment (CI/CD).
8. **Version control systems**
   - **Git**: GitHub, GitLab, or Bitbucket for version control.
   - **Subversion (SVN)**: For legacy systems.
9. **Build and automation tools**
   - **Maven/Gradle**: For Java build automation.
   - **MSBuild**: For .NET applications.
   - **Jenkins/GitLab CI/CD**: For automated testing and deployment.
10. **Testing tools**
    - **Unit testing**: JUnit, NUnit, PyTest.
    - **Integration testing**: Postman, SoapUI.
    - **End-to-end testing**: Selenium, Cypress.
11. **Application servers**
    - **Apache Tomcat**: Lightweight server for Java applications.
    - **JBoss/WildFly**: Java EE applications.
    - **Microsoft IIS**: For .NET applications.
12. **Security tools**
    - **OAuth2 and JSON Web Tokens (JWT)**: For authentication and authorization.
    - **OWASP dependency-check**: vulnerability scanner.
    - **Spring security**: To protect Java applications.
13. **Containerization and orchestration**
    - **Docker**: For creating isolated environments.
    - **Kubernetes**: For container orchestration.
14. **Cloud platforms**
    - **Amazon Web Services (AWS)**: growing system hosting.
    - **Microsoft Azure**: Enterprise integration.
    - **Google Cloud Platform (GCP)**: When AI/ML and data-intensive applications are required.

This platform is scalable, maintainable, and secure, and it has supported contemporary development patterns such as microservices, DevOps, and CI/CD.

## 2.2 Eclipse integrated development environment

**Step 1: Download Eclipse Installer**

1. **Go to the official Eclipse website**:
   Visit https://www.eclipse.org.
2. Go to the Downloads section:
   Select the download button on the homepage.
3. **Select your version**:
   Select the most recent version of the Eclipse IDE or a certain one, like the Eclipse IDE Java Developers.
4. **Choose the Installer**:
   Download the correct installer for your operating system:
   - **Windows**: .exe file
   - **Mac**: .dmg file
   - **Linux**: .tar.gz file

**Step 2: Launch the Installer**

1. **Set the downloaded file**:
   Go to your "Downloads" folder and find the Eclipse installer.
2. **Run the Installer**: Either(.exe/.dmg/.tar.gz files)

**Step 3: Select the Eclipse IDE package and click install**
**Step 4: Accept licenses**

1. **Review licenses**:
   Read through the licenses and agreements.
2. **Accept terms**:

   Check the box to accept the terms and click "Accept."

**Step 5: Wait for installation**

1. **Installation process**:
   The installer will download the required components and set up the IDE.
2. **Progress indicator**:

   You'll see a progress bar. Wait until the installation completes.

**Step 6: Launch Eclipse**

1. **Start Eclipse**:
   After installation, click on the "Launch" button in the installer.
2. **Workspace setup**:
   - Choose a location or use the default one, and click "Launch."

**Step 7: Verify installation**

1. **Check Eclipse Version**:
   Go to Help > About Eclipse to verify the installed version.

2. **Create a sample project**:
   - Go to File > New > Java Project.
   - Test by creating a basic program to ensure the IDE is working correctly.

**Optional steps**

1. **Install plugins**:
   - Go to Help > Eclipse Marketplace to install additional plugins like PyDev, Maven, or Git integration.
2. **Configure JDK**:
   - Go to Window > Preferences > Java > Installed JREs.
   - Add the JDK path if it's not already configured.

## 2.3 Apache Tomcat installation and integration to Eclipse integrated development environment

**Part 1: Installing Apache Tomcat**

**Step 1: Download Apache Tomcat**

1. Go to the official Apache Tomcat website: https://tomcat.apache.org.
2. Click on "**Download**".
3. Select the version compatible with your system and project requirements (e.g., **Tomcat 10**, **Tomcat 9**).
4. Under **Binary Distributions**, download the ZIP file for **Windows/Linux** or the TAR.GZ file for **Mac/Linux**.

**Step 2: Extract Apache Tomcat**

1. Extract the file:
   - **Windows**: Use a tool like WinRAR or 7-Zip.
   - **Linux/Mac**: Use tar -xvzfapache-tomcat-<version>.tar.gz.
2. Move the extracted folder to a desired location.

**Step 3: Verify installation**

1. Open the extracted folder and navigate to the **bin** directory.
2. Run the startup script:
   - **Windows**: Double-click startup.bat.
   - **Linux/Mac**: Use ./startup.sh.
     - Open a web browser and go to: http://localhost:8080. If you see the Tomcat homepage, the installation is successful.

**Part 2: Integrating Tomcat with Eclipse**

**Step 1: Launch Eclipse**

1. Open your Eclipse IDE.

2. Go to the **"Servers"** tab at the bottom of the IDE. (If you don't see it, go to **Window** > **Show View** > **Servers**).

**Step 2: Add a new server**

1. In the Servers tab, click the **"No servers are available. Click this link to create a new server."** message or right-click and select Servers tab, click the**"No server"**.
2. In the **New Server** wizard:
   - Select **Apache** > **Tomcat vX.X Server** (choose the version you installed).
   - Click **Next**.

**Step 3: Configure Tomcat installation directory**

1. In the **Tomcat installation directory** field:
   - Browse to the location where you extracted Tomcat (e.g., C:\Apache\Tomcat or /opt/Tomcat).
2. Click **Finish**.

**Part 3: Deploy and run a web application**
**Step 1: Create a Dynamic Web Project**

1. Go to **File** > **New** > **Dynamic Web Project**.
2. Enter a project name (e.g., MyWebApp) and click **Finish**.

**Step 2: Add the project to the server**

1. In the **Servers** tab, right-click on the Tomcat server and select **"Add and Remove."**
2. Select your project and click **Add** >.
3. Click **Finish**.

**Step 3: Start the server**

1. Right-click on the Tomcat server in the **Servers** tab.
2. Click **Start** to launch the server.
3. Once started, open a browser and go to http://localhost:8080/YourProjectName.

**Part 4: Optional configurations**
**Step 1: Modify server port**

1. Double-click the Tomcat server in the **Servers** tab.
2. Change the HTTP port (default is 8080) if needed.

**Step 2: Debug mode**

1. Right-click the Tomcat server and select **Debug** to enable debugging during development.

## 2.4 Spring Security and OAuth2 and JSON Web Tokens integration to Eclipse integrated development environment

**Step 1: Create a Spring Boot project**

1. Open Eclipse IDE.
2. Go to File > New > Spring Starter Project.
3. Provide the following:
   - **Project name**: SpringSecurityOAuth2JWT
   - **Type**: Maven
   - **Java version**: 11 or above (if supported).
   - **Dependencies**:
   - Spring Web
   - Spring Security
   - Spring Boot DevTools
   - OAuth2 Resource Server
   - Spring Data JPA
   - H2 Database (or other database options).
4. Click Finish to generate the project.

**Step 2: Add dependencies to pom.xml**

1. Open the pom.xml file and add the required dependencies.
2. Save the file and wait for Maven to resolve the dependencies.

**Step 3: Configure application.properties**
Add the properties to src/main/resources/application.properties:
**Step 4: Create a JwtUtils Utility Class**
Add a utility class for JWT token generation and validation.
**Step 5: Configure Spring Security**
Create a new SecurityConfig class to enable OAuth2 and JWT authentication.
**Step 6: Create a controller**
Create a REST controller to test secured and unsecured endpoints.
**Step 7: Test the application**

1. **Run the application**:
   - Right-click on the project and select Run As > Spring Boot App.
2. **Access endpoints**:
   - Public endpoint: http://localhost:8080/api/public/hello
   - Private endpoint: http://localhost:8080/api/private/hello
   - Pass a valid JWT token in the Authorization header as Bearer <token>.

Now the readers have integrated Spring Security, OAuth2, and JWT into Eclipse. They can secure APIs and test authentication seamlessly.

## 2.5 Maven integration to Eclipse

**Step 1: Ensure Eclipse IDE has Maven installed**

1. **Verify Maven support**:
   - Open Eclipse IDE.
   - Go to Help > About Eclipse IDE.
   - Look for the Maven logo or "Maven Integration for Eclipse" in the installed features.
2. **Install Maven plugin (if not available)**:
   - Go to Help > Eclipse Marketplace.
   - Search for "Maven Integration for Eclipse" (also known as m2e).
   - Click Install, and follow the installation wizard.

**Step 2: Configure Maven in Eclipse**

1. **Open Maven Preferences**:
   - Go to Window > Preferences.
   - Navigate to Maven > Installations.
2. **Add External Maven (optional)**:
   - If you want to use an external Maven installation:
   - Download Maven from Apache Maven.
   - Extract the Maven files to a folder (e.g., C:\Maven).
   - In Eclipse, click Add, browse to the extracted Maven directory, and select it.
   - Click Apply and Close.

**Step 3: Create a Maven project in Eclipse**

1. **Create a New Maven project**:
   - Go to File > New > Project.
   - Select Maven > Maven Project and click Next.
2. **Select project location**:
   - Choose "Create a simple project (skip archetype selection)" if you don't want a predefined template.
   - Alternatively, select an archetype (e.g., maven-archetype-webapp) to use a predefined structure.
   - Click Next.
3. **Provide project details**:
   - Enter the following details:
   - **Group Id**: A unique identifier for your project (e.g., com.example).
   - **Artifact Id**: Your project's name.
   - **Version**: The version of your project (default is 0.0.1-SNAPSHOT).
   - Click **Finish**.
4. **Maven project created**:
   - Your Maven project structure will now appear in Eclipse with the pom.xml file.

**Step 4: Add dependencies in pom.xml**

1. Open the pom.xml file and add the required dependencies
2. Save the file. Maven will download the dependencies automatically.

**Step 5: Build and run Maven project**

1. **Build the project**:
   - Right-click the project in the Project Explorer.
   - Select Run As > Maven Build.
   - Enter a goal (e.g., clean install) and click Run.
2. **Run the project**:
   - If it's a web application, deploy it to a server (e.g., Apache Tomcat).
   - If it's a simple Java application, right-click and select Run As > Java Application.

**Step 6: Configure Maven repository**

1. **Default Maven repository**:
   - By default, Maven uses the .m2/repository folder in your user's home directory to store dependencies.
2. **Custom repository (optional)**:
   - To use a custom repository, open the settings.xml file located in the Maven/conf folder or .m2 directory.
   - Add the <localRepository> tag:
   - <localRepository>C:/CustomMavenRepository</localRepository>

**Step 7: Update Maven project**

If dependencies or plugins don't download correctly:

1. Right-click the Maven project.
2. Select Maven > Update Project.
3. Check the Force Update of Snapshots/Releases box.
4. Click OK.

## 2.6 Spring Boot integration to Eclipse

**Step 1: Install the Spring Tools (STS) plugin in Eclipse**

1. **Open Eclipse**:
   - Go to Help > Eclipse Marketplace.
2. **Search for STS (Spring Tools)**:
   - Type Spring Tools 4 in the search box.
   - Select Spring Tools 4 (for Spring Boot) and click Install.
3. **Follow the installation wizard**:
   - Accept the license agreement and complete the installation.
   - Restart Eclipse after the installation is complete.

**Step 2: Create a new Spring Boot project**

1. **Open New Spring Starter Project Wizard**:
   - Go to File > New > Spring Starter Project.
2. **Configure project details**:
   - **Name**: Enter your project name (e.g., SpringBootApp).
   - **Type**: Maven.
   - **Group**: Enter a group ID (e.g., com.example).
   - **Artifact**: Enter an artifact ID (e.g., springbootapp).
   - **Version**: Use the default (e.g., 0.0.1-SNAPSHOT).
   - **Package**: Enter the base package name(e.g.,com.example.springbootapp).
3. **Add dependencies**:
   - Click **Next** and select dependencies such as:
   - **Spring Web**: For building REST APIs.
   - **Spring Boot DevTools**: For automatic reloads.
   - **Spring Data JPA**: For database interaction.
   - **H2 Database**: For in-memory database support.
4. **Finish**:
   - Click Finish.

**Step 3: Verify the project structure**

1. The project will be created with the following structure:
2. src/main/java
3. └── com.example.springbootapp
4. └── SpringbootappApplication.java (Main class)
5. src/main/resources
6. └── application.properties (Configuration file)
7. The pom.xml file will have the necessary dependencies.

**Step 4: Configure the application.properties**

1. Add the configuration for a simple Spring Boot application insrc/main/resources/application.properties.

**Step 5: Add a REST controller**

1. Write the REST controller program

**Step 6: Run the application**

1. Right-click on the project in Eclipse.
2. Select Run As > Spring Boot App.
3. The application will start, and the console will display a message similar to:
4. Tomcat started on port(s): 8080 (http)
5. Started SpringbootappApplication in 3.456 seconds (JVM running for 4.123)

**Step 7: Test the application**

1. Open a browser or Postman.
2. Navigate to http://localhost:8080/hello.
3. You should see the response: Hello, Spring Boot!.

**Step 8: Add more features**

You can now extend your Spring Boot application by adding:

- **Database integration** with JPA and repositories.
- **Custom configurations** in the application.properties file.
- **Additional dependencies** in pom.xml for advanced functionality.

## 2.7 Hibernate integration to Eclipse

**Step 1: Install Hibernate Tools in Eclipse**

1. **Open Eclipse**:
   - Go to Help > Eclipse Marketplace.
2. **Search for Hibernate Tools**:
   - In the Eclipse Marketplace window, search for Hibernate Tools.
   - Click Go, and find Hibernate Tools in the search results.
3. **Install Hibernate Tools**:
   - Click Install next to Hibernate Tools.
   - Follow the installation prompts and restart Eclipse when prompted.

**Step 2: Create a New Dynamic Web Project**

1. **Create a new project**:
   - Go to File > New > Dynamic Web Project.
2. **Enter project name**:
   - Enter a project name (e.g., HibernateDemo).
   - Click Finish.

**Step 3: Configure Hibernate dependencies**

1. **Add Hibernate JARs manually** (for Java projects, not Web projects):
   - Right-click the project in Project Explorer.
   - Select Properties > Java Build Path.
   - Go to the Libraries tab and click Add External JARs.
   - Download the necessary Hibernate libraries (you can get them from Hibernate releases).
   - Add the following JARs:
   - hibernate-core-x.x.x.Final.jar
   - hibernate-commons-annotations-x.x.x.Final.jar
   - hibernate-jpa-2.1-api-x.x.x.Final.jar

- slf4j-api-x.x.x.jar
- slf4j-simple-x.x.x.jar (optional, for logging)

2. **Alternatively, use Maven** (Recommended):
   - Right-click the project and choose Configure > Convert to Maven Project.
   - Add Hibernate dependencies in the pom.xml file.
   - Save the pom.xml file. Maven will automatically download and add the dependencies to your project.

**Step 4: Configure Hibernate configuration file**

1. **Create Hibernate configuration file (hibernate.cfg.xml):**
   - Right-click the **src** folder and select **New > Folder**. Name it resources.
   - Right-click the resources folder and choose **New > File**. Name it hibernate.cfg.xml.
   - Add the required configuration to hibernate.cfg.xml:

**Step 5: Create an Entity Class**

1. **Create an Entity Class**:
   - Right-click src/main/java and select New > Class. Name it Student.
   - Add annotations to make it a Hibernate entity:

**Step 6: Create a Hibernate Utility Class**

1. **Create a Hibernate Utility Class to configure the session factory:**

**Step 7: Create a Test Class to run Hibernate**

Create a Test Class to test Hibernate functionality:

**Step 8: Run the project**

1. **Run the Test Class**:
   - Right-click on HibernateTest.java and select Run As > Java Application.
2. **Verify database**:
   - Check the MySQL database (yourdb) for the student table. The Student record should be inserted.

**Step 9: (Optional) Configure Hibernate with Spring**

If you want to integrate Hibernate with Spring, you can configure Hibernate with Spring's SessionFactory and DataSource beans in your Spring configuration.

Hibernate integration is now complete in Eclipse.

## 2.8 pom.xml file

The pom.xml (Project Object Model) file is a fundamental part of a Maven-based project in Java. It is an XML file that contains configuration information for your Maven project.

The pom.xml file defines the structure of the project, its dependencies, plugins, goals, and other configurations, allowing Maven to manage the build lifecycle and project dependencies.

**Key sections of pom.xml**

1. **Project coordinates (group, artifact, version):** The project coordinates uniquely identify the project in the Maven repository. These are typically set by the project's creator and are used for version control, artifact management, and dependency resolution.
2. <groupId>com.example</groupId><!- A unique identifier for the group ->
3. <artifactId>my-project</artifactId><!- The name of the artifact ->
4. <version>1.0-SNAPSHOT</version><!- Version of the artifact ->
    - groupId: Defines the group to which the project belongs. This is often a reverse domain name (e.g., com.example).
    - artifactId: The name of the artifact (project or module).
    - version: The version of the artifact. SNAPSHOT indicates a development version, whereas other versions indicate stable releases.
5. **Packaging type:** This defines the type of artifact that Maven will generate (e.g., JAR, WAR, EAR).
6. <packaging>jar</packaging><!- Can be 'jar', 'war', 'ear', etc. ->
7. **Dependencies:** This section defines the libraries or dependencies your project needs. Each dependency is defined by a <dependency> tag that includes the groupId, artifactId, and version of the library.
    - Maven will download these dependencies from the central Maven repository or from custom repositories defined in the pom.xml file.
    - Dependencies can also have scopes (e.g., compile, test, runtime), indicating when they are needed.
8. **Repositories:** This section defines external repositories from which dependencies will be downloaded, aside from the default Maven Central repository.
9. **Build configuration:** The build section configures how the project will be built.
    - sourceDirectory: Specifies the location of the Java source files.
    - plugins: Declares Maven plugins offering auxiliary functionality, e.g., compiling the source code or executing unit tests.
10. **Plugin management**: This is the same as the <build> section but deals with plugin versions and configuration for all submodules within a multimodule project.
11. **Properties**: The properties section declares custom properties that can be used anywhere within the pom.xml file. It helps you avoid hardcoding values and makes version management or other duplicated settings simpler.
12. **Profiles**: Maven's profiles enable you to tailor the build for varying environments. You might, for instance, need to set up different settings for a production environment compared to a development environment.
13. **Parent project**: In a multimodule project, the parent tag can be used to inherit the common configuration and dependencies from the parent pom.xml. This reduces repetitive configurations for each module.

14. **Dependency management**: Like dependencies, but in place of explicitly declaring the dependencies, this part enables you to manage the dependencies across several modules by declaring the versions and scope at a more elevated level.

    Example:
    ```
    <dependencyManagement>
    <dependencies>
    <dependency>
    <groupId>org.apache.commons</groupId>
    <artifactId>commons-lang3</artifactId>
    <version>3.12.0</version>
    </dependency>
    </dependencies>
    </dependencyManagement>
    ```

15. **Parent versioning**: This can prove useful for automating versioning of your project. For instance, Maven enables you to define versions of some plugins.

    Example:
    ```
    <versioning>
    <releaseVersion>1.0.0</releaseVersion>
    <nextSnapshotVersion>1.1.0-SNAPSHOT</nextSnapshotVersion>
    </versioning>
    ```

**How Maven uses pom.xml**

1. Dependency management: Maven downloads and takes care of project dependencies defined in the pom.xml file automatically.
2. Build lifecycle: As you execute Maven commands (i.e., mvn clean install), Maven uses the pom.xml file to establish how to construct the project and its lifecycle phases.
3. Project versioning: Maven manages and follows project versions and dependencies, such that dependencies become simpler to keep up to date over time.

The pom.xml file is important in specifying the configuration, dependencies, and build process for Maven projects, and automates much of Java development.

## 2.9 application.properties file

- The application.properties file is widely utilized in Spring Boot applications to set different properties concerning the behavior of the application, environment configurations, and external integrations. It is one of the most important features for externalizing configuration in Spring Boot applications, allowing developers to keep application settings independent of the code.
  **Structure of application.properties**

- Every line in the application.properties file is a key-value pair, where the key is the name of the configuration and the value is the value that has been assigned to the configuration. This enables developers to personalize many things about the application, including database connection properties, logging settings, and server settings.
- The common sections in an application.properties file:
  1. **Server configuration**
     These settings determine the behavior of the application relative to the embedded server (e.g., Tomcat, Jetty, Undertow) and the network.
     server.port: Designates the port on which the Spring Boot application will execute. The default is 8080, but can be overridden to any other available port.**server.servlet.context-path**: Sets the context path (the base URL) for the application. For example, setting it to /myapp means that the application will be accessible at http://localhost:8080/myapp.
  2. **Spring profiles**
     Spring Profiles are used to define different configurations for different environments (e.g., development, production).
     spring.profiles.active=dev
     - **spring.profiles.active**: Specifies the active profile that Spring Boot should use. This can be useful for loading different configurations based on the environment (e.g., dev, prod, test).
  3. **Database configuration**
     Database-related properties are configured to connect the application to a database. Typically, these settings include the database URL, username, password, and driver class name.
     - **spring.datasource.url**: Specifies the database URL.
     - **spring.datasource.username** and **spring.datasource.password**: Provide credentials for database authentication.
     - **spring.jpa.hibernate.ddl-auto**: Defines the schema management strategy (e.g., update, validate, create, none). update automatically updates the database schema to match the entities.
     - **spring.jpa.show-sql**: If set to true, this will print SQL queries generated by Hibernate to the console.
  4. **Logging configuration**
     You can configure logging levels and output formats in application.properties. Spring Boot uses Logback as the default logging framework.
     - **logging.level.<logger_name>**: Sets the logging level for a specific logger (e.g., DEBUG, INFO, ERROR, etc.). In this example, all logs from the Spring Web package (org.springframework.web) will be at the DEBUG level.
     - **logging.file.name**: Specifies the name of the log file where the logs will be written.
  5. **Spring MVC configuration**
     Spring Boot applications often need customization for the web layer, such as message source configuration or view resolver settings.

- **spring.mvc.view.prefix**: Defines the directory where the views are located.
- **spring.mvc.view.suffix**: Specifies the file extension for view files.

6. **Cache configuration**

   Caching settings can be configured for Spring Boot applications, including cache type and expiration settings.

   spring.cache.type=simple

   - **spring.cache.type**: Specifies the caching provider. Options include simple, ehcache, redis, etc.

7. **Security configuration**

   Security-related properties define how Spring Security is configured in the application, such as the user authentication, authorization, and password encryption.

   - **spring.security.user.name** and **spring.security.user.password**: Define the default username and password for basic authentication. This can be used to set up an in-memory user store for simple applications.

8. **Mail server configuration**

   Properties for setting up an email service using Spring Boot's mail support.

   - **spring.mail.host**: Specifies the mail server host.
   - **spring.mail.port**: Defines the port for the mail server (587 is commonly used for SMTP with STARTTLS).
   - **spring.mail.username** and **spring.mail.password**: Used for authentication to the email service.

9. **Actuator configuration**

   Spring Boot's Actuator module provides various production-ready features like health checks and metrics.

   - **management.endpoints.web.exposure.include**: Controls which endpoints are exposed via the web interface (e.g., health, info, and metrics).
   - **management.endpoint.health.show-details**: Configures whether detailed health information is shown.

10. **Custom properties**

    You can also define custom properties to store your application-specific configurations.

    - **app.name** and **app.version**: These are user-defined properties that can be accessed in the application code or used to configure behavior within the application.

11. **External configuration (e.g., AWS, Kafka, etc.)**

    Spring Boot lets you configure external services and integrations like Kafka, AWS, etc., through the application.properties file.

    - spring.kafka.bootstrap-servers: Specifies the URLs of Kafka brokers.
    - aws.access-key-id and aws.secret-access-key: Specify credentials for AWS services.

**Using properties in code**

You can refer to the properties declared in application.propertiesusing @Value or @ConfigurationProperties annotations.

The application.properties file is also vital in the configuration of a Spring Boot application in a centralized and externalized way. With it, you are able to easily administer settings in different environments, customize application behavior, and add external services like databases, security and messaging. It is an effective and versatile way of separating configuration and code.

## 2.10 settings.xml

The environments.xml file is used in settings that affect the behavior of Maven, including the location of the repositories, the settings of the plugins, profiles and other environment settings. Such a file is found in the{Maven_Home}/conf/ directory (global settings) or ${user.home}/.m2/ directory (user settings).

Important features of the settings.xml file:

- Repository configuration: To define repositories of dependencies and so on.
- Mirrors: This defines the way in which Maven retrieves dependencies via the remote repositories.
- Profiles: Describes different environments that can be called upon in specific circumstances.
- Proxy configuration: Configures the access of remote repositories by Maven when accessed via a proxy server.
- Servers: Stores log information and properties, which are used to authenticate the user upon accessing specific repositories.
- Active profiles: Specifies the default or specific profiles that become active.

settings.xml file:

1. **<settings> Root Element**
   <settings> is the root element within the settings.xml file and surrounds all the rest of the settings.

```
<settings>
<!- Configuration details go here ->
</settings>
```

2. Local repository configuration
   The <localRepository> tag is used to indicate the path to the local repository where Maven places downloaded dependencies and plugins. Maven defaults to using the.m2/repository directory in the home directory of the user, but you can alter it if you need to.

```
<localRepository>/path/to/your/local/repo</localRepository>
```

3. Mirrors
   Maven employs mirrors to retrieve artifacts from remote repositories. You can define mirrors in the settings.xml file to define which mirror Maven should use for downloading artifacts.

- <id>: A mirror identifier.
- <mirrorOf>: Identifies the repository this mirror is for (e.g., central).
- <url>: The URL of the mirror repository.
- <blocked>: Maven will block usage of this mirror if set to true.

4. Profiles
Profiles in settings.xml enable you to specify a set of configurations that can be enabled under a specific condition. Profiles can be utilized to alter settings such as repositories, plugin versions, and other build parameters.
    - <id>: The profile identifier.
    - <activation>: Specifies what activates the profile. For instance, it could be activated by default or only under certain circumstances, such as operating system or a file's existence.
    no<activeByDefault>: A boolean indicating if this profile must be activated by default. It is possible for profiles to benefit from managing alternative environments such as development, test, and production.
5. Servers
The <servers> element keeps authentication information (e.g., username and password) for Maven repositories. It enables you to supply credentials to private repositories or other facilities.
    - <id>: Server identifier. You use this ID in the repository configuration in your pom.xml to reference the server by a repository.
    - <username> and <password>: Supply credentials for accessing the repository.
    This element assists in the safe handling of repository credentials when connecting to private repositories.
6. Proxies
When Maven is in front of a proxy, you can set up proxy configurations within the settings.xml file so Maven can access the remote repositories by going through the proxy.
    - <id>: An identifying name for the proxy setup.
    - <active>: It is active when set to true.
    - <protocol>: The protocol such as http or https.
    - <host> and <port>: Proxy server address and port.
    - <username> and <password>: Provide the proxy server authentication credentials.
    - <nonProxyHosts>: A comma-separated list of hosts that must be exempted from the proxy.
    This is useful when you are working within corporate environments that necessitate the use of a proxy to access the internet.
7. Plugin groups
Here, you can define plugin groups that Maven can utilize during the resolution of plugins.

```
<pluginGroups>
<pluginGroup>com.example.plugins</pluginGroup>
</pluginGroups>
```

- <pluginGroup>: Defines the group IDs for the plugins that must be taken into consideration during plugin resolution.

8. Active profiles

   The <activeProfiles> element specifies which profiles are active by default for a specific Maven installation. You can define default profiles to prevent you from having to include them on the command line every time you execute Maven.

```
<activeProfiles>
<activeProfile>development</activeProfile>
</activeProfiles>
```

   - <activeProfile>: Specifies the profiles that should be active.

The settings.xml file is a critical configuration file for controlling Maven's behavior and handling complicated development environments.

## 2.11 hibernate.cfg.xml file

The hibernate.cfg.xml file is a core configuration file for Hibernate, the Java ORM (Object-Relational Mapping) framework. It contains essential configurations for setting up the Hibernate session factory, including database connection details, dialect, caching, and other Hibernate-specific settings.

**Basic structure of hibernate.cfg.xml**

The basic structure of the hibernate.cfg.xml file includes the following key sections:

- The root element <hibernate-configuration>
- <session-factory> element where Hibernate settings are defined

```
<hibernate-configuration>
<session-factory>
<!– Configuration properties go here –>
</session-factory>
</hibernate-configuration>
```

1. **<hibernate-configuration> Root Element**

   It is the base component of the configuration file that encloses the configuration of the session factory. All the Hibernate configurations are contained in this element.

```
<hibernate-configuration>
<session-factory>
<!– Hibernate configuration properties go here –>
</session-factory>
</hibernate-configuration>
```

2. **<session-factory> Element**
   The key element in hibernate.cfg.xml is the element the session-factory. It also holds a range of property settings that Hibernate requires to initialize and set up the Session Factory, which is the collection that interacts with the database.
3. **Database connection properties**
   These properties contain the database connection information, such as the JDBC URL, username, password and the JDBC driver class.
   - **hibernate.connection.driver_class**: The full-qualified name of the JDBC driver (e.g. the com.mysql.cj.jdbc.Driver of MySQL).
   - **hibernate.connection.url**: The database URL to connect with (e.g., jdbc:mysql://localhost:3306/mydatabase).
   - **hibernate.connection.username**: This is the username forthe database.
   - **hibernate.connection.password**: The user name of the database user.
4. **Dialect**
   The dialect used in the database is defined in the hibernate.dialect property, which enables Hibernate to produce the SQL that is optimized for the database being utilized. Hibernate supports multiple databases, such as MySQL, PostgreSQL, Oracle, etc.
   - **hibernate.dialect**: Specifies the SQL dialect for the database, such as org.hibernate.dialect.MySQL8Dialect for MySQL or org.hibernate.dialect.PostgreSQLDialect for PostgreSQL.
5. **Show SQL**
   This property controls whether Hibernate should log the SQL statements it generates. This can be useful for debugging or development purposes.
   - **hibernate.show_sql**: Set to true to print SQL statements in the console.
6. **Format SQL**
   The hibernate.format_sql property controls whether Hibernate formats the generated SQL for better readability.
   - **hibernate.format_sql**: Set to true to format SQL queries (e.g., for easier debugging).
7. **hibernate.hbm2ddl.auto**
   This property controls the automatic generation of the database schema. Hibernate can automatically generate, update, or validate the database schema based on entity mappings.
   - **hibernate.hbm2ddl.auto**: Specifies how Hibernate handles the schema:
   - create: Drops the schema and creates a new one at startup.
   - update: Updates the schema to match the entity mappings.
   - validate: Validates the schema without modifying it.
   - none: Does not modify the schema.
8. **Connection pooling**
   Hibernate supports connection pooling, which improves performance by reusing database connections. The connection pool is usually configured via hibernate.c3p0.* properties (if using the C3P0 connection pool).

- **hibernate.c3p0.min_size**: Minimum number of connections in the pool.
- **hibernate.c3p0.max_size**: Maximum number of connections in the pool.
- **hibernate.c3p0.timeout**: Time (in seconds) to wait before considering a connection as idle.
- **hibernate.c3p0.max_statements**: The maximum number of cached prepared statements.

9. **Cache settings**
   Hibernate supports first and second-level caching for better performance. Cache-related settings can be added to the configuration file.
   - **hibernate.cache.use_second_level_cache**: Set to true to enable second-level caching.
   - **hibernate.cache.region.factory_class**: Specifies the caching provider, such as EhCacheRegionFactory.
10. **Transaction factory**
    This setting defines how transactions are managed within Hibernate.

```
<property
name="hibernate.transaction.factory_class">org.hibernate.transaction.JDBCTransaction-
Factory</property>
```

   - **hibernate.transaction.factory_class**: Specifies the transaction factory. JDBCTransactionFactory is a basic option, but you can use JTA for container-managed transactions in Java EE.
11. **Annotated classes/entity mappings**
    This section defines which Java classes should be treated as Hibernate entities.
    - **<mapping class="com.example.model.User"/>**: Maps a Java class (User) to a database table. Hibernate will use reflection to map the fields of the User class to columns in the database.
12. **Java Database Connectivity (JDBC) batch processing**
    Hibernate can use batch processing to execute multiple SQL statements in a single round-trip to the database, which can improve performance in large-scale applications.
    - **hibernate.jdbc.batch_size**: Defines the batch size for JDBC operations.
    - **hibernate.order_inserts**: If set to true, it will order insert statements to minimize foreign key constraint violations.
    - **hibernate.order_updates**: If set to true, it will order update statements.

The hibernate.cfg.xml file is a key configuration file for setting up Hibernate's environment, including database connection settings, caching, transaction management, and entity mappings. Proper configuration ensures Hibernate interacts efficiently with the underlying database, and it helps with performance optimization, security, and error handling.

## 2.12 Java Development Kit (JDK) integration to Eclipse

**Step 1: Download and install JDK**

1. **Download the JDK:**

- Visit the official Oracle website or the OpenJDK website and download the JDK version you want (e.g., JDK 8, JDK 11, JDK 17).
- Select the appropriate version based on the specific operating system.
- Follow the instructions on the website to complete the download and installation process.

2. **Install the JDK**:
   - After downloading, follow the installation instructions provided by Oracle or OpenJDK.
   - For Windows: Run the installer and follow the setup wizard to install the JDK.
   - For macOS: Mount the .dmg file and follow the installation prompts.
   - For Linux: Use package managers like apt (Ubuntu) or yum (CentOS) for installation.
3. **Verify JDK installation**:
   - Open a command prompt/terminal.
   - Run the command:
   - java -version

Prints the version number of the JDK installed on a specific system.

**Step 2: Set up JDK in Eclipse**

1. **Launch Eclipse IDE**:
   - Open Eclipse IDE. If you haven't installed it yet, download and install the latest version from Eclipse Downloads.
2. **Open Preferences**:
   - In Eclipse, go to the **"Window"** menu (on Windows/Linux) or **"Eclipse"** menu (on macOS) at the top of the screen.
   - Select **Preferences** (under the "General" section).
3. **Add JDK to Eclipse**:
   - In the Preferences window, expand **Java** and click on **Installed JREs.**
   - Click the **Add External JARs** button or **Add JDK** (depending on your Eclipse version).
   - Select the JDK folder where the JDK is installed (for example, C:\Program Files\Java \jdk-17 on Windows or /Library/Java/JavaVirtualMachines/jdk-17.jdk/Contents/Home on macOS).
   - After selecting the JDK folder, click **OK** or **Finish.**
4. **Set the JDK as the default JRE**:
   - In the same **Installed JREs** window, select the newly added JDK and click the **Apply and Close** button.
   - This sets the selected JDK as the default Java Runtime Environment (JRE) for your Eclipse workspace.

**Step 3: Create a Java Project using the integrated JDK**

1. **Create a New Java Project**:
   - In Eclipse, go to **File → New → Java Project.**
   - Name the project (e.g., MyFirstJavaProject) and click **Finish.**

2. **Configure JDK for your project** (optional):
   - If your project needs a specific version of the JDK, you can configure it individually for that project.
   - Right-click on your project in the **Project Explorer** and select **Properties**.
   - In the **Java Build Path** section, go to the **Libraries** tab.
   - Click Add Library → JRE System Library.
   - Select the installed JDK and click **Finish**.

**Step 4: Verify JDK setup by creating a simple Java class**

1. **Create a simple Java class**:
   - Right-click on src → New → Class.
   - Name the class (e.g., test), and check the box to include the public static void main (String[] args) method.
   - Click Finish.
2. **Write sample code**:

In the test.java class, add a simple System.out.println() statement:

```
public class test {
public static void main(String[] args) {
System.out.println("testing");
}
}
```

1. **Run the Java program**:
   - Right-click on the HelloWorld.java file and select Run As → Java Application.
   - The Console window at the bottom should display Hello, World!, indicating that the JDK is properly integrated and working.

**Step 5: Additional configuration (optional)**

- **Setting up multiple JDK versions**: If you need to switch between multiple JDKs in Eclipse, you can add other JDK versions by repeating the steps in Step 2.
- **JDK updates**: Ensure that you regularly check for updates to your JDK to stay up-to-date with new features and security patches.

By doing so, you will have successfully incorporated the JDK into Eclipse and set it up to build, create, and execute Java projects

## 2.13 Integrate cloud platform into Eclipse

Adding a cloud platform (such as AWS, Google Cloud, or IBM Cloud) to the Eclipse IDE may differ based on the cloud platform you want to use.

Procedure for AWS Integration to Eclipse

**Step 1: Install the AWS Toolkit for Eclipse**

1. **Open Eclipse IDE**: Launch the Eclipse IDE where you want to integrate AWS.
2. **Install AWS Toolkit for Eclipse**:
   - Go to the **Help** menu.
   - Select **Eclipse Marketplace.**
   - In the **Eclipse Marketplace** dialog, type AWS Toolkit in the search bar and press Enter.
   - Find **AWS Toolkit for Eclipse** in the search results and click the **Install** button next to it.
   - Follow the installation prompts. After installation, Eclipse may prompt you to restart the IDE. Click **Restart Now.**

**Step 2: Set up AWS credentials**

1. **Create an AWS account** (if you don't have one):
   - Visit AWSwebsite and sign up for an account.
2. **Create an IAM user with Programmatic access**:
   - Go to the AWS Management Console and navigate to **IAM** (Identity and Access Management).
   - Under **Users**, click on **Add user.**
   - Set the **User name** and choose **Programmatic access.**
   - Assign **permissions** (for simplicity, you can assign AdministratorAccess or create a custom policy based on your requirements).
   - Click **Next: Tags** and then **Review,** and finally **Create user.**
   - **Save** the **Access Key ID** and **Secret Access Key**.
3. **Configure AWS credentials in Eclipse**:
   - In Eclipse, go to **Window** → **Preferences.**
   - In the Preferences window, expand **AWS Toolkit** and select **Credentials.**
   - Click on Add and enter your **Access Key ID** and **Secret Access Key** that you saved earlier.
   - After entering the credentials, click **OK.**

**Step 3: Create a new AWS project in Eclipse**

1. **Create a New Java Project**:
   - Go to **File** → **New** → **Java Project.**
   - Enter the **project name** (e.g., MyAWSProject) and click **Finish.**
2. **Configure the AWS SDK for Java**:
   - Right-click on the newly created project and select **Properties.**
   - Under **Java Build Path**, go to the **Libraries** tab.
   - Click **Add External JARs.**
   - Navigate to the **AWS SDK for Java** libraries (you can download these from the AWS SDK for Java page) or use Maven for automatic dependency management (explained below).

**Step 4: Use AWS SDK in the project**

1. **Add AWS SDK dependency** (optional):
   - If you're using **Maven** in your project, you can add the AWS SDK dependency to your pom.xml file:
   - This will automatically download and manage the AWS SDK libraries for your project.
2. **Write AWS code**:
   - Create a new Java class (e.g., AWSDemo.java).
   - Write code to interact with AWS services.
3. **Run the application**:
   - Right-click on your Java class and select **Run As → Java Application**.
   - You should see the output listing your S3 buckets (if you have any).

**Step 5: Access AWS resources from Eclipse**

1. **AWS Explorer**:
   - AWS Toolkit adds a new view called **AWS Explorer**. To access it, go to **Window → Show View → AWS Explorer**.
   - Interact with your AWS resources (S3 buckets, EC2 instances, Lambda functions, etc.) directly from Eclipse.
   - You can right-click on AWS resources in the AWS Explorer to perform various actions, such as uploading files to S3 or starting/stopping EC2 instances.

**Step 6: Deploy AWS Lambda Functions (optional)**

1. **Create AWS Lambda Function**:
   - Right-click on your project and select **New → Other → AWS → AWS Lambda Function**.
   - Follow the wizard to create and deploy a Lambda function.
2. **Invoke Lambda Function**:
   - You can use the AWS SDK or AWS Explorer to invoke your Lambda functions.

**Step 7: Additional cloud platforms (Google Cloud, IBM Cloud)**

If you want to integrate other cloud platforms, such as **Google Cloud** or **IBM Cloud**, the procedure is similar:

- Install the appropriate toolkit for the cloud platform (e.g., **Google Cloud Tools for Eclipse or IBM Cloud Tools for Eclipse**).
- **Authenticate** and set up credentials as per the platform's instructions.
- **Write code** to interact with cloud services (e.g., Google Cloud Storage, IBM Watson, etc.).

By following these steps, you can integrate AWS (or other cloud platforms) into your Eclipse IDE, allowing you to easily interact with cloud services, manage resources, and build cloud-based applications. If you're working with specific services like Lambda, S3, or EC2, the integration steps may vary slightly, but the general process remains consistent.

## 2.14 What is web.xml?

web.xml is the Servlet API deployment descriptor for Java web applications. It is a fundamental part of configuring a web application and is placed in the WEB-INF directory of the application. It holds data on how the web application responds, such as servlet mappings, filters, listeners, and additional configuration parameters the application requires in order to be operational within a servlet container (e.g., Apache Tomcat).

**Key components of web.xml**

The most important pieces that are utilized in web.xml:

**1.** <web-app>: The root element of the web.xml file. It specifies the web application version and any necessary configurations.

```
<web-app xmlns="http://java.sun.com/xml/ns/javaee"
xmlns:xsi="http://www.w3.org/2001/XMLSchema-instance"
xsi:schemaLocation="http://java.sun.com/xml/ns/javaee
http://java.sun.com/xml/ns/javaee/web-app_3_0.xsd"
version="3.0">
</web-app>
```

**2.** <servlet>: This defines a servlet in the application. A servlet is a Java class that processes HTTP requests and generates responses.

```
<servlet>
<servlet-name>dispatcher</servlet-name>
<servlet-class>org.springframework.web.servlet.DispatcherServlet</servlet-class>
<load-on-startup>1</load-on-startup>
</servlet>
```

**3.** <servlet-mapping>: This maps a URL pattern to a servlet. When the servlet container receives a request that matches the URL pattern, the corresponding servlet is invoked.

**4.** <filter>: This defines a filter that can intercept requests before they reach the servlet and/or manipulate responses before they are sent to the client.

**5.** <filter-mapping>: This specifies which filters apply to which servlet or URL pattern.

**6.** <listener>: This specifies an event listener class that listens for certain events like application startup, shutdown, and session creation or destruction.

**7.** <error-page>: This specifies customized error pages for processing certain error codes or exceptions.

**8.** <welcome-file-list>: This indicates the page to display by default when the user is at the web application root.

**Usage of web.xml for Spring MVC**

Procedure to configure a Spring MVC application using web.xml:

1. Define the DispatcherServlet:
   - Configure the DispatcherServlet in web.xml, which is the main controller for handling HTTP requests in a Spring MVC web application.

- The DispatcherServlet should be mapped to the root URL (/), ensuring that all requests are handled by Spring's dispatcher.

2. Character encoding filter:
    - Configure a filter to ensure that the encoding of HTTP requests and responses is set correctly (e.g., UTF-8).
3. ContextLoaderListener:
    - The ContextLoaderListener is responsible for initializing the Spring application context and managing the lifecycle of beans for the application.

## 2.15 What is spring-mvc-servlet.xml?

Spring-mvc-servlet.xml is the Spring configuration file that is typically used in a Spring MVC application to configure the application's components, such as controllers, view resolvers, message converters, and other Spring beans. The DispatcherServlet (the front controller of the Spring MVC) uses this XML file to create and configure the Spring application context to process the HTTP requests.

This file is mentioned in the web.xml file in the Spring MVC application to load the Spring configuration and receive the mapping of the HTTP requests to controllers and views.

**Key components of spring-mvc-servlet.xml**

The important elements and setup choices that might generally occur in a spring-mvc-servlet.xml document:

1. Component scan: Enables component scanning to automatically detect Spring beans (like controllers, services, and repositories).

```
<context:component-scan base-package="com.example.controller"/>
```

2. View resolver: Configures a view resolver to map logical view names (like "home") to actual view files (e.g., JSP files).

```
<bean
class="org.springframework.web.servlet.view.InternalResourceViewResolver">
<property name="prefix" value="/WEB-INF/views/"/>
<property name="suffix" value=".jsp"/>
</bean>
```

3. Handler mapping: Specifies how Spring MVC will map HTTP requests to handler methods in controllers. By default, Dispatcher Servlet automatically maps HTTP requests to methods based on the @RequestMapping annotation, but custom mappings can be configured here.

```
<bean class="org.springframework.web.servlet.handler.BeanNameUrlHandlerMapping"/>
```

1. Message converters: Configures the message converters for handling different types of requests and responses (e.g., JSON, XML).

```
<bean class="org.springframework.http.converter.json.
MappingJackson2HttpMessageConverter"/>
```

1. Locale resolver: Defines how the application handles locale settings (such as internationalization).

```
<bean class="org.springframework.web.servlet.i18n.SessionLocaleResolver"/>
```

6. Custom filters and interceptors: Spring MVC configures custom filters and interceptors that can perform tasks like logging, authentication, or preprocessing HTTP requests.

```
<mvc:interceptors>
<bean class="com.example.interceptor.CustomInterceptor"/>
</mvc:interceptors>
```

7. Static resource handling: Configures handling for static resources like CSS, JavaScript, and images.

```
<mvc:resources mapping="/resources/**" location="/WEB-INF/resources/"/>
```

1. DispatcherServlet configuration: In Spring, DispatcherServlet is responsible for dispatching requests to the appropriate controllers. Configure this in web.xml, but spring-mvc-servlet.xml contains other important settings related to how requests are handled.

## 2.16 Conclusion

In this chapter, readers have gained practical experience in setting up a comprehensive development environment for enterprise applications. They have learned to install and configure Eclipse IDE, integrate essential tools and frameworks such as Apache Tomcat, Spring Security, OAuth2, JWT, Maven, Spring Boot, and Hibernate, and manage critical configuration files. Additionally, readers have understood the importance of integrating the JDK and connecting to cloud platforms. With this setup, developers are now equipped to embark on building robust and scalable enterprise applications.

## Bibliography

Eclipse Foundation. (2024). Eclipse IDE documentation. https://www.eclipse.org

Apache. (2024). Apache Tomcat documentation. https://tomcat.apache.org

Apache Maven. (2024). Maven documentation. https://maven.apache.org/guides

Oracle. (2024). JDK documentation. https://docs.oracle.com/en/java/

Spring. (2024). Spring Boot documentation. https://docs.spring.io/spring-boot/docs/current/reference/html/

Spring Security. (2024). https://docs.spring.io/spring-security/reference/

OAuth. (2024). OAuth 2.0 Framework. https://oauth.net/2/

JWT. (2024). JSON Web Token. https://jwt.io/introduction

Amazon AWS. (2024). AWS Toolkit for Eclipse. https://aws.amazon.com/eclipse/

Hibernate. (2024). Hibernate Configuration Guide. https://hibernate.org

# 3 Introduction to Spring Framework

## 3.1 Spring Model-View-Controller

A simplified Spring Model-View-Controller (MVC) architecture diagram:

Components of Spring MVC:

1. Client request:
   - The initial request sent by the client (browser, mobile app, etc.) that invokes a specific action on the server.
2. DispatcherServlet (Front Controller):
   - The core component of Spring MVC. It is the first point of entry for all requests and delegates them to appropriate handlers. It manages the entire workflow of handling the request and response.
   - It is responsible for routing requests, processing them, and rendering the final response.
3. HandlerMapping:
   - The HandlerMapping determines which controller method should handle the incoming request based on the URL pattern and other parameters.
   - It resolves the appropriate handler (Controller) to process the request.
4. Controller:
   - A component that is responsible for handling the business logic of the request. The controller receives the user input, processes it, and returns the ModelAndView.
   - It maps user requests to corresponding controller methods using annotations like @ RequestMapping or more specific ones like @GetMapping, @PostMapping.
5. Model (Plain Old Java Object):
   - The model represents the data of the application. It is typically a Plain Old Java Object (POJO) that holds data that needs to be processed by the controller.
   - The model is populated by the controller and passed to the view for rendering.
6. ViewResolver:
   - The ViewResolver resolves the logical view name returned by the controller into an actual view (e.g., a JavaServer Pages [JSP] file or Thymeleaf template).
   - It determines which view template should be rendered based on the returned name.
7. View:
   - The view is responsible for rendering the final output (e.g., HTML, JSON, XML) to the client.
   - The view is rendered using technologies like JSP, Thymeleaf, or other template engines.
8. Model object:
   - It is the actual data that the controller passes to the view for rendering. The controller populates this model object (typically a JavaBean or POJO) with data and passes it to the view for rendering.

**Mastering Java Full Stack Development. DOI: https://doi.org/10.1016/B978-0-443-51683-2.00011-4**

9. Data binding:
   - Data binding involves converting the user input from the web form (request parameters) into Java objects (model). The Spring framework automatically binds incoming data to the model object (usually via form submission or request parameters).

   Workflow:

1. The client sends a request (e.g., HTTP GET or POST).
2. The DispatcherServlet receives the request and consults the HandlerMapping to determine which Controller method to call.
3. The Controller processes the request, handles business logic, and prepares the Model (data).
4. The ViewResolver takes the logical name of the view returned by the controller and resolves it into an actual view (e.g., JSP, Thymeleaf).
5. The View is rendered with the model data and returned as a response to the client (Fig. 3-1).

## 3.2 Spring MVC Web Application Architecture

Here is a simplified Spring MVC Web Application Architecture diagram (Fig. 3-2):
Components:

1. Client (Browser):
   - The client (typically a web browser) sends an HTTP request to the server. This request could be to fetch a resource or submit data.
2. DispatcherServlet (Front Controller):
   - The core component of Spring MVC that intercepts all incoming requests. It acts as a central controller and is responsible for dispatching the request to the appropriate handler (controller).
3. HandlerMapping:
   - Responsible for mapping the incoming request to the correct controller method based on the URL, HTTP method (GET/POST), and other parameters.

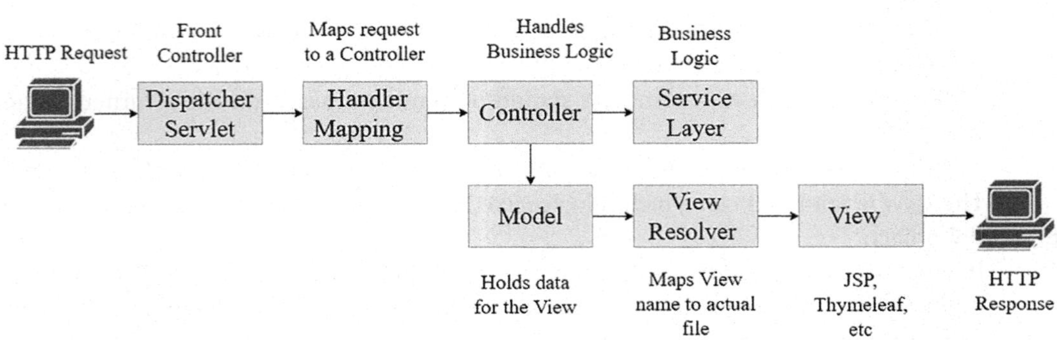


**FIGURE 3–1** Spring Model-View-Controller architecture. *JSP*, JavaServer Pages.

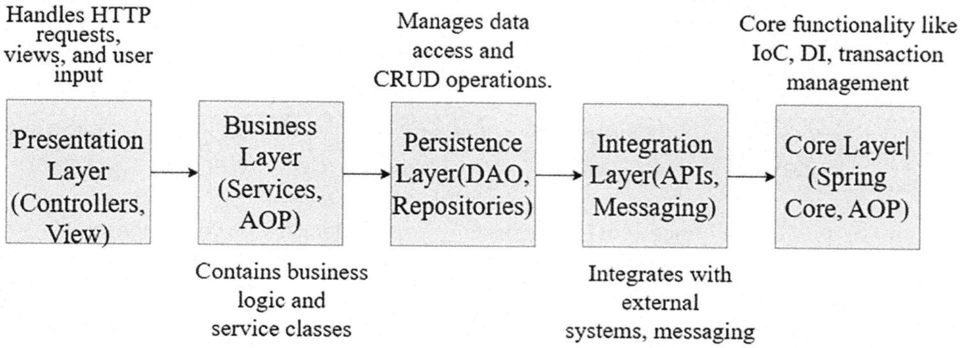


**FIGURE 3–2** Spring MVC Web Application Architecture. *AOP*, Aspect-Oriented Programming; *CRUD*, Create, Read, Update, Delete; *DAO*; Data Access Object; *DI*, dependency injection; *IoC*, Inversion of Control.

4. Controller:
   - The controller contains the business logic for handling the request. It processes the user input, interacts with the service layer, and prepares a model for the view.
5. Model (Plain Old Java Object or Data Transfer Object):
   - The model is a data object (usually a Plain Old Java Object or Data Transfer Object [DTO]). It holds the data that will be displayed to the user or used in the response. The controller prepares the model based on the request data.
6. Service Layer:
   - The Service Layer contains business logic and service methods that interact with the data access layer. It acts as an intermediary between the controller and the data access layer, ensuring business rules are applied.
7. Data access layer (DAO/Repository):
   - The data access layer provides the methods to interact with the database. It contains the Data Access Object (DAO) or Repository pattern, which abstracts database operations (CRUD - Create, Read, Update, Delete) to communicate with the database.
8. Database (MySQL, MongoDB, etc.):
   - The database stores the application's data. It can be any relational database , like MySQL or a NoSQL database like MongoDB. The data access layer interacts with the database to retrieve, store, or modify data.
9. ViewResolver:
   - Once the controller has prepared the model and business logic, the ViewResolver is responsible for resolving the view (JSP, Thymeleaf, etc.) and passing the model data to be rendered on the client side.
10. View:
    - The view is a template that displays the model data. It is responsible for rendering HTML, JSON, or any other format to the client. Technologies like JSP or Thymeleaf are commonly used to generate the response view (Figs. 3–3–3–4).

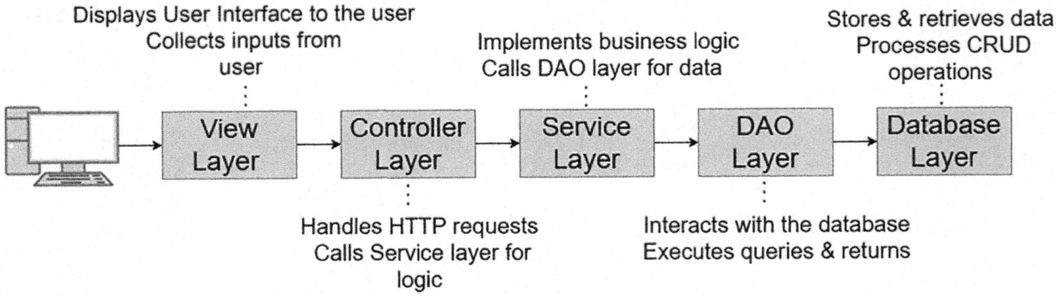


**FIGURE 3–3** Spring Model-View-Controller Layered Architecture. *CRUD*, Create, Read, Update, Delete; *DAO*; Data Access Object.

Workflow:

1. Client sends a request (HTTP GET/POST) to the server.
2. DispatcherServlet handles the request and consults HandlerMapping to choose the appropriate Controller.
3. The Controller processes the request, communicates with the Service Layer, and prepares a Model with the data.
4. The Service Layer processes business logic and interacts with the data access layer to fetch or store data.
5. The data access layer communicates with the database to access or insert the data according to the need.
6. The Model is then passed back by the Controller to the ViewResolver, which translates the Model into a view (such as JSP or Thymeleaf).
7. View transforms the information and transmits the answer to the Client.

## 3.3 Spring Framework layers

Application development in the Spring Framework architecture is abstracted and modularized into several layers. These layers are used in tandem to simplify the development of enterprise applications by offering structure, lessening code, and fostering flexibility.

1. **Presentation layer**
   - Purpose:
   - Handles the user interface and user interactions.
   - Processes HTTP requests and returns HTTP responses.
   - Components:
   - Controllers (e.g., @Controller, @RestController) manage user requests.
   - The response is rendered to the user by the use of views (e.g., JSP, Thymeleaf, or FreeMarker).
   - Spring modules:
   - Spring Web: Provides basic web functionalities like multipart file upload.

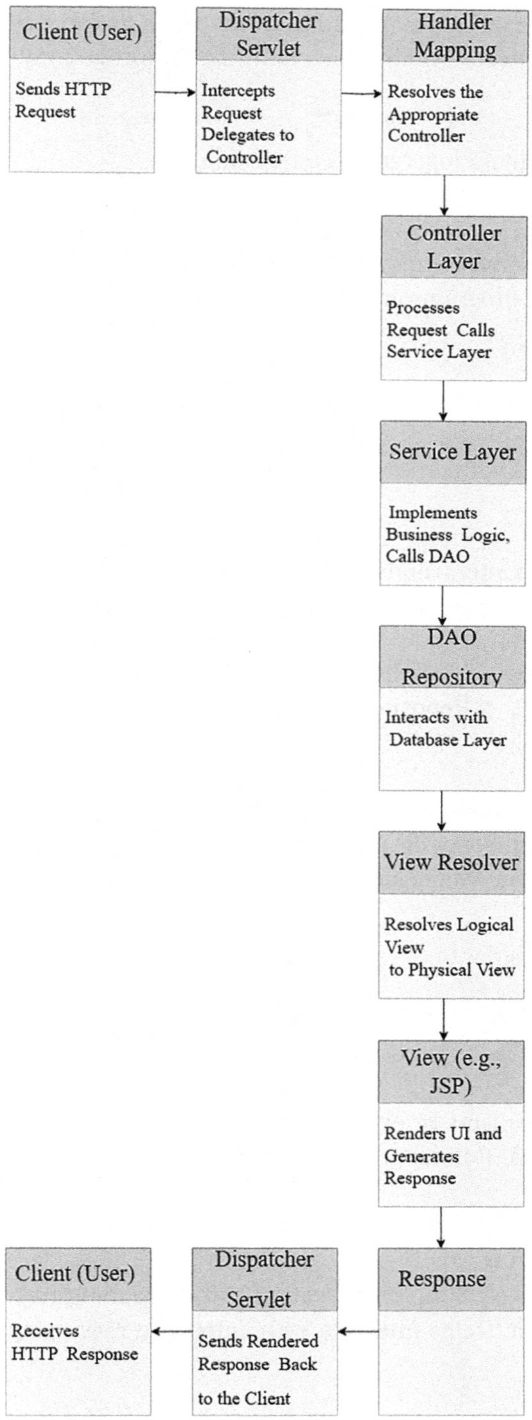


**FIGURE 3–4** HTTP request response flow. *DAO*, Data Access Object; *JSP*, JavaServer Pages.

- Spring Web MVC: an implementation of the MVC design pattern.
- Spring Web Reactive: Asynchronous and reactive programming models.

2. **Business layer**
   - Purpose:
   - Contains the business logic of the application.
   - Processes data and applies rules as per business requirements.
   - Components:
   - Services (e.g., @Service annotated classes) encapsulate business logic.
   - Aspect-Oriented Programming (AOP) is often used here to handle cross-cutting concerns.
   - Spring modules:
   - Spring Core: Provides dependency injection (DI) and bean management to support the business layer.
   - Spring AOP: Deals with cross-cutting issues such as logging, transactions, and security.
3. **Persistence layer**
   - Purpose:
   - Manages database interactions, such as creating, reading, updating, and deleting records.
   - Offers a distinct separation of business logic and data access logic.
   - Components:
   - DAOs (Data Access Objects): Encapsulate database operations.
   - Repositories (e.g., @Repository annotated classes): Provide access to persistence mechanisms.
   - Spring modules:
   - Spring JDBC: Simplifies working with relational databases.
   - Spring ORM: Integrates ORM frameworks like Hibernate and JPA.
   - Spring Transaction Management: Declarative or programmatic transaction management.
4. **Integration layer**
   - Purpose:
   - Communication with other systems or external resources, for example, messaging systems, REST APIs, or third-party services.
   - Components:
   - Messaging mechanisms or external APIs.
   - Messaging queues, JMS, or RESTful web services.
   - Spring modules:
   - Spring Messaging: Provides support for asynchronous messaging and integration with messaging platforms.
   - Spring Web Services: Simplifies creating and consuming web services.
   - Spring Integration: Helps integrate with enterprise messaging systems.
5. **Core layer**
   - Purpose:
   - Forms the foundation of the Spring Framework.

- Provides the IoC container and DI functionality for the entire framework.
- Components:
- BeanFactory and ApplicationContext for managing beans and configurations.
- Lifecycle management and DI of the application.
- Spring modules:
- Spring Core: Handles basic IoC and DI functionalities.
- Spring Context: Extends the Core module by providing features like event propagation and internationalization.
- Spring SpEL (Spring Expression Language): Provides querying and manipulation of objects at runtime.

**Key characteristics of each layer**

1. Separation of concerns: It is modular and maintainable code with each layer having a specific purpose.
2. Loose coupling: DI enables the communication between the components of the different layers without tight coupling.
3. Reusability: A component of one layer can be reused in several projects.

## 3.4 Spring Architecture working procedure

The architecture of Spring is such that it is meant to offer a lightweight and modular application structure when it comes to developing enterprise applications. A typical Spring application is designed in a layered manner with the flow of data towards the interaction with the user, business logic, data persistence, and external communication being managed by specific components. This isolation of concern assists in preserving clarity, modularity, and testability.

**Step 1: User input (Presentation Layer)**

The Presentation Layer is involved when a user deals with the application. In the case of a web application, this usually comes at a web layer, whereby the HTTP requests are received. These requests are processed by the Spring Web MVC framework, which is a component of the Presentation Layer and directs them to the correct Controller. Annotated with either the element of annotation controller or rest controller, a controller method receives the incoming HTTP request, authenticates input data, and packages it to be processed by other methods.

The process of request flow starts when the user inputs data (e.g., filling in a form or an API request). This data is presented to the Controller, which may leave the processing of this data to Business Layer services.

Step 2: Business Logic Processing (Business Layer)

After making the request to the Business Layer, it is the Service Layer that is in charge of the main application logic. This layer handles the actual business rules and operations of the application, which are usually contained in service classes with the annotation of @Service. The service type is able to manipulate information, invoke business policies, and control the circulation of information in and out of the other layers.

At this level, the Business Layer may invoke certain methods of Repositories or classes of the DAO in the Persistence Layer in case it has to get or save some data. The AOP module may also enter the picture in this layer and take care of cross-cutting concerns, including logging, transactional management, and security checks. An example could be where a service approach is encircled by a transaction border, making sure that any changes in the database would occur in an atomic manner.

Step 3: Data Access (Persistence Layer)

The application interacts with the database or other data storage systems in the Persistence Layer. These layers hold DAOs (Data Access Objects) or Repositories (often annotated with annotations) holding CRUD operations. These database interactions are commonly managed through the Spring JDBC, Spring ORM (Hibernate/JPA) or the Spring Data JPA and offer abstraction of raw JDBC code and lessen code.

Business Layer forwards its request to the Persistence Layer, which communicates with the database to read, write, or store data. When the business logic involves the retrieval of data, the data are sent back to the Business Layer.

Step 4: External System (Integration Layer) interaction.

In the event that the application requires connecting to external systems (e.g. making calls to third-party APIs, processing messages or connecting to other microservices), the Integration Layer will do so. This layer may utilize Spring Integration, Spring Messaging or Spring Web Services to deal with interactions with other services or systems. To give an example, in case the business logic in the Business Layer has to access external data, the Integration Layer makes a network call to the external service, obtains the data and forwards it to the Business Layer to be further processed.

Step 5: Go back to the Presentation Layer (Output)

Lastly, after the Business Layer and, possibly, Persistence Layer processes have been completed with the data, the output is fed back to the Controller within the Presentation Layer. This may be as a model object, or in the case of a RESTful API, as JSON data. The Controller then writes the necessary view (when there are web applications) or makes a reply (when there are RESTful services).

In case it is a web-based request, the response may be sent to a view template (e.g., JSP, Thymeleaf) where it will be rendered and made available to the user. In case of an API call, the information is formatted as an API response in either JSON or XML format. In the whole process, Core Layer (including Spring Core and Spring Context) is the one that deals with the beans and dependencies of the application, ensuring that all the elements are properly constructed and connected through DI. ApplicationContext is the main point of controlling the beans and settings to make sure that the different layers of the application are not tightly related but tightly integrated.

The process is also flawless as the Inversion of Control (IoC) and DI capabilities of Spring take care of the dependencies among various parts and levels of the application. The architecture permits flexibility in the configuration and expansion of the application, and so it is quite straightforward to substitute the parts or introduce new ones without affecting the remaining parts of the system.

Advantages of Spring MVC Architecture

1. Separation of concerns:
   - Clarity in the roles of Model, View, and Controller.
2. Flexibility:
   - Multiple view technologies (e.g., JSP, Thymeleaf, PDF, Excel).
3. Ease of testing:
   - Business logic and controllers can be tested separately.
4. Integration:
   - Can be easily interoperable with other modules of Spring, such as Spring Data, and so on.
5. Scalability:
   - Designed for modern web applications with robust request-handling capabilities.

This architecture ensures maintainability and extensibility, making it a widely used choice for web application development.

## 3.5 HTTP Request and HTTP Response

In a Spring web application, **HttpRequest** and **HttpResponse** objects play a critical role in handling client requests and sending back responses. These are standard objects in the Servlet API, but Spring MVC provides a more flexible way to work with them through **controllers** and **HandlerMappings**.

Flow of HTTP Request and HTTP Response in Spring MVC:

1. **Client sends HTTP request**:
   - A client (browser or any other HTTP client) sends an HTTP request to a Spring application. The request typically includes:
   - The **URL**(for routing).
   - **HTTP method** (GET, POST, etc.).
   - **Headers** (to specify content types, authentication, etc.).
   - **Body** (in case of POST, PUT requests containing data).
2. **DispatcherServlet**:
   - The **DispatcherServlet** is the front controller in the Spring MVC architecture. It is mapped to handle all incoming requests (configured in web.xml or Spring Boot auto-configures it for you).
   - The DispatcherServlet intercepts the HTTP request and forwards it to the appropriate **HandlerMapping** based on the request's **URL**.
3. **HandlerMapping**:
   - **HandlerMapping** is responsible for determining which controller should handle the request.
   - It maps the incoming HTTP request to a **Controller** or **Handler** method based on the URL and HTTP method.

4. **Controller**:
   - The controller method is invoked by Spring MVC. The HttpServletRequest and HttpServletResponse objects can be accessed directly as method arguments in the controller.

```
@RequestMapping("/greet")
public String greet(HttpServletRequest request, HttpServletResponse response) {
// You can manipulate request or response objects here
String name = request.getParameter("name");
response.setStatus(HttpServletResponse.SC_OK);
return "greetView";
}
```

- **HttpServletRequest** provides access to request parameters, headers, attributes, etc.
- **HttpServletResponse** is used to set response codes, headers, cookies, and content.

1. **ViewResolver**:
   - After the controller method executes, Spring MVC resolves the view to be used to render the response. It can be either a **JSP, HTML, Thymeleaf**, etc., depending on the configuration and return type of the controller.
   - The view is rendered, and the HTTP response body is populated with the data (e.g., HTML content, JSON).
2. **HTTP response sent to client**:
   - Once the view is rendered, the **HttpServletResponse** object is populated with the appropriate data. Spring then sends the response back to the client.
   - Response status (e.g., 200 OK, 404 Not Found).
   - Response headers (e.g., Content-Type, Cache-Control).
   - Response body (e.g., rendered HTML, JSON data).

Spring MVC provides an easy-to-use mechanism for handling HttpRequest and HttpResponse in a web application. The DispatcherServlet, acting as an interceptor, receives the request, decides what controller to pass it through and processes the response. It is very configurable and allows one to customize the way requests and responses are processed, and is all over the top of the underlying Servlet API.

For a non-web application using Spring (such as a Spring-based desktop application or a console application), the flow is slightly different because there is no web layer involved. DI and IoC still apply, and Spring manages beans and their lifecycle.

For a command-line application, the flow starts from the main method where Spring is initialized, beans are injected, business logic is executed, and the results are printed to the console.

## 3.6 Specific files in Spring MVC

In **Spring MVC architecture**, the layers consist of specific files that serve different purposes. Each layer is responsible for a certain aspect of the application's functionality.

1. **Presentation Layer (View Layer)**
   This layer is responsible for the User Interface (UI)and the presentation of the data. It receives user input, passes it to the controller, and displays the results.
   **Files in the Presentation Layer**:
   - **WEB-INF/web.xml**:
   - Configures the **DispatcherServlet** and other necessary web components like filters.
   - The **DispatcherServlet** is the main entry point for processing HTTP requests.
   - **WEB-INF/dispatcher-servlet.xml** (or Java-based configuration):
   - Configures Spring MVC-specific beans such as **view resolvers**, **handler mappings**, and **controllers**.
   - **View files** (JSP, Thymeleaf, etc.):
   - **JSP** files (or **Thymeleaf** templates) are responsible for rendering the final HTML view.
   - Stored under **/WEB-INF/views/** or configured path.
   - Example: **home.jsp**, **login.jsp**, etc.
   - **Static Resources**:
   - **CSS, JavaScript, and Images** files are stored in the **/static/** or **/public/** directories.
2. **Controller Layer**
   The **Controller Layer** manages user input, processes it, and returns a **ModelAndView** (data and view name) to the **DispatcherServlet**.
   **Files in the Controller Layer**:
   - **Controller Classes**:
   - Java classes annotated with @Controller or @RestController.
   - These classes handle HTTP requests and return appropriate responses.
   - Example: HomeController.java, LoginController.java, etc.
3. **Service Layer (Business Logic Layer)**
   The **Service Layer** contains the business logic of the application. It performs the necessary operations (like calculations, transformations, validations) and interacts with the **Persistence Layer** for data operations.
   **Files in the Service Layer**:
   - **Service Classes**:
   - Annotated with @Service.
   - Contain the business logic and serve as intermediaries between the **Controller Layer** and **Persistence Layer**.
   - Example: UserService.java, ProductService.java.
4. **Persistence Layer (DAO Layer)**
   The **Persistence Layer** interacts with the database and handles data storage, retrieval, and manipulation using **JPA**, **Hibernate**, or other data access technologies.
   **Files in the Persistence Layer**:
   - **Repository Classes**:
   - Classes annotated with @Repository (for JPA or Hibernate-based DAO).
   - Used to perform CRUD operations on the database.

- Example: UserRepository.java, ProductRepository.java.
- **Entity Classes**:
- Classes annotated with @Entity that represent database tables.
- Example: User.java, Product.java.
- **Configuration for Data Source**:
- In **application.properties** or **application.yml**, the configuration for connecting to the database (JDBC URL, username, password, etc.) is specified.

5. **Configuration Layer**
   The **Configuration Layer** contains classes and files responsible for application-wide configuration, such as database connections, bean definitions, and other application-wide settings.
   **Files in the Configuration Layer**:
   - **application.properties** or **application.yml**:
   - Used to configure beans, database connections, logging settings, and other properties required across the application.
   - **@Configuration classes**:
   - Java classes annotated with @Configuration where Spring Beans are defined and configured.
   - Example: AppConfig.java, WebConfig.java.
   - **pom.xml** or **build.gradle**:
   - Dependency management, plugin management, and lifecycle management of the Spring MVC application (Table 3–1)

It is a highly structured design that implements a clean separation of concerns, with each layer having a defined responsibility. This scaling method enables the application to be easier to manage, test, and scale.

**Table 3–1** Layers and their roles.

| Layer | Files | Role/action |
|---|---|---|
| Presentation Layer | WEB-INF/web.xml, dispatcher-servlet.xml, JSP files | Handle user input and present data (UI). |
| Controller Layer | Java classes annotated with @Controller, @RestController | Handle HTTP requests, call the Service Layer, return ModelAndView. |
| Service Layer | Java classes annotated with @Service | Contains business logic, call Persistence Layer for data manipulation. |
| Persistence Layer | Java classes annotated with @Repository, @Entity | Interact with the database, perform CRUD operations. |
| Configuration Layer | application.properties, pom.xml, @Configuration | Provide application-wide settings, bean configurations, and dependencies. |

*CRUD*, Create, Read, Update, Delete; *JSP*, JavaServer Pages.

## 3.7 Inversion of Control

IoC is a software development principle where object creation, configuration, and lifecycle management are delegated to a container or framework, rather than being done manually in the application.

Need for IoC in Spring:

1. Decoupling components:
   IoC helps to enforce loose coupling by controlling dependencies, which minimizes the dependency between the components.
2. Improved testability:
   Dependencies can be mocked or replaced using objects that are easily controlled externally to do unit testing.
3. Centralized configuration:
   IoC enables the central control of the creation of objects and dependencies, having a cleaner and more maintainable configuration.
4. Simplified code:
   The dependency creation and management code is smaller, and more emphasis is put on business logic.
5. Scalability and flexibility:

IoC provides more flexibility to changes in applications since dependencies can be changed outside the dependent class without modifying it.

Key characteristics of IoC:

1. Inversion of responsibility:
   The responsibility Inversion takes place when the initiator of a service is the one whose actions are being observed. The task of developing and maintaining objects is inverted and transferred to the IoC container.
2. Decoupling: Encourages loose coupling among the classes, because the dependencies are not created directly in the code.
3. Configuration management:

Brings configuration of objects (e.g., XML, annotations, Java-based configuration) into the center, rendering applications easier to maintain.

Examples of IoC Containers:

- Spring Framework: This consists of a powerful DI and lifecycle management IoC container.
- EJB Containers: Enterprise Java Beans (EJB) also has IoC.

Benefits of IoC:

1. Reduced code:
   The code is made easier since it does not need manual dependency management.
2. Enhanced testability:
   Mocks and replacements are easy to make dependencies, which makes it easy to unit test.

3. Flexibility:

   Enables configuration and dependency management of objects.
   4. Reusability:
   Encourages re-use and modularity.
   Types of IoC in Spring:
   Spring is a framework that supports two kinds of mechanisms of IoC:

1. Dependency injection:
   Under this mechanism, the dependencies reach objects in the container in the following ways:
   - Constructor injection: The dependencies are specified using the constructor.
   - Setter injection: Dependencies are established with the help of setter methods.
   - Field injection: The annotations are used to directly inject dependencies into fields (e.g., @Autowired).
2. Event-based IoC:

This entails object-to-object communication by events in which events are published and subscribed to by the relevant components. It allows dynamic behavior without binding the components tightly together.

**Specific types of IoC in Spring and their usage**

1. **Constructor Injection**
   - Dependencies are also given during the creation of the objects in the form of a class constructor.
   - Tended to use as mandatory dependencies to make sure that the object is fully initialized.
   - **Usage:**
   - Guarantees permanence with dependencies being given at the creation of the objects.

   **Syntax**:
   ```
   public class MyClass {
   private final Dependency dependency;
   // Constructor Injection
   public MyClass(Dependency dependency) {
   this.dependency = dependency;
   }
   }
   ```

2. **Setter Injection**
   - Dependencies are injected with public setter methods once the object has been created.
   - Appropriate for optional dependencies or where values have to change. **Usage:**
   - Allows dependencies to be partially initialized and changed.

- Offers flexibility of optional properties.

**Syntax**:

```
public class MyClass {
private Dependencydependency;
// Setter Injection
public void setDependency(Dependency dependency) {
this.dependency = dependency;
}
}
```

3. **Field Injection**
   - Dependencies are injected directly on the field of the classes with the annotations, such as those of the annotation @Autowired.
   - Eliminates the explicit setter or constructor methods.

   **Usage**:

   - Simple and concise for small projects or prototype-level development.
   - Should not be tested, since it makes it hard to mock dependencies.

   **Syntax**:

```
public class MyClass {
@Autowired
private Dependencydependency;
}
```

4. **Event-based IoC**
   - Components communicate by means of events. The IoC container also provides communication through publishing events to listeners.
   - Enables the separation of components through the rejection of the method call

   **Usage**:

   - Ideal in situations where dynamic behavior is needed, such as asynchronous processing or UI notification.
   - Typically used together with ApplicationEventPublisher and ApplicationListener.

**Syntax**:

```
// Event definition
public class CustomEvent extends ApplicationEvent {
public CustomEvent(Object source) {
super(source);
}
}
// Publisher
@Component
```

```
public class EventPublisher {
@Autowired
private ApplicationEventPublisherpublisher;
public void publishEvent() {
publisher.publishEvent(new CustomEvent(this));
}
}
// Listener
@Component
public class EventListener implements ApplicationListener<CustomEvent> {
@Override
public void onApplicationEvent(CustomEventevent) {
System.out.println("Event received: " + event);
}
}
```

**Working of IoC in Spring**

IoC is a design concept in the Spring framework to control the lifecycle of the objects (beans) and their dependencies. The object creation and dependency management are not provided in the application code, but in the IoC container. The IoC container is the focal point that configures, instantiates, and wires beans according to the configuration metadata of the application.

Spring has an IoC mechanism that operates in the following way:

1. Configuration metadata loading:
   The IoC container interprets the configuration metadata, which denotes the beans, their properties and relationships. This metadata may be made available either in XML files, Java annotations, or Java configuration classes.
2. Bean definition parsing
   The container reads the configuration in order to determine the classes that are to be instantiated, their dependencies and the nature of DI (constructor, setter, or field injection).
3. Bean instantiation:
   The beans are instantiated by the container depending on the metadata. In case there are dependencies on a bean, the container will address them at this stage.
4. Dependency injection:
   The IoC container injects the required dependencies into the beans as specified. This injection can be done via constructors, setters, or directly into fields using annotations like @Autowired.
5. Bean lifecycle management:
   The container manages the lifecycle of beans, including initialization (@PostConstruct or init-method), usage, and destruction (@PreDestroy or destroy-method).
6. Bean registry:
   All instantiated and wired beans are stored in the container's bean registry. When a bean is requested, the container retrieves it from this registry.

7. Application execution:

Once the container is initialized and beans are fully configured, the application can use these beans to perform business logic. The container ensures that beans are always in a ready-to-use state (Fig. 3–5)

**Flowchart: IoC working in Spring**

Here is a diagram to illustrate the working of IoC in Spring:

**Inversion of Control procedure**

The IoC mechanism in Spring allows the container to manage object creation, DI, and the lifecycle of objects (known as beans) (Fig. 3–6).

1. **Core components of IoC in Spring**
    - **IoC Container:** The heart of IoC in Spring, responsible for managing beans and their dependencies. Spring provides two types of IoC containers:
    - **BeanFactory:** A lightweight container, used for simple applications.
    - **ApplicationContext:** A more feature-rich container used for enterprise applications.
    - **Beans:** Objects managed by the IoC container. These are defined in the Spring configuration (XML, annotations, or Java-based).
    - **Configuration Metadata:** Defines how beans should be created, wired, and managed. Configuration can be:
    - XML-based
    - Annotation-based
    - Java-based
2. **Steps in the working of IoC**

    **Step 1: Read Configuration Metadata**
    - The IoC container reads the metadata (e.g., XML file, annotations, or Java config) to understand the beans, their properties, and dependencies.
    - Example: **XML configuration**
    - <bean class="com.example.MyClass">
    - <property name="dependency" ref="dependencyBean" />
    - </bean>
    - <bean class="com.example.Dependency" />

    **Step 2: Create and register Beans**

- The container scans the configuration and creates instances of all defined beans. These instances are stored in the container's **bean registry**.

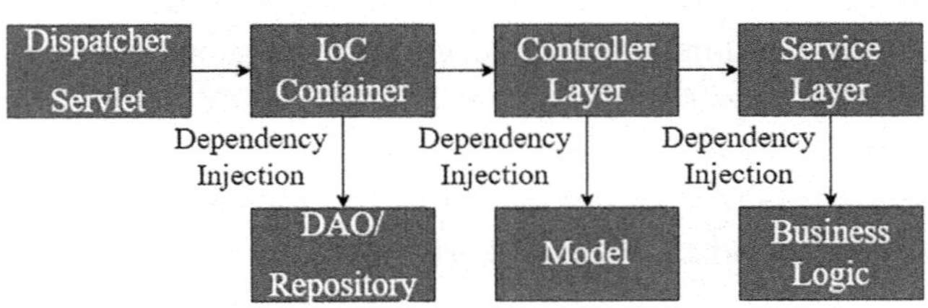


**FIGURE 3–5** Inversion of Control (*IoC*) working in Spring. *DAO*, Data Access Object.

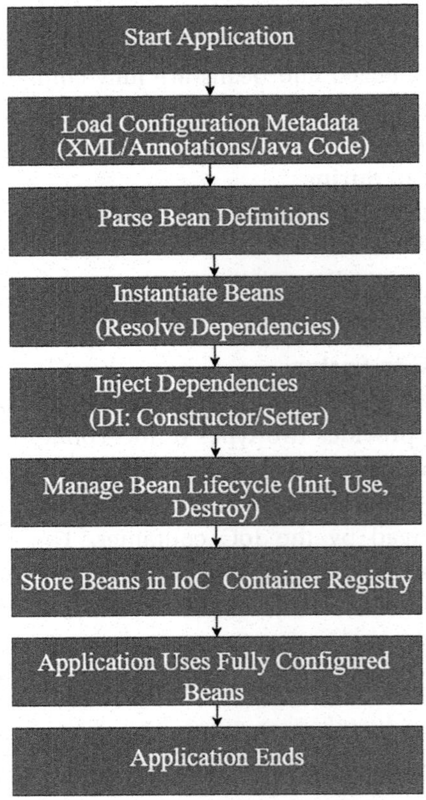


FIGURE 3–6 Inversion of Control (*IoC*) flowchart. *DI*, dependency injection.

**Step 3: Resolve dependencies**

- The IoC container identifies and resolves dependencies for each bean based on:
- **Constructor injection:** Inject dependencies through the bean's constructor.
- **Setter injection:** Use setter methods to inject dependencies.
- **Field injection:** Use annotations like @Autowired to inject dependencies into fields.

**Step 4: Manage Bean lifecycle**

- The IoC container manages the lifecycle of beans, which involves:
  1. **Instantiation:** Creating the bean.
  2. **Property setting:** Injecting dependencies.
  3. **Post-processing:** Applying custom logic (e.g., @PostConstruct methods).
  4. **Bean Initialization:** Calling initialization callbacks (e.g., init-method or InitializingBean).
  5. **Destruction:** Calling destruction callbacks (e.g., destroy-method or DisposableBean).

**Step 5: Provide Beans on request**

- When the application requests a bean from the container, it retrieves the corresponding object from the bean registry, fully configured and ready to use.

3. **Lifecycle management of Beans in IoC**
   - **Singleton scope:** A single instance of the bean is created and shared throughout the application.
   - **Prototype scope:** A new instance of the bean is created each time it is requested.
   - **Other scopes:** Request, Session, Application (used in web applications).

**Advantages of IoC**:

1. **Loose coupling:** Reduces direct dependencies between classes.
2. **Centralized configuration:** Makes it easier to manage and modify beans.
3. **Enhanced testability:** Facilitates dependency mocking for testing.
4. **Lifecycle management:** Automatically handles initialization and destruction of beans.

**Types of IoC containers in Spring: BeanFactory versus ApplicationContext**

Spring provides two primary types of IoC containers for managing beans and their dependencies: **BeanFactory**and**ApplicationContext**.Both are IoC containers, but vary in capabilities, scope, and applications.

1. **BeanFactory**

   The lowest level of IoC container in Spring is the Bean factory, which is used in simple dependencies. It sluggishly loads beans and offers the bare minimum of the IoC features.

   **Key characteristics**:
   - Lazy initialization: Beans are lazy-created and are not created until they are called upon (on-demand).
   - Minimal features: Does not offer advanced features such as event propagation, AOP, or internationalization.
   - Lightweight: It can be used where there is a constraint on memory or where the applications are straightforward.

   **Usage**:
   - Best used in resources where resource utilization is important, like mobile or embedded systems.
   - Only basic and standalone applications should be recommended.

   **Common implementations**:
   - XmlBeanFactory (Deprecated): Parses bean definitions to an XML file.

   **Example syntax**:

   ```
   Resource resource = new ClassPathResource("beans.xml");
   BeanFactory factory = new XmlBeanFactory(resource);
   MyClassobj = (MyClass) factory.getBean("myBean");
   ```

2. **ApplicationContext**

   ApplicationContext is a more feature-oriented IoC container, which is enterprise application-friendly. It is an extension of the Beanfactory.

**Key characteristics**:

- Eager initialization: Beans get generated upon the container start-up (default), and this is better for the performance of an application where the bean is used frequently.
- **Advanced features:** Provides:
- Event propagation
- Declarative AOP support
- Message resource handling (for internationalization)
- Application-layer context (web integration)
- **Integration support:** Easily integrates with Spring's MVC, security, and ORM modules.

**Usage**:

- Favored as an enterprise-level application that has complex features and integration abilities.

**Common implementations**:

- ClassPathXmlApplicationContext: Bean definitions in an XML file in the classpath are loaded.
- FileSystemXmlApplicationContext: Bean definitions are loaded in an XML file within the file system.
- AnnotationConfigApplicationContext: Loads bean definitions in classes that are configured using Java.

**Example syntax**:

ApplicationContext context = new ClassPathXmlApplicationContext("beans.xml");
MyClassobj = (MyClass) context.getBean("myBean"); Table 3–2

When to use:

- Use **BeanFactory**:
- For simple applications with limited memory and no need for advanced features.
- When it is necessary to use lazy-inited to maximize startup time.
- Use **ApplicationContext**:
- Applications of large-scale, enterprise level applications that need such features as event handling, internationalization, AOP, and integration with other Spring modules.

**Table 3–2** BeanFactory versus ApplicationContext Comparison.

| Feature | BeanFactory | ApplicationContext |
|---|---|---|
| Initialization | Lazy (on-demand) | Eager (at container startup) |
| Event handling | Not supported | Supported |
| AOP integration | Limited | Fully supported |
| Internationalization | Not supported | Supported |
| Resource management | Manual | Automatic |
| Web application support | Not suitable | Suitable for enterprise-level apps |
| Preferred usage | Lightweight or simple applications | Enterprise applications with advanced features |

*AOP*, Aspect-Oriented Programming.

## 3.8 Dependency injection

IoC is implemented by the use of a design pattern known as DI. In DI, the role of defining and injecting dependencies of an object is given to an outsourced entity (e.g., an IoC container) rather than the object itself. This enables the objects to concentrate only on their functionality as compared to dealing with dependencies. DI during Spring is done by injecting dependencies as constructors, setters or fields depending on configuration metadata (XML, annotations, or Java classes) (Table 3-3).

DI requirement.

1. Loose coupling:
   DI enhances decoupling between the parts of the code, which is more flexible and maintainable.
2. Improved testability:
   Dependencies can easily be mocked or easily replaced, which means smooth unit testing.
3. Centralized configuration: Dependencies are established in a single place (e.g., Spring configuration) and are easier to manage.
4. Reusability and maintainability: Components can also be used in other applications, as they do not have dependencies on themselves.
5. Decoupled object lifecycle:

   The IoC container creates and destroys objects, which enables improved control of resources.

   **Types of dependency injection in Spring**

   DI has three distinct types in spring; each type has peculiarities and areas of application.

These types are used to determine the way dependencies are injected into objects (beans) by the IoC container.

1. Constructor-based dependency injection.
   Dependencies are made available in the form of class constructors. The IoC container invokes the class constructor with the required dependencies as arguments.

**Table 3–3** Dependency injection (DI) and Inversion of Control (IoC) Difference.

| Aspect | DI | IoC |
|---|---|---|
| Definition | A specific design pattern for injecting dependencies into objects. | A broader principle where control of object creation and lifecycle is inverted. |
| Focus | Focuses on how dependencies are provided to an object. | Focuses on who controls the object creation and dependency management. |
| Implementation | DI is one of the ways to implement IoC. | IoC can be implemented using various patterns, including DI, service locators, etc. |
| Granularity | Granular, dealing with object-level dependencies. | High-level concept managing the entire application context. |
| Scope | Limited to dependency management. | Manages both dependency injection and the object lifecycle. |

**Key characteristics**:

- Mandatory dependencies are injected at the time of object creation.
- Ensures immutability since dependencies are final after the object is constructed.
- Commonly used for injecting required dependencies.

**Syntax**:
```
public class MyClass {
private Dependency dep;
public MyClass(Dependency dep) {
this.dep = dep; // Constructor Injection
}
}
```

2. **Setter-based dependency injection**

Dependencies are provided through public setter methods after the object is created. The IoC container calls the setter methods to inject the dependencies.

**Key characteristics**:

- Suitable for optional dependencies.
- Provides flexibility, as dependencies can be modified after the object is created.
- Used when objects have many optional properties.

**Syntax**:
```
public class MyClass {
private Dependency dep;
public void setDependency(Dependency dep) {
this.dep = dep; // Setter Injection
}
}
```

3. **Field-based dependency injection**

Dependencies are injected directly into the fields of a class using annotations such as @Autowired. This type is available only with annotation-based configuration.

**Key characteristics**:

- Simplifies code by eliminating the need for constructors or setter methods.
- Can inject private fields, but this may lead to reduced testability.
- Primarily used with annotations (@Autowired).

**Syntax**:
```
public class MyClass {
@Autowired
private Dependency dep; // Field Injection
}
```
Table 3–4

**Configuration of dependency injection types in Spring**

Spring provides multiple ways to configure DI using XML, annotations, or Java-based configurations.

**Table 3–4** Dependency injection types comparison.

| Type | Use case | Advantages | Disadvantages |
|---|---|---|---|
| Constructor | For mandatory, immutable dependencies. | Ensures all required dependencies are provided. | Not suitable for many optional properties. |
| Setter | For optional or modifiable dependencies. | Flexible and easy to modify after creation. | May lead to incomplete or inconsistent state. |
| Field | For simple configurations with annotations. | Simplifies code and avoids boilerplate. | Reduces testability and breaks encapsulation. |

1. **Constructor-based dependency injection**
   **XML configuration**:
   In XML configuration, the dependencies are injected using the <constructor-arg> element.

```
<bean class="com.example.MyClass">
<constructor-arg ref="dependency" />
</bean>
<bean class="com.example.Dependency" />
```

- The <constructor-arg> element specifies which dependency (bean) to inject into the constructor of MyClass.
  **Annotation configuration**:

  For constructor-based DI with annotations, use @Autowired on the constructor.

```
@Component
public class MyClass {
private final Dependency dependency;
@Autowired
public MyClass(Dependency dependency) {
this.dependency = dependency; // Constructor Injection
}
}
```

- Spring will automatically detect and inject the required dependency when the bean is created.
  **Java-based configuration**:

  In Java-based configuration, use @Bean and constructor injection via constructor parameters.

```
@Configuration
public class AppConfig {
@Bean
public MyClassmyClass() {
return new MyClass(dependency()); // Constructor Injection
}
@Bean
```

```
public Dependency dependency() {
return new Dependency();
}
}
```

2. **Setter-based dependency injection**
   **XML configuration**:

   In XML configuration, setter-based DI is configured using the <property> element.

```
<bean class="com.example.MyClass">
<property name="dependency" ref="dependency" />
</bean>
<bean class="com.example.Dependency" />
```

   - The <property> element specifies which property of the MyClass bean will have its setter method called to inject the dependency.
     **Annotation configuration**:
     With annotations, setter-based DI is configured using @Autowired on the setter method.

```
@Component
public class MyClass {
private Dependency dependency;
@Autowired
public void setDependency(Dependency dependency) {
this.dependency = dependency; // Setter Injection
}
}
```

   - Spring will call the setter method to inject the dependency automatically.
     **Java-based configuration**:

     In Java configuration, setter-based DI can be configured via setter methods.

```
@Configuration
public class AppConfig {
@Bean
public MyClassmyClass() {
MyClassmyClass = new MyClass();
myClass.setDependency(dependency()); // Setter Injection
return myClass;
}
@Bean
public Dependency dependency() {
return new Dependency();
}
}
```

**Table 3–5** Dependency injection (DI) configuration methods.

| DI type | XML configuration | Annotation configuration | Java-based configuration |
|---|---|---|---|
| Constructor-based | <constructor-arg ref="dependency" /> | @Autowired on constructor | @Bean with constructor parameters |
| Setter-based | <property name="dependency" ref="dependency" /> | @Autowired on setter method | Manually call setter in @Bean method |
| Field-based | Not directly supported in XML | @Autowired on fields | Enabled by @ComponentScan with @Autowired fields |

3. **Field-based dependency injection**
   **XML configuration**:

   Field injection cannot be configured directly in XML because XML relies on method-based configuration (either constructor or setter). It is possible to configure field injection using annotations and scanning.
   **Annotation configuration**:

   In annotation-based configuration, field-based DI is configured using @Autowired directly on the fields.

```
@Component
public class MyClass {
@Autowired
private Dependency dependency; // Field Injection
}
```

   - Spring will inject the dependency directly into the field when the bean is created.
     **Java-based configuration**:

     With Java-based configuration, field injection can be configured using reflection or by enabling component scanning.

```
@Configuration
@ComponentScan(basePackages = "com.example")
public class AppConfig {
// No need to manually configure field injection in Java-based config.
}
```

   - By enabling component scanning (@ComponentScan), Spring automatically injects the dependencies into the fields annotated with @Autowired (Table 3–5).

## 3.9 Aspect-Oriented Programming in Spring

AOP in Spring is a powerful feature that allows you to define and modularize cross-cutting concerns (like logging, transaction management, security, etc.) separately from the core business logic of your application. By using AOP, you can apply the same behavior to multiple parts of your application without repeating the code, thus making the code cleaner, more maintainable, and easier to manage.

Spring AOP is implemented using the proxy-based approach. In Spring, AOP is primarily used to implement "cross-cutting concerns" like:

- Logging
- Transaction management
- Security
- Performance monitoring
- Exception handling

With Spring AOP, you can inject additional behavior into your existing code in a declarative way without modifying the code itself.

**Categories of AOP in Spring**

AOP in Spring involves several important concepts that help define how cross-cutting concerns are implemented. These include:

1. **Aspect**
2. **Join Point**
3. **Pointcut**
4. **Advice**
5. **Weaving**
6. **Target Object (or Join Point Target)**
7. **Proxy**

1. **Aspect**:
   An **Aspect** is a modularized cross-cutting concern. It is a class that contains logic related to a specific concern (e.g., logging, transaction handling, or performance monitoring) that cuts across multiple classes. The aspect is applied to specific methods or classes in the application.
   - In Spring, an aspect is usually defined as a class annotated with @Aspect.
2. **Join point**:
   A **join point** is a point in the execution flow of the application where an aspect can be applied. It represents a specific location in the program, such as the execution of a method, object construction, field access, etc. In Spring AOP, the join point is typically method execution.
3. **Pointcut**:
   A **pointcut** is an expression that defines the conditions under which an aspect should be applied. It is used to match specific join points. A pointcut defines which methods will be intercepted by the aspect. It is often specified using AspectJ's expression language or Spring AOP annotations.
   - Example of pointcut expression: execution(com.example.service.(.)) which matches all methods in com.example.service package.

4. **Advice**:
   **Advice** is the action or logic that gets executed at a specific join point (as defined by the pointcut). There are several types of advice, each executed at different points in the join point lifecycle:
   - **Before Advice**: Executes before the target method.
   - **After Advice**: Executes after the target method execution, regardless of its outcome.
   - **After Returning Advice**: Executes after the target method returns successfully.
   - **After Throwing Advice**: Executes if the target method throws an exception.
   - **Around Advice**: Surrounds the target method execution. It can decide whether to proceed with the method execution, modify the result, or even skip the method execution entirely.
5. **Weaving**:
   **Weaving** is the process of linking aspects with the target objects to create a new proxy object. This happens at different times:
   - **Compile-time Weaving**: Done when the source code is compiled.
   - **Load-time Weaving**: Done when the classes are loaded into the JVM.
   - **Runtime Weaving**: In Spring, this weaving happens at runtime using dynamic proxies.
6. **Target Object (or Join Point Target)**:
   The **Target Object** is the object to which the aspect is applied. This object contains the method execution (or other join points) that the aspect will modify.
7. **Proxy**:
   A **Proxy** is a wrapper around the target object. In Spring AOP, proxies are created at runtime using dynamic proxy generation. These proxies allow Spring AOP to apply the advice (cross-cutting concerns) to the target object.
   - **JDK Dynamic Proxies**: Used when the target object implements an interface.
   - **CGLIB Proxies**: Used when the target object does not implement an interface (i.e., a subclass is created).

**Categories of AOP Advice in Spring**

Spring AOP defines several types of advice, each executed at different stages of a method execution:

1. **Before Advice**:
   - Runs **before** the target method is invoked.
   - It cannot prevent the method execution.
2. **After Advice**:
   - Runs **after** the target method, regardless of the method's success or failure.
3. **After Returning Advice**:
   - Runs **after** the target method completes successfully (i.e., without throwing exceptions).
4. **After Throwing Advice**:
   - Runs **after** the target method throws an exception.
5. **Around Advice**:
   - Surrounds the target method invocation. It has full control over whether the method is executed or not.

- It can modify the return value or handle exceptions.
- It is the most powerful type of advice, as it can prevent the method from being called.

## 3.10 Spring modules

The **Spring Framework** is designed to address several key needs in enterprise application development. Each **Spring module** serves a specific purpose to simplify different aspects of application development, making it easier to build, maintain, and scale applications. List of **Spring modules**:

1. **Core container modules**
   The modules are the most fundamental ones in the Spring Framework:
   a. Spring Core module:
      - It is the basic component of the Spring Framework. It offers the fundamental functionality required by Spring, which includes:
        o BeanFactory: The main interface of Spring IoC container. o DI: A dependency management between objects. o IoC: The main principle of Spring container, which is to transfer the power of creating and controlling objects to the framework rather than the application.

   b. Spring Beans module:
      For example, beans will be managed in the Spring IoC container by this module. • It offers bean lifecycle management functionality, DI features and bean configuration either through XML or annotations.

   c. Spring Context module:
      The Spring Context module is based on the core module and offers a richer version of the IoC container.
      It promotes internationalization, propagation of events, integrations using application layer, and configuration to the environment.
      ApplicationContext interface is the interface around which this module will center, and this interface is the one that will initialize beans and the way they will interact.

   d. Spring Expression Language (SpEL):
      Object graphs: Object graphs can be queried and manipulated by SpEL. • It is incredibly popular with Spring setups (XML, annotations, etc.) and can provide dynamically loaded values into an object.

2. **Access/integration modules of data.**
   These modules offer full support in dealing with databases and integrating with other enterprise systems:
   a. Java Database Connectivity module:
      - Makes it easier to work with relational databases with JDBC (Java Database Connectivity). It comes with support of JDBC templates, exception translation, and connection pooling.

b. Object-Relational Mapping module:
   - Offers support to integrate with the popular Object-Relational Mapping (ORM) frameworks such as Hibernate, JPA, and JDO.
   - It provides an ORM configuration simplification and transaction management in Spring.

c. Java Message Service module:
   - Allows message integration and queue management through Java Message Service (JMS).
   - It gives JMS template and listener containers to make working with JMS easier.

d. Transactions module:
   - Declarative and programmatic transaction management to integrate with JDBC, JPA, Hibernate, JMS, and others.

     Spring is used to manage transactions in both distributed and local transactions.

3. **Web modules**

   These modules are aimed at web application construction and support of enterprise functionality of the RESTful services and integration with popular web frameworks:

   a. **Spring Web module**:
      - Offers the basic platform for creating web applications with Servlets.
      - Has DispatcherServlet, which forwards the HTTP requests to the relevant handler beans.

   b. **Spring Web MVC module**:
      - An advanced Model-View-Controller (MVC) web application architecture.
      - It has characteristics such as controller control, view resolution, and form control.

   c. **Spring Web Flow module**:
      - Provides support for **web flows**, allowing the management of the state of web applications and orchestrating complex page flows.
      - Used for **stateful web applications** with complex workflows.

   d. **Spring WebSocket module**:
      - Provides integration with **WebSockets**, allowing real-time, bidirectional communication between the client and the server.
      - Supports **websocket endpoints** and **message broker** for communication.

   e. **Spring REST (Spring Web Services) module**:
      - Supports building **RESTful services** with annotations and easy integration with Spring-based applications.
      - Includes **REST controllers, message converters**, and **request/response mapping**.

4. **Aspect-Oriented Programming module**
   - AOP in Spring is used to separate **cross-cutting concerns** (such as logging, transaction management, and security) from business logic.
   - It allows developers to define **aspects** that can be applied to different parts of an application.
   - Spring AOP is based on **dynamic proxies** and works in combination with other modules to manage concerns such as **logging**, **security**, and **transactions**.

5. **Security module**
   - Provides support for **authentication** and **authorization**.
   - It includes **security filters**, **authentication providers**, and **role-based access control (RBAC)**.
   - Integrates with multiple security protocols such as **LDAP**, **OAuth2**, and **JWT** for securing web applications and APIs.
6. **Testing module**
   - The Spring **Testing** module is used to write unit and integration tests for Spring-based applications.
   - It provides **JUnit** and **TestNG** integration and simplifies writing tests using **mocking** and **dependency injection**.
   - It has the annotation of running the Spring Boot tests with the annotation of SpringBootTest.
7. **Messaging module**
   - It is a module of integration with message brokers and queue-based systems such as RabbitMQ, ActiveMQ, or Kafka.
   - It supports **JMS**, **AMQP**, **Kafka**, and **STOMP** messaging protocols.
8. **Spring Boot**
   - While not a core module of the traditional Spring Framework, **Spring Boot** simplifies Spring-based application development by providing:
   - **Auto-configuration**: Automatically configures the application based on the dependencies.
   - **Embedded servers**: Includes embedded **Tomcat**, **Jetty**, and **Undertow** for running web applications without needing an external server.
   - **Spring Boot Starter**: Provides a collection of pre-configured dependencies for different tasks (e.g., web development, data access, etc.).
9. **Spring Cloud**
   - Spring Cloud is a set of tools and modules designed for building **cloud-native applications** and microservices.
   - It provides integration with **cloud platforms** (e.g., AWS, Azure), **service discovery**, **configuration management**, **circuit breakers**, and more.
10. **Spring Data**
    - The **Spring Data** module simplifies **data access** and integration with various **databases** (relational, NoSQL).
    - It includes projects like **Spring Data JPA**, **Spring Data MongoDB**, **Spring Data Redis**, etc., to provide easier data access through repositories and simplified queries.

## 3.11 Spring Beans

In Spring, a **Bean** is an object that is managed by the **Spring IoC container**. These beans are the fundamental building blocks of a Spring application. Beans can be any Java object that is created, configured, and managed by the Spring container.

The process of **bean creation** is defined by **DI**, and the lifecycle of a bean is controlled by the Spring container.

### Categories of Spring Beans

Spring beans can be categorized based on their **lifecycle** and **scope**.

1. **Based on lifecycle**

   a. **Singleton Bean**

   - A Singleton bean is the default scope for Spring beans. Only one instance of the bean is created and shared across the entire Spring container.
   - Singleton beans are used when you need a single, shared instance of a bean across multiple requests.

   **Syntax**:

   ```
   <bean class="com.example.MyClass" scope="singleton"/>
   ```

   or using annotations:

   ```
   @Component
   @Scope("singleton")
   public class MyClass { }
   ```

   b. **Prototype Bean**

   - A new instance of the bean is created every time it is requested from the container.
   - Prototype beans are useful when you want a new instance each time, for example, for stateful objects.

   **Syntax**:

   ```
   <bean class="com.example.MyClass" scope="prototype"/>
   ```

   or using annotations:

   ```
   @Component
   @Scope("prototype")
   public class MyClass { }
   ```

   c. **Request Bean (Web Context)**

   - This scope is used for request-scoped beans in web applications.

   **Syntax**:

   ```
   <bean class="com.example.MyClass" scope="request"/>
   ```

   or using annotations:

   ```
   @Component
   @Scope("request")
   public class MyClass { }
   ```

   d. **Session Bean (Web Context)**

   - This scope is used when you need to store data for the entire duration of a user's session.

   **Syntax**:

   ```
   <bean class="com.example.MyClass" scope="session"/>
   ```

   or using annotations:

```
@Component
@Scope("session")
public class MyClass { }
```

e. **Application Bean (Web Context)**
- A new bean is created for the entire **servlet context** (i.e., for the entire web application).
- It's used when you want a bean that will live for the entire duration of the web application.

**Syntax**:
```
<bean class="com.example.MyClass" scope="application"/>
```
or using annotations:
```
@Component
@Scope("application")
public class MyClass { }
```

f. **Custom Scope Bean**
- You can create a custom scope for your Spring beans by implementing the Scope interface.
- This is used when you want a scope that doesn't fit into the standard scopes (singleton, prototype, etc.).

**Syntax**: Define a custom scope using configuration or annotations.
```
@Component
@Scope("custom")
public class MyClass { }
```

2. **Based on Bean configuration type**

a. **XML-based configuration**
- Beans are defined in **XML configuration files**.
- Traditional Spring application configuration.

**Syntax**:
```
<beans xmlns="http://www.springframework.org/schema/beans"
xmlns:xsi="http://www.w3.org/2001/XMLSchema-instance"
xsi:schemaLocation="http://www.springframework.org/schema/beans
http://www.springframework.org/schema/beans/spring-beans-3.0.xsd">
<bean class="com.example.MyClass">
<property name="property" value="value"/>
</bean>
</beans>
```

b. **Annotation-based configuration**
- Beans are defined using **annotations** in Java classes, which are scanned by Spring.
- It's a more modern, concise configuration style that uses **@Component**, **@Service**, **@Repository**, **@Controller**, etc.

**Syntax**:

```
@Component
public class MyClass {
@Autowired
private AnotherClassanotherClass;
}
```

c. **Java-based configuration (Java Config)**
   - Beans are configured using Java classes with **@Configuration** and **@Bean** annotations.
   - A more flexible and type-safe configuration approach using Java code.

   **Syntax:**

```
@Configuration
public class AppConfig {
@Bean
public MyClassmyBean() {
return new MyClass();
}
}
```

3. **Spring Bean lifecycle categories**
   a. **Instantiating Bean**
      - The bean is created by the Spring container during initialization.
      - **Lifecycle Method**: @PostConstruct, init-method
   b. **Initializing Bean**
      - The bean is initialized after it is created and its dependencies are injected.
      - **Lifecycle Method**: @PostConstruct, init-method
   c. **Destroying Bean**
      - The bean is destroyed when the container is shut down or the scope of the bean ends.
      - **Lifecycle method**: @PreDestroy, destroy-method

**Spring beans configuration**

Configuring Spring beans in a specific context depends on how you want to manage their lifecycle, scope, and dependencies.

1. **XML-based configuration**

   In XML-based configuration, beans are defined in an XML file and can be configured with properties, constructor arguments, and DIs.

   a. **Bean configuration in Singleton Scope (Default)**

      Singleton is the default scope, so if you do not specify the scope, it will create only one instance of the bean.

b. **Bean configuration in Prototype Scope**
   A new instance of the bean will be created every time it's requested from the container.
   **Example:**

```
<bean class="com.example.MyClass" scope="prototype"/>
```

c. **Bean configuration with Constructor Injection**
   You can define dependencies to be injected into the bean through its constructor.
d. **Bean configuration with Property Injection**
   You can inject dependencies through setter methods or directly into fields (when using annotations).

2. **Annotation-based configuration**
   With annotation-based configuration, Spring uses classpath scanning to automatically detect beans and their dependencies. Beans can be configured using annotations like **@Component, @Service, @Repository**, etc.
   a. **Defining a Bean with @Component**
      This is a general-purpose annotation used to define beans in Spring.

      **Example**:

```
@Component
public class MyClass {
// Class body
}
```

   b. **Defining a Bean with @Scope (Singleton, Prototype, etc.)**
      You can specify the scope of the bean using the @Scope annotation.

      **Example**:

```
@Component
@Scope("prototype")
public class MyClass {
// Class body
}
```

   c. **Defining a Bean with @Autowired (Dependency Injection)**
      Use @Autowired to inject dependencies into a bean.

      **Example**:

```
@Component
public class MyClass {
@Autowired
private AnotherClassanotherClass;
}
```

   d. **Defining Beans for Specialization with @Service, @Repository, @Controller**
      These annotations are specialized forms of **@Component** used to indicate the role of the bean in the application.

**Example:**

```
@Service
public class MyService {
// Service logic
}
@Repository
public class MyRepository {
// Data Access logic
}
@Controller
public class MyController {
// Web Controller logic
}
```

3. **Java-based configuration (Java Config)**
   In Java-based configuration, Spring beans are defined using Java classes annotated with **@Configuration** and the **@Bean** annotation to define bean methods.
   a. **Defining a Bean using @Configuration and @Bean**
      You can define beans in Java config files and configure their dependencies.
   b. **Defining Beans with Constructor Injection in Java Config**
      You can configure constructor-based DI.
   c. **Defining Beans with Setter Injection in Java Config**
      If you want to use setter-based DI, you can configure it as follows:

      **Example**:
```
@Configuration
public class AppConfig {
@Bean
public MyClassmyClass() {
MyClassmyClass = new MyClass();
myClass.setSomeProperty("Some value");
return myClass;
}
}
```

   d. **Scope in Java Config (Prototype, Singleton, etc.)**
      You can configure the scope of beans in Java config using @Scope.

      **Example**:
```
@Configuration
public class AppConfig {
@Bean
@Scope("prototype")
```

```
public MyClassmyClass() {
return new MyClass();
}
}
```

4. **Profiles in Spring**
   You can define beans for different environments or profiles using @Profile.
   a. **Defining Beans for Specific Profiles**

   With profiles, you can define beans for different environments (e.g., development, production).
   **Spring Bean contexts**
   The most common contexts to configure Spring beans:

- **ApplicationContext**: The central interface to provide configuration for Spring-based applications. It is used for retrieving beans and setting their configurations.
- ClassPathXmlApplicationContext (XML-based configuration)
- AnnotationConfigApplicationContext (Annotation-based configuration)
- GenericWebApplicationContext (Web-based applications)
- **WebApplicationContext**: Used in web applications. Beans are scoped to HTTP requests or sessions, and it also integrates with Spring MVC.

## Bibliography

IBM. (2024). MVC architecture overview. https://www.ibm.com/docs

Oracle. (2024). HTTP protocol overview. https://developer.mozilla.org/en-US/docs/Web/HTTP

Spring. (2024). AOP documentation. https://docs.spring.io/spring-framework/reference/core/aop/

Spring. (2024). Dependency injection docs. https://docs.spring.io

Spring. (2024). IoC container docs. https://docs.spring.io/spring-framework/reference/core/beans/

Spring. (2024). Spring MVC documentation. https://docs.spring.io/spring-framework/reference/web/webmvc/

Walls, C. (2022). *Spring in action*. Simon and Schuster, 3–459.

4

# Understanding Hibernate Object-Relational Mapping

## 4.1 Hibernate Object-Relational Mapping

Hibernate Object-Relational Mapping (ORM) is a framework that gives a connection between the object-oriented domain model and the relational database. Hibernate provides the transformation of Java objects into SQL statements to facilitate the CRUD (Create, Read, Update, Delete) operations as well as the converse.

## 4.2 Hibernate Object-Relational Mapping architecture

Hibernate ORM architecture can be designed in a way that it is able to manage interaction between Java and relational databases, and it consists of several major components that interact with one another to make the work of data management easier.

Hibernate ORM architecture flowchart

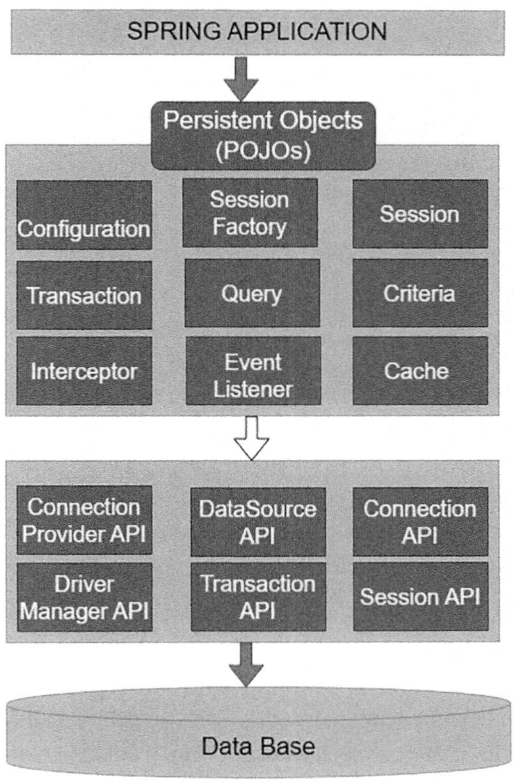


Mastering Java Full Stack Development. DOI: https://doi.org/10.1016/B978-0-443-51683-2.00009-6

Figure Hibernate ORM architecture

### 4.2.1 Core components of Hibernate Object-Relational Mapping

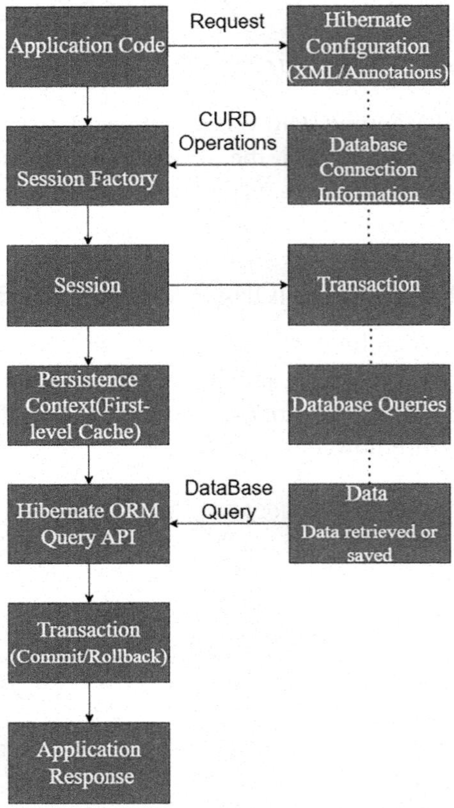


1. Configuration:
   - This component reads and processes configuration files such as hibernate.cfg.xml or hibernate.properties. It has database connection information, Hibernate property, and class mapping.
   - Key Responsibilities:
     - Load database settings (URL, username, password, dialect, etc.).
     - Specify mappings of entity classes to database tables.
   - Example Syntax:

```
<hibernate-configuration>
<session-factory>
<property name="hibernate.connection.url">jdbc:mysql://localhost:3306/mydb</property>
<property name="hibernate.connection.username">root</property>
```

```
<property name="hibernate.connection.password">password</property>
<property name="hibernate.dialect">org.hibernate.dialect.MySQLDialect</property>
</session-factory>
</hibernate-configuration>
```

2. SessionFactory:
   - It is a Session object factory, which offers a thread-safe means of managing database sessions.
   - Key Responsibilities:
     - Create Session instances for database interactions.
     - Cache data for better performance (second-level caching).
   - Initialization:
     - Built once during application startup and used throughout the application's lifecycle.
   - Example Syntax:

```
sessionfactoryscessionfactory=new Configuration.
.configure("hibernate.cfg.xml")
.buildSessionFactory();
```

3. Session:
   - A lightweight, one-thread database interaction object.
   - Key Responsibilities:
     - Perform CRUD operations on database entities.
     - Manage the transaction context.
     - Provide methods like save(), update(), delete(), and get().
   - Example Syntax:

```
Session session=sessionFactory.openSession();
Transaction tx=session.beginTransaction();
// Perform operations
session.save(entity);
tx.commit();
session.close();
```

4. Transaction:
   - Boundaries of transaction in the database and atomicity of the operations are enforced.
   - Key Responsibilities:
     - Commit, roll back, or start transactions.
     - Assure reliable and consistent database state.
   - Example Syntax:

```
Transaction transaction=session.beginTransaction;
session.save(entity);
transaction.commit();
```

5. Query and Criteria API:
    - Offers ways of querying the database.
    - Query API:
        - Used to either run HQL (Hibernate Query Language) or native SQL queries.
    - Criteria API:
        - Applied in developing queries in an object-oriented way.
    - Example Syntax:

      HQL Query:

```
Query query=session.createQuery("FROM Employee WHERE id=:id");
query.setParameter("id", 1);
List results=query.list();
Criteria API:
Criteriabuildercb=session getcriteriabuilder;
CriteriaQuery <Employee>cq=cb.createQuery(Employee.class);
Root <Employee> root=cq.from(Employee.class);
cq.select(root).where(cb.equal(root.get("id"), 1));
List <Employee>results=session. createQuery (cq). getResultList();
```

6. Entity:
    - Represents a Java class corresponding to a database relation.
    - Key Responsibilities:
        - Specify database table structure and relationship in annotations or XML.
    - Example Syntax:

```
@Entity
@Table(name="EMPLOYEE")
public class Employee {
@Id
GeneratedValue(strategy=GenerationType.IDENTITY)
private Long id;
@Column(name="NAME")
private String name;
// Getters and Setters
}
```

7. Hibernate Query Language (HQL):
    - The Hibernate object-oriented query language to become familiar with the objects, rather than database tables.

- Key Responsibilities:
  - Simplify complex queries that involve an object reference.
- Example Syntax:
  String hql="FROM Employee WHERE name=:name;
  Query query=session.createQuery(hql);
  query.setParameter("name", "rani");
  List results=query.list();

8. Cache:
   - Hibernate has two caching levels to maximize performance:
     - First-Level Cache: By default, session-level cache that is turned on by default.
     - Second-Level Cache: Optional cache that stores information between sessions.
   - Key Responsibilities:
     - Equalize the database hits.
9. Connection Provider:
   - Purpose:
     - Ensures the database connection pool.
   - Key Responsibilities:
     - Make database connections efficient.
10. Interceptor:
    - Purpose:
      - Event processing, such as save, delete, update, etc.

- Example Syntax:
  sessionFactory.withOptions().interceptor(new MyInterceptor()).openSession();
  Hibernate ORM elements collaborate in order to abstract the database operation, ease the development, and guarantee a solid performance.

# 4.3 Hibernate Object-Relational Mapping architecture

## 4.3.1 Layers in Hibernate ORM architecture

The Hibernate ORM architecture can be split into a number of layers that help in the process of data management and communication with the database.

1. Configuration Layer:
   - This layer reads the details of the Hibernate configuration (typically of the hibernate.cfg.xml file or annotations) and sets the connection properties to the database. It contains such settings as database dialect, JDBC driver, and connection pooling configuration.

2. SessionFactory Layer:
   - This is a thread-safe object that creates Session objects. It is set up once and applied throughout the application.
   - It is also a factory of Session objects and offers means of configuring and optimizing database connections.
3. Session Layer:
   - A Session is a unit of work of communicating with the database. It is applied to CRUD operations.
   - The Session also offers cache through Persistence Context (first-level cache) to minimize interactions with the database.
4. Transaction Layer:
   - This layer handles the transaction limits (begin, commit, and rollback). It also guarantees consistency and integrity of the data because it makes sure that either there is full success or rollback of database operations in case of an error.
   - Session objects are linked with transaction objects to manage the activities of databases.
5. Query Layer:
   - The interaction with the database is done by the Query layer by way of HQL or Criteria Queries.
6. Persistence Layer:
   - The Persistence layer is charged with the role of maintaining the object state. Hibernate converts the Java objects into the database tables and is used to assure that the modifications in the Java objects are reflected in the database.
   - This layer operates with the Session and Transaction layers to execute CRUD operations while maintaining a synchronization of changes with the database.
7. JDBC Layer:
   - The JDBC layer will communicate with the database.
8. Application Layer:
   - The Business logic is located in the Application layer.
   - The Application layer interacts with the Hibernate ORM framework and manages database interactions with the help of the SessionFactory, the Session, and the Transaction layers.

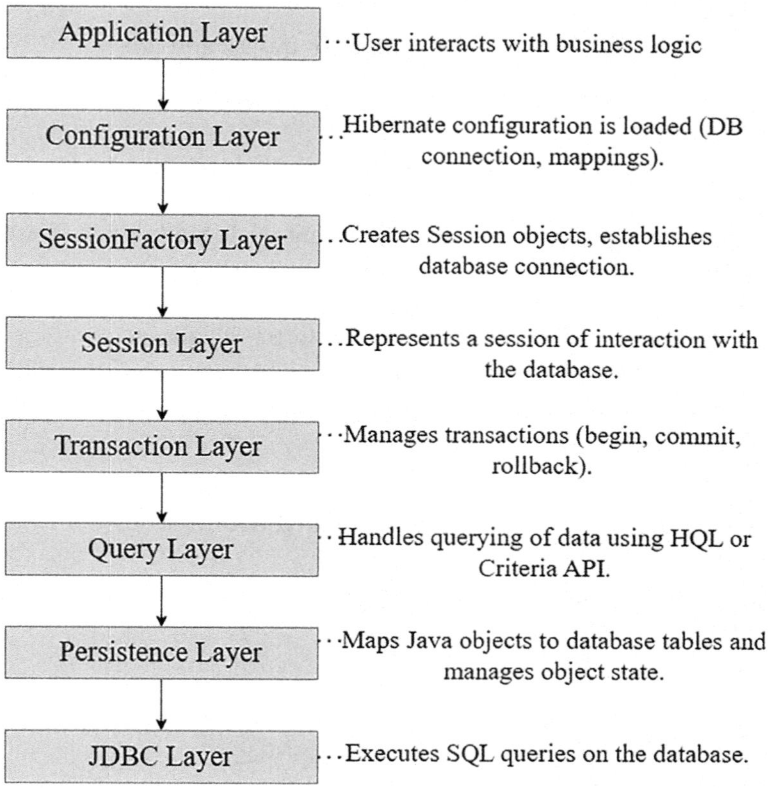


## 4.4 Hiberante Object-Relational Mapping lifecycle

The following are the description of Hibernate lifecycle and the flowchart:

### 4.4.1 One ensures that the hardware is set up to support the software

1. Configuration and Initialization:
   - The Hibernate system begins with configuration. This usually entails the generating of a SessionFactory by Hibernate configuration files (hibernate.cfg.xml or annotations).
2. Session Creation:
   - To create a session, one calls the openSession method of the SessionFactory. The interface of the application and the database is primarily the session.
3. Transaction Start:
   - Hibernate also involves transactions in order to do any operations in the database. In order to start a transaction, the session invokes the beginTransaction method.

### 4.4.2 Create, Read, Update Delete operations

The various operations that can be done within the transaction are:

- Save/Update: Writing or revising objects in the database with such actions as save, update, or saveOrUpdate.
- Fetch: Get the entities of the database through HQL (Hibernate Query Language) or Criteria API.
- Delete: By removing objects in a database using such methods as delete()Transaction Commit/Rollback:
  - If all operations are successful, the transaction is committed using the commit() method. This makes all changes permanent in the database.
  - If any issue arises, the transaction can be rolled back using the rollback() method, undoing any changes made during the transaction.

### 4.4.3 Session closure

- After the transaction is either committed or rolled back, the session is closed using the close() method.
- This step is important to release database connections and free up resources.

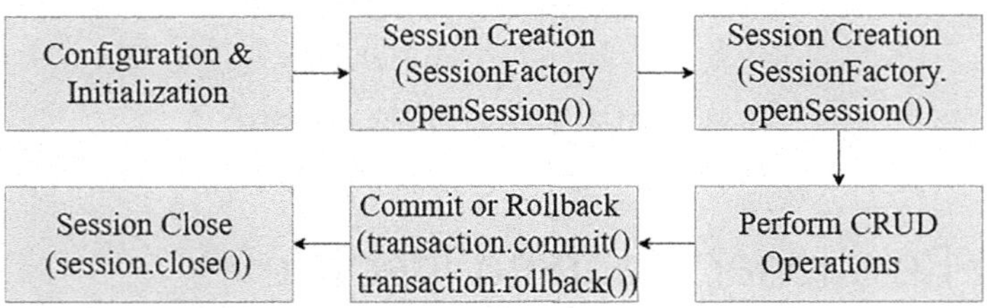


### 4.4.4 Components of the flow

1. Configuration and Initialization:
   - Hibernate is configured using a configuration file (hibernate.cfg.xml) or annotations. This step initializes the SessionFactory object that will handle database connections.
2. Session Creation:
   - A Session object is created from the SessionFactory. The Session object is used for all interactions with the database.
3. Start Transaction:
   - Before any database operation is performed, a transaction is started. This transaction ensures that all database operations within it are handled atomically.
4. Perform CRUD Operations:
   - The application performs various database operations using the session. These operations are generally related to the persistence of Java objects (CRUD).

5. Commit or Rollback:
   - Once the CRUD operations are complete, the transaction is either committed (if successful) or rolled back (if an error occurs). This step ensures data consistency and integrity.
6. Session Close:
   - After the transaction is finished, the session is closed to release resources, such as database connections, and to avoid memory leaks.

## 4.5 Spring Hibernate Object-Relational Mapping configuration

1. Hibernate ORM Configuration:

**(a) Hibernate Configuration File** (hibernate.cfg.xml)

This file provides basic configurations for Hibernate ORM, such as database connection details, dialect, and other Hibernate-specific properties.

- Syntax for Hibernate Configuration:

```
<hibernate-configuration>
<session-factory>
<!- Hibernate Database connection properties ->
<property name="hibernate.dialect">org.hibernate.dialect.MySQLDialect</property>
<property name="hibernate.connection.driver_class">com.mysql.cj.jdbc.Driver</property>
<property name="hibernate.connection.url">jdbc:mysql://localhost:3306/your_db</property>
<property name="hibernate.connection.username">root</property>
<property name="hibernate.connection.password">password</property>
<!- Hibernate JDBC and SQL properties ->
<property name="hibernate.show_sql">true</property>
<property name="hibernate.hbm2ddl.auto">update</property>
<!- Entity Classes to be mapped ->
<mapping class="com.example.YourEntity"/>
</session-factory>
</hibernate-configuration>
```

2. Spring Configuration with Hibernate ORM:

**(a) Spring Configuration File** (applicationContext.xml):

This is the core configuration file for Spring's application context where beans are defined and wired together. It includes Hibernate session factory, data source configuration, and transaction management.

- Syntax for Spring Hibernate Configuration:

```
<beans xmlns="http://www.springframework.org/schema/beans"
xmlns:xsi="http://www.w3.org/2001/XMLSchema-instance"
```

```
xsi:schemaLocation="http://www.springframework.org/schema/beans
http://www.springframework.org/schema/beans/spring-beans.xsd">
<!- DataSource configuration ->
<bean class="org.apache.commons.dbcp2.BasicDataSource">
<property name="driverClassName" value="com.mysql.cj.jdbc.Driver"/>
<property name="url" value="jdbc:mysql://localhost:3306/your_db"/>
<property name="username" value="root"/>
<property name="password" value="password"/>
</bean>
<!- SessionFactory configuration ->
<bean class="org.springframework.orm.hibernate5.LocalSessionFactoryBean">
<property name="dataSource" ref="dataSource"/>
<property name="hibernateProperties">
<props>
<prop key="hibernate.dialect">org.hibernate.dialect.MySQLDialect</prop>
<prop key="hibernate.show_sql">true</prop>
<prop key="hibernate.hbm2ddl.auto">update</prop>
</props>
</property>
<property name="packagesToScan" value="com.example"/>
</bean>
<!- TransactionManager configuration ->
<bean class="org.springframework.orm.hibernate5.HibernateTransactionManager">
<property name="sessionFactory" ref="sessionFactory"/>
</bean>
</beans>
```

**3.** Java-Based Configuration:

Java-based configuration uses @Configuration and @Bean annotations to define and configure beans programmatically.

(a) Hibernate Java Configuration Class:

- Syntax for Spring Hibernate Java-Based Configuration:

```
@Configuration
@EnableTransactionManagement
@ComponentScan(basePackages="com.example")
public class HibernateConfig {
@Bean
public DataSourcedataSource() {
BasicDataSourcedataSource=new BasicDataSource();
dataSource.setDriverClassName("com.mysql.cj.jdbc.Driver");
dataSource.setUrl("jdbc:mysql://localhost:3306/your_db");
```

```
dataSource.setUsername("root");
dataSource.setPassword("password");
return dataSource;
}
@Bean
public LocalSessionFactoryBeansessionFactory() {
LocalSessionFactoryBeansessionFactory=new LocalSessionFactoryBean();
sessionFactory.setDataSource(dataSource());
sessionFactory.setPackagesToScan("com.example");
sessionFactory.setHibernateProperties(hibernateProperties());
return sessionFactory;
}
@Bean
public HibernateTransactionManagertransactionManager() {
HibernateTransactionManagertransactionManager=new HibernateTransactionManager();
transactionManager.setSessionFactory(sessionFactory().getObject());
return transactionManager;
}
private Properties hibernateProperties() {
Properties properties=new Properties();
properties.put("hibernate.dialect", "org.hibernate.dialect.MySQLDialect");
properties.put("hibernate.show_sql", "true");
properties.put("hibernate.hbm2ddl.auto", "update");
return properties;
}
}
```

**4.** Annotation-Based Configuration:

In annotation-based configuration, we use annotations like @Component, @Autowired, @ Entity, etc., for configuring beans directly in the application class.

- Syntax for Annotation-based Spring Hibernate Configuration:

```
@Configuration
@EnableTransactionManagement
@ComponentScan(basePackages="com.example")
public class AppConfig {
@Bean
public DataSourcedataSource() {
DriverManagerDataSourcedataSource=new DriverManagerDataSource();
dataSource.setDriverClassName("com.mysql.cj.jdbc.Driver");
dataSource.setUrl("jdbc:mysql://localhost:3306/your_db");
dataSource.setUsername("root");
```

```
dataSource.setPassword("password");
return dataSource;
}
@Bean
public LocalSessionFactoryBeansessionFactory() {
LocalSessionFactoryBeansessionFactory=new LocalSessionFactoryBean();
sessionFactory.setDataSource(dataSource());
sessionFactory.setPackagesToScan("com.example");
sessionFactory.setHibernateProperties(hibernateProperties());
return sessionFactory;
}
@Bean
public HibernateTransactionManagertransactionManager() {
HibernateTransactionManagertransactionManager=new HibernateTransactionManager();
transactionManager.setSessionFactory(sessionFactory().getObject());
return transactionManager;
}
private Properties hibernateProperties() {
Properties properties=new Properties();
properties.put("hibernate.dialect", "org.hibernate.dialect.MySQLDialect");
properties.put("hibernate.show_sql", "true");
properties.put("hibernate.hbm2ddl.auto", "update");
return properties;
}
}
```

Each approach can be used depending on the project requirements, with Java-based and Annotation configurations being more widely adopted in newer Spring applications due to their flexibility and cleaner code.

**Hibernate and Spring Integration** refers to the seamless combination of the **Hibernate ORM framework** for data persistence with the **Spring Framework** for dependency injection, transaction management, and other features. By integrating Hibernate with Spring, developers can simplify data access and transaction management, while taking advantage of both frameworks' strengths.

## 4.5.1 Benefits of integrating Spring with Hibernate

**1** Loose Coupling:

- By using Spring's dependency injection (DI) mechanism, the coupling between the application's components and Hibernate is reduced. The SessionFactory and DataSource are managed by Spring, and Hibernate-specific configurations are abstracted away.

**2** Declarative Transaction Management:

- Spring allows you to manage transactions declaratively using annotations (@Transactional) or XML configuration. You no longer need to manage transactions manually within your code.

**3** HibernateTemplate:

- Spring's HibernateTemplate simplifies the use of Hibernate. It manages sessions and transactions, reducing the amount of boilerplate code required for common tasks like saving, updating, or querying objects.

**4** Exception Translation:

- Spring provides consistent exception handling. Hibernate exceptions are automatically converted to Spring's DataAccessException exceptions, which are unchecked and offer a higher-level abstraction for error handling.

## 4.5.2 Steps for integrating Spring with Hibernate

**1.** Configuration in Spring XML:
   - **SessionFactory Bean**: The SessionFactory is defined in the Spring configuration file, and Spring manages it.
   - **Transaction Manager**: A PlatformTransactionManager (e.g., Hibernate Transaction Manager) is used to manage transactions across Hibernate sessions.

**Example:** (XML configuration for Spring and Hibernate Integration):

```
<bean class="org.apache.commons.dbcp2.BasicDataSource">
<property name="driverClassName" value="com.mysql.cj.jdbc.Driver"/>
<property name="url" value="jdbc:mysql://localhost:3306/mydb"/>
<property name="username" value="root"/>
<property name="password" value="password"/>
</bean>
<bean class="org.springframework.orm.hibernate5.LocalSessionFactoryBean">
<property name="dataSource" ref="dataSource"/>
<property name="hibernateProperties">
<props>
<prop key="hibernate.dialect">org.hibernate.dialect.MySQLDialect</prop>
<prop key="hibernate.show_sql">true</prop>
<prop key="hibernate.hbm2ddl.auto">update</prop>
</props>
</property>
<property name="packagesToScan" value="com.example"/>
</bean>
<bean class="org.springframework.orm.hibernate5.HibernateTransactionManager">
<property name="sessionFactory" ref="sessionFactory"/>
</bean>
```

2. Java Configuration Example:
   For Java-based configuration, you can use annotations to define the beans and configurations.

**Example:** (Java-based configuration for Spring and Hibernate Integration):

```
@Configuration
@EnableTransactionManagement
@ComponentScan(basePackages="com.example")
public class HibernateConfig {
@Bean
public DataSourcedataSource() {
BasicDataSourcedataSource=new BasicDataSource();
dataSource.setDriverClassName("com.mysql.cj.jdbc.Driver");
dataSource.setUrl("jdbc:mysql://localhost:3306/mydb");
dataSource.setUsername("root");
dataSource.setPassword("password");
return dataSource;
}
@Bean
public LocalSessionFactoryBeansessionFactory() {
LocalSessionFactoryBeansessionFactory=new LocalSessionFactoryBean();
sessionFactory.setDataSource(dataSource());
sessionFactory.setPackagesToScan("com.example");
sessionFactory.setHibernateProperties(hibernateProperties());
return sessionFactory;
}
@Bean
public HibernateTransactionManagertransactionManager() {
HibernateTransactionManagertransactionManager=new HibernateTransactionManager();
transactionManager.setSessionFactory(sessionFactory().getObject());
return transactionManager;
}
private Properties hibernateProperties() {
Properties properties=new Properties();
properties.put("hibernate.dialect", "org.hibernate.dialect.MySQLDialect");
properties.put("hibernate.show_sql", "true");
properties.put("hibernate.hbm2ddl.auto", "update");
return properties;
}
}
```

**3.** Using @Transactional for Transaction Management:
You can use the @Transactional annotation to manage transactions declaratively. This eliminates the need to manually handle session commit or rollback.

**Example:** (Usage of @Transactional annotation):

```
@Service
public class UserService {
@Autowired
private UserDaouserDao;
@Transactional
public void saveUser(User user) {
userDao.save(user);
}
@Transactional(readOnly=true)
public List<User>getUsers() {
return userDao.getAllUsers();
}
}
```

**4.** HibernateTemplate for Simplified Operations:

Spring provides HibernateTemplate as a higher-level abstraction for Hibernate. It simplifies interactions with the Hibernate session and reduces the need for explicit session management.

**Example:** :

```
public class UserDao {
@Autowired
private HibernateTemplatehibernateTemplate;
public void save(User user) {
hibernateTemplate.save(user);
}
public List<User>getAllUsers() {
return hibernateTemplate.loadAll(User.class);
}
}
```

### 4.5.3 Data flow in Hibernate and Spring integration

1. User Input: The application receives user input, such as a request to save or retrieve data.
2. Service Layer: The service layer, annotated with @Transactional, delegates the operation to the DAO (Data Access Object) layer.

3 DAO Layer: The DAO layer interacts with the Hibernate session to perform CRUD operations using Hibernate APIs or HibernateTemplate.
4 Session Management: Spring manages the session and transaction through the HibernateTransactionManager. The transaction is automatically committed or rolled back depending on the success or failure of the operation.
5 Database Operation: Hibernate maps the Java object to a database table and performs the operation (e.g., insert, update, delete, select).
6 Result: After the transaction is completed, the result is returned to the service layer, which sends it back to the user.

## 4.6 Hibernate Object-Relational Mapping data type

Hibernate ORM provides a wide range of data types for mapping Java types to SQL database column types. These are referred to as **Hibernate Types** and are categorized into four main groups:

1. Basic (Built-in) Data Types:
   These types are the most commonly used and map basic Java types to corresponding SQL types.

| Hibernate type | Java type | SQL type |
|---|---|---|
| string | java.lang.String | VARCHAR |
| boolean | boolean or Boolean | BOOLEAN or BIT |
| byte | byte or Byte | TINYINT |
| short | short or Short | SMALLINT |
| int or integer | int or Integer | INTEGER |
| long | long or Long | BIGINT |
| float | float or Float | FLOAT |
| double | double or Double | DOUBLE |
| big_decimal | java.math.BigDecimal | NUMERIC or DECIMAL |
| date | java.util.Date | DATE |
| time | java.util.Date | TIME |
| timestamp | java.util.Date | TIMESTAMP |
| binary | byte[] | VARBINARY |
| blob | java.sql.Blob | BLOB |

| | | |
|---|---|---|
| clob | java.sql.Clob | CLOB |
| uuid | java.util.UUID | UUID |
| text | java.lang.String | TEXT |

**2.** Collection Types:
Hibernate supports mapping Java collections (e.g., List, Set, Map) to relational database tables. These require a collection mapping.

| Hibernate type | Java collection | Description |
|---|---|---|
| List | java.util.List | Maps to an ordered collection. |
| Set | java.util.Set | Maps to a collection with unique values. |
| Map | java.util.Map | Maps keys to values. |
| Bag | java.util.Collection | Maps an unordered collection with duplicates. |

To map collection types, the corresponding annotations or XML configuration must specify the relationship (@OneToMany, @ManyToMany, etc.) and the type of collection.

**3.** Date and Time Types:
Hibernate supports the mapping of Java date and time types to appropriate SQL types.

| Hibernate type | Java type | SQL type |
|---|---|---|
| date | java.util.Date | DATE |
| time | java.util.Date | TIME |
| timestamp | java.util.Date or java.sql.Timestamp | TIMESTAMP |
| local_date | java.time.LocalDate | DATE |
| local_time | java.time.LocalTime | TIME |
| local_date_time | java.time.LocalDateTime | TIMESTAMP |
| offset_date_time | java.time.OffsetDateTime | TIMESTAMP |
| zoned_date_time | java.time.ZonedDateTime | TIMESTAMP |
| duration | java.time.Duration | BIGINT |

**4.** Custom/User-Defined Types:

Hibernate allows developers to define custom data types when the built-in types do not suffice. This is achieved by implementing UserType or CompositeUserType.

Example of a Custom Data Type:

- Imagine you want to map a custom Java class (Address) to a database structure.

### 4.6.1 Steps to create a custom data type

1. Implement the UserType interface.
2. Override its methods such as nullSafeSet(), nullSafeGet(), and deepCopy().
3. Register the custom type in Hibernate.

```
public class AddressUserType implements UserType {
// Implement UserType methods for custom mapping
}
Usage:
@Type(type="com.example.AddressUserType")
private Address address;
```

**5.** Enumerated Types:

Hibernate allows you to map enums to database columns.

| Hibernate type | Java type | SQL type |
|---|---|---|
| enum | java.lang.Enum | VARCHAR or INTEGER |

- Use the @Enumerated annotation to specify whether the enum should be stored as a String or Ordinal (integer).

```
Example:
@Enumerated(EnumType.STRING)
private Status status;
```

**6.** Hibernate Annotations for Data Types:

- Use Hibernate annotations such as @Column, @Lob, and @Temporal to specify additional details about how Java types map to SQL.

```
Examples:
Basic String Mapping:
@Column(name="name", length=255, nullable=false)
private String name;
Date Mapping:
@Temporal(TemporalType.TIMESTAMP)
@Column(name="created_date")
private Date createdDate;
Lob (Large Object) Mapping:
```

```
@Lob
@Column(name="profile_picture")
private byte[] profilePicture;
```

Hibernate provides a rich set of built-in data types to cover almost every standard Java type. It also supports user-defined types for specific use cases. Proper configuration of these data types ensures a smooth mapping between Java objects and SQL tables, reducing the complexity of database interactions.

In Hibernate ORM, **user-defined types** are custom types created by developers when the built-in Hibernate types are not sufficient to map specific Java objects to database columns. These custom types are implemented using the UserType or CompositeUserType interfaces provided by Hibernate. User-defined types allow you to control how complex objects or nonstandard data types are stored and retrieved from the database.

### 4.6.2 Why use user-defined types?

1 To handle custom data structures like Address, Point, or any composite data type.
2 To map nonstandard database types (e.g., JSON, XML, or proprietary types).
3 To encapsulate specific logic for transforming data between Java and SQL representations.

### 4.6.3 Steps to create user-defined types in Hibernate

**1.** Implement the UserType Interface:

The UserType interface is used for simple custom types. It requires implementing the following methods:

| Method | Description |
|---|---|
| nullSafeGet() | Extracts the value of the column from the ResultSet. |
| nullSafeSet() | Binds the Java object to a SQL statement. |
| deepCopy() | Creates a deep copy of the custom type. |
| equals() | Compares two instances of the custom type for equality. |
| hashCode() | Generates a hash code for the custom type. |
| returnedClass() | Returns the Java class type of the custom type. |
| sqlTypes() | Specifies the SQL column types that the custom type maps to. |
| assemble() / disassemble() | Supports Hibernate's second-level cache and serialization. |
| replace() | Handles merging detached objects with persistence context during updates. |

### 4.6.4 CompositeUserType

For more complex custom types, you can use the CompositeUserType interface. It is used when the custom type involves multiple columns in the database.

### 4.6.5 Advantages of user-defined types in Hibernate

1. Encapsulation: Allows encapsulating custom mapping logic in one place.
2. Flexibility: Provides full control over how Java objects map to database columns.
3. Reusability: Custom types can be reused across multiple entities.
4. Extensibility: Extends Hibernate's capabilities to handle complex types or proprietary formats.

By defining user-defined types, Hibernate enables mapping between custom Java objects and database structures in a way that is clean, efficient, and maintainable.

## 4.7 Identifiers in Hibernate Object-Relational Mapping

In Hibernate ORM, **identifiers** refer to the unique key or primary key that is used to identify an entity object within the database. Hibernate requires every entity to have an identifier to manage data uniquely. These identifiers are mapped to a specific database column that acts as the primary key.

### 4.7.1 Need for identifiers in Hibernate

1. Uniqueness: To uniquely identify records in the database.
2. Persistence Context: Hibernate uses identifiers to map Java objects to database rows during transactions.
3. Primary Key Mapping: To maintain the relationship between entities (e.g., foreign key references).
4. Efficient Caching: Hibernate uses identifiers to retrieve cached entities.

### 4.7.2 Types of identifiers in Hibernate

Identifiers in Hibernate can be defined in two ways:

1. Simple Identifiers: Single-column primary key.
2. Composite Identifiers: Combination of multiple columns as a primary key.

### 4.7.3 Generating identifiers in Hibernate

Hibernate provides multiple strategies to generate identifiers. These strategies are specified using the @GeneratedValue annotation with the strategy attribute.

### 4.7.4 Identifier generation strategies

| Strategy | Description |
|---|---|
| AUTO | Automatically selects the generation strategy based on the database dialect. |
| IDENTITY | Uses the database's identity column (e.g., AUTO_INCREMENT in MySQL). |
| SEQUENCE | Uses a database sequence to generate unique values (e.g., NEXTVAL in PostgreSQL, Oracle). |
| TABLE | Uses a database table to store and generate unique values. |
| UUID | Generates a universally unique identifier. |

### *4.7.4.1 Syntax for identifiers*

**1.** Simple Identifier:

```
@Entity
public class Employee {
@Id
@GeneratedValue(strategy=GenerationType.IDENTITY)
private Long id;
private String name;
// Getters and Setters
}
```

**2.** Composite Identifier:

For composite keys, you need to define a separate class to hold the key values.

### *4.7.4.2 Composite key class*

```
@Embeddable
public class EmployeeKey implements Serializable {
private String departmentId;
private Long employeeNumber;
// Getters, Setters, equals(), and hashCode() methods
}
```

### *4.7.4.3 Entity class with composite key*

```
@Entity
public class Employee {
@EmbeddedId
private EmployeeKey id;
private String name;
// Getters and Setters
}
```

#### 4.7.4.4 Configuring identifiers in XML

If you're using XML-based configuration, identifiers are defined using the <id> tag.

Example:

```
<class name="Employee" table="EMPLOYEE">
<id name="id" column="EMPLOYEE_ID">
<generator class="identity" />
</id>
<property name="name" column="EMPLOYEE_NAME" />
</class>
```

#### 4.7.4.5 Primary key mapping in relationships

Hibernate identifiers play a crucial role in managing relationships between entities:

- **One-to-One**: Identifiers are used to associate the primary key of one entity with another.
- **One-to-Many/Many-to-One**: Identifiers act as foreign keys to establish the relationship.

## 4.8 Keys in Hibernate Object-Relational Mapping

In Hibernate ORM, keys are important in determining the way data is uniquely identified and operated in the database. Hibernate has two keys: Primary Keys and Foreign Keys. Every type is useful in different situations, and Hibernate offers a lot of annotations and XML configurations in order to deal with such keys.

### 4.8.1 Types of keys in Hibernate

**1** Primary Key:

- A primary key is used to uniquely identify each record in a table.
- In Hibernate, primary keys are mapped using the @Id annotation.
- Composite keys (keys made of multiple columns) can also be used, defined with @ EmbeddedId or @IdClass.

**2** Foreign Key:

- A foreign key is used to establish a relationship between two tables.
- In Hibernate, foreign keys are managed using annotations like @OneToOne, @ OneToMany, @ManyToOne, and @ManyToMany.

### 4.8.2 Primary key in Hibernate

#### 4.8.2.1 Single primary key

This involves a single column acting as the primary key for the table.

#### *4.8.2.2 Syntax*

```
@Entity
public class Employee {
@Id
@GeneratedValue(strategy=GenerationType.IDENTITY) // Auto-generates the key
private Long id;
private String name;
// Getters and Setters
}
```

#### *4.8.2.3 Composite primary key*

When multiple columns together act as a primary key.

#### *4.8.2.4 Approaches*

1 Using @EmbeddedId:

- A separate class is created to represent the composite key.

#### *4.8.2.5 Composite key class*

```
@Embeddable
public class EmployeeKey implements Serializable {
private String departmentId;
private Long employeeNumber;
// Getters, Setters, equals(), and hashCode() methods
}
```

#### *4.8.2.6 Entity class*

```
@Entity
public class Employee {
@EmbeddedId
private EmployeeKey id;
private String name;
// Getters and Setters
}
```

1 Using @IdClass:

- The composite key class is specified using the @IdClass annotation.

#### *4.8.2.7 Composite key class*

```
public class EmployeeKey implements Serializable {
private String departmentId;
private Long employeeNumber;
```

```
// Getters, Setters, equals(), and hashCode() methods
}
```

#### *4.8.2.8 Entity class*

```
@Entity
@IdClass(EmployeeKey.class)
public class Employee {
@Id
private String departmentId;
@Id
private Long employeeNumber;
private String name;
// Getters and Setters
}
```

#### *4.8.2.9 Foreign keys in Hibernate*

Foreign keys establish relationships between entities and are defined using association mappings.

### 4.8.3 One-to-one relationship

#### *4.8.3.1 Syntax*

```
@Entity
public class Employee {
@Id
@GeneratedValue(strategy=GenerationType.IDENTITY)
private Long id;
@OneToOne
@JoinColumn(name="address_id") // Foreign key column
private Address address;
// Getters and Setters
}
```

### 4.8.4 One-to-many relationship

#### *4.8.4.1 Syntax*

```
@Entity
public class Department {
@Id
@GeneratedValue(strategy=GenerationType.IDENTITY)
private Long id;
```

```
@OneToMany(mappedBy="department")
private List<Employee> employees;
// Getters and Setters
}
```

## 4.8.5 Many-to-one relationship

### *4.8.5.1 Syntax*

```
@Entity
public class Employee {
@Id
@GeneratedValue(strategy=GenerationType.IDENTITY)
private Long id;
@ManyToOne
@JoinColumn(name="department_id") // Foreign key column
private Department department;
// Getters and Setters
}
```

## 4.8.6 Many-to-many relationship

### *4.8.6.1 Syntax*

```
@Entity
public class Student {
@Id
@GeneratedValue(strategy=GenerationType.IDENTITY)
private Long id;
@ManyToMany
@JoinTable
(
name="student_course",
joinColumns=@JoinColumn(name="student_id"), // Foreign key from Student
inverseJoinColumns=@JoinColumn(name="course_id") // Foreign key from Course
)
private List<Course> courses;
// Getters and Setters
}
```

### *4.8.6.2 Keys in XML configuration*

If you are using XML for configuration instead of annotations:

#### *4.8.6.3 Primary key*

```
<class name="Employee" table="EMPLOYEE">
<id name="id" column="EMPLOYEE_ID">
<generator class="identity" />
</id>
</class>
```

#### *4.8.6.4 Foreign key (one-to-many)*

```
<class name="Department" table="DEPARTMENT">
<id name="id" column="DEPARTMENT_ID">
<generator class="identity" />
</id>
<set name="employees" inverse="true" cascade="all">
<key column="DEPARTMENT_ID"/>
<one-to-many class="Employee"/>
</set>
</class>
```

## Bibliography

Bauer, C. (2005). *Hibernate in action.*

Hibernate. (2024). ORM Documentation. https://hibernate.org/orm/documentation/.

IBM. (2024). ORM Concepts. https://www.ibm.com/docs.

Oracle. (2024). JDBC Documentation. https://docs.oracle.com/javase/tutorial/jdbc/.

Red Hat. (2024). Hibernate Guide. https://access.redhat.com/documentation.

Spring. (2024). Spring ORM Docs. https://docs.spring.io.

# 5

# Building a simple Create, Read, Update, and Delete application with Spring Boot and Hibernate

## 5.1 Introduction

In this chapter, the author is going to develop a basic CRUD (Create, Read, Update, and Delete) system based on Spring Boot and Hibernate Object-Relational Mapping (ORM). The Hibernate is a well-known ORM that makes the interaction between Java applications and databases easier through mapping to database tables. This chapter starts by giving a summary of CRUD operations in Hibernate and then configuring the connections with different databases. The combination of Spring Boot with Hibernate is then addressed and how the two technologies simplify data persistence. Also, Hibernate ORM lifecycle on CRUD operations is discussed as well as the database connectivity and SQL dialects. This chapter also discusses how entity classes are created, utility configuration is done, and how Data Access Object (DAO) classes are used to efficiently manage database operations. At the end, learners would have a lucid idea of how to combine Hibernate ORM with Spring Boot to achieve smooth operations with the database (Table 5–1).

## 5.2 Create, Read, Update, and Delete operations in Hibernate Object-Relational Mapping

CRUD operations are the standard operations of Create, Read, Update, and Delete, which are the fundamental building blocks of using a database. These operations are used in the case of Hibernate ORM to manipulate data in relational databases in Java object form rather than writing SQL queries.

CRUD operations are as follows:

1. Create: Inserting new records into the database.
2. Read: Retrieving data from the database.
3. Update: Modifying existing records in the database.
4. Delete: Elimination of records in the database.

Hibernate offers an easy and object-oriented way of executing such operations, with the support of its Session API and Hibernate Query Language (HQL).

Mastering Java Full Stack Development. DOI: https://doi.org/10.1016/B978-0-443-51683-2.00005-9

**Table 5–1** SQL dialects with their corresponding database and Hibernate class.

| Database | Hibernate dialect class | Usage example |
|---|---|---|
| MySQL | org.hibernate.dialect.MySQLDialect | MySQL version 4.x and earlier |
| MySQL 5.x or later | org.hibernate.dialect.MySQL5Dialect | Use for MySQL 5.x |
| PostgreSQL | org.hibernate.dialect.PostgreSQLDialect | PostgreSQL 9.x or later |
| Oracle 10 g | org.hibernate.dialect.Oracle10gDialect | For Oracle 10 g |
| Oracle 12c | org.hibernate.dialect.Oracle12cDialect | For Oracle 12c |
| Microsoft SQL Server | org.hibernate.dialect.SQLServerDialect | Use for SQL Server 2000 |
| SQL Server 2012+ | org.hibernate.dialect.SQLServer2012Dialect | Use for SQL Server 2012 and later |
| SQLite | org.hibernate.dialect.SQLiteDialect | Use for SQLite |
| DB2 | org.hibernate.dialect.DB2Dialect | Use for IBM DB2 |
| H2 | org.hibernate.dialect.H2Dialect | Use for H2 in-memory database |
| MariaDB | org.hibernate.dialect.MariaDBDialect | Use for MariaDB |
| Sybase | org.hibernate.dialect.SybaseDialect | Use for Sybase |

### 5.2.1 Why are Create, Read, Update, and Delete operations needed in Hibernate Object-Relational Mapping?

1. Easy Data Processing: Hibernate removes the issue of writing SQL queries to perform simple data operations in the database, allowing developers to concentrate on business code rather than interacting with the database.
2. Object-Oriented Approach: CRUD operations in Hibernate operate on Java objects (entities) directly, thereby being easy to use by developers and lessening the impedance difference between the object-oriented concept and relational one.
3. Database Independence: Hibernate is also able to support multiple databases, and CRUD operations are also similar across various database systems. This does not require writing queries differently in various databases.
4. Automatic Transaction Management: Hibernate also handles transactions effectively when making CRUD operations, and it also guarantees atomicity and consistency.
5. Caching to Performance: Hibernate has a caching strategy (first-level and second-level caches) that enhances performance when performing CRUD operations to reduce database access.
6. Lazy Loading and Eager Fetching: Hibernate gives the option of control over the manner in which the associated information is loaded on a fine-grained basis during CRUD operations to optimize memory operations and performance.
7. Relationships Handling: Hibernate eases CRUD operations on relational entities (e.g., one-to-many, many-to-many) through cascading, which simplifies the handling of detailed data models.

## 5.3 Operations

1. Create Operation (Insert):

   The Create option adds a record in the database. Hibernate offers the save method and the persist method toward this end.

- save(): Saves the object to the database and gives the created identifier (primary key).
- persist(): Same as save, except that it does not return a value. It is normally applied where the object is required to move between a transient and persistent state.

**Syntax**

```
Session session = sessionFactory.openSession(); // Open a session
Transaction transaction = session.beginTransaction(); // Begin a transaction
session.save(object); // Save the object (returns generated ID)
session.persist(object); // Persist the object (no return value)
transaction.commit(); // Commit the transaction
session.close(); // Close the session
```

2. Read Operation (Retrieve):

Read operation retrieves data in the database. Hibernate has many approaches to record retrieval.

- get(): Accesses an entity via a primary key. Checks null in case the entity is not located.
- load(): Just like get, except that it returns a proxy object. Rethrows in the event that the entity cannot be found.
- HQL: You can use it to run queries in an object-oriented syntax.
- Criteria API: A programmatic method of using queries.

**Syntax**

a) Fetch by Primary Key

```
session.get(EntityClass.class, primaryKey); // Fetch entity or null if not found
session.load(EntityClass.class, primaryKey); // Fetch proxy or throw exception if not found
```

b) Using HQL

```
Query query = session.createQuery("FROM EntityClass WHERE fieldName =:value");
query.setParameter("value", value);
List<EntityClass> results = query.getResultList(); // Fetch multiple results
EntityClasssingleResult = query.getSingleResult(); // Fetch single result
```

c) Using Criteria API

```
CriteriaBuilder builder = session.getCriteriaBuilder();
CriteriaQuery<EntityClass> criteria = builder.createQuery(EntityClass.class);
Root<EntityClass> root = criteria.from(EntityClass.class);
criteria.select(root).where(builder.equal(root.get("fieldName"), value));
List<EntityClass> results = session.createQuery(criteria).getResultList();
```

3. Update Operation:

The Update operation modifies existing records in the database. Hibernate provides the update() and merge() methods for this purpose.

- update(): Updates a detached entity (an entity not associated with the current session).
- Merge(): Merges changes in a detached entity into a managed entity.

**Syntax**

```
Session session = sessionFactory.openSession(); // Open a session
Transaction transaction = session.beginTransaction(); // Begin a transaction
```

session.update(object); // Update an existing object
session.merge(object); // Merge changes to a detached object
transaction.commit(); // Commit the transaction
session.close(); // Close the session

4. Delete Operation:

   The Delete operation removes records from the database. Hibernate provides the delete() method to delete entities.

   - delete(): Removes an entity from the database. The entity must first be fetched into the session.

   **Syntax**

   Session session = sessionFactory.openSession(); // Open a session
   Transaction transaction = session.beginTransaction(); // Begin a transaction
   session.delete(object); // Delete the object from the database
   transaction.commit(); // Commit the transaction
   session.close(); // Close the session

Hibernate simplifies the implementation of these operations by abstracting the underlying SQL and providing an object-oriented approach for interacting with the database.

## 5.4 Connection configuration for various databases using Hiberate Object-Relational Mapping

1. MySQL:
   - hibernate.connection.driver_class: Specifies the JDBC driver class used to connect to MySQL.
   - hibernate.connection.url: The JDBC URL for the MySQL database. It includes the host, port, and database name (localhost:3306/your_database_name).
   - hibernate.connection.username: Username to connect to the MySQL database.
   - hibernate.connection.password: Password for the specified username.
   - hibernate.dialect: Specifies the Hibernate dialect for MySQL (e.g., MySQL5Dialect for MySQL 5.x).
2. JDBC:
   - hibernate.connection.driver_class: JDBC driver class for MySQL.
   - hibernate.connection.url: JDBC URL for connecting to MySQL.
   - hibernate.connection.username: Username for MySQL.
   - hibernate.connection.password: Password for the MySQL username.
   - hibernate.dialect: Specifies the Hibernate dialect. For MySQL, you can use MySQLDialect.
   - hibernate.c3p0.min_size: Specifies the minimum number of connections in the connection pool (C3P0 connection pool).
   - hibernate.c3p0.max_size: Specifies the maximum number of connections in the pool.
3. MongoDB (Using Hibernate OGM):
   - hibernate.ogm.datastore.provider: Specifies the provider for the datastore, in this case, MongoDB.

- hibernate.ogm.datastore.host: The hostname or IP address of the MongoDB server (localhost if running locally).
- hibernate.ogm.datastore.port: The port for MongoDB (default 27017).
- hibernate.ogm.datastore.database: The name of the MongoDB database.
- hibernate.ogm.mongodb.database: Another way to specify the MongoDB database.
- hibernate.ogm.transaction.manager_lookup_class: Specifies the transaction manager class for Hibernate OGM (Object/Grid Mapper) to manage transactions for MongoDB. Hibernate Object/Grid Mapper (OGM) extends Hibernate for NoSQL databases like MongoDB. This configuration is for setting up a connection to MongoDB.

**4.** PostgreSQL:
   - hibernate.connection.driver_class: Specifies the PostgreSQL JDBC driver class (org.postgresql.Driver).
   - hibernate.connection.url: The JDBC URL for PostgreSQL (jdbc:postgresql://localhost:5432/your_database_name). It includes the host (localhost), port (5432), and the database name.
   - hibernate.connection.username: Username to access the PostgreSQL database.
   - hibernate.connection.password: Password for the PostgreSQL username.
   - hibernate.dialect: Specifies the Hibernate dialect for PostgreSQL (PostgreSQLDialect).

These properties allow Hibernate to establish a connection with various types of databases (MySQL, PostgreSQL, and MongoDB) and manage the interactions seamlessly through ORM.

## 5.5 Integration of Spring with Hibernate Object-Relational Mapping using Create, Read, Update, and Delete operations

Spring and Hibernate integration allows developers to combine the strengths of the Spring Framework (dependency injection, transaction management) and Hibernate ORM. This integration is commonly used to build scalable and efficient data-driven applications.

### 5.5.1 Key steps for integration

**1.** Configure Hibernate in Spring:
   - Set up Hibernate as a dependency in your project.
   - Use Spring's configuration to manage Hibernate'sSessionFactory and transaction management.

**2.** Define Entity Classes:
   - Create entity classes annotated with JPA annotations like @Entity and @Table.

**3.** Set Up a DAO Layer:
   - Use the Session object from Hibernate to perform CRUD operations.

**4.** Enable Transaction Management:
   - Use Spring's @Transactional annotation to manage transactions seamlessly.

Configuration and Syntax

1. Dependencies (Maven or Gradle):
   Add Spring and Hibernate dependencies in pom.xml (Maven):

```
<dependency>
<groupId>org.springframework</groupId>
<artifactId>spring-orm</artifactId>
<version>5.x.x</version>
</dependency>
<dependency>
<groupId>org.hibernate</groupId>
<artifactId>hibernate-core</artifactId>
<version>5.x.x</version>
</dependency>
<dependency>
<groupId>javax.persistence</groupId>
<artifactId>javax.persistence-api</artifactId>
<version>2.x</version>
</dependency>
<dependency>
<groupId>org.springframework.boot</groupId>
<artifactId>spring-boot-starter-data-jpa</artifactId>
<version>2.x</version>
</dependency>
```

2. Hibernate Configuration:
   Use application.properties for database and Hibernate settings:

```
spring.datasource.url=jdbc:mysql://localhost:3306/your_database
spring.datasource.username=root
spring.datasource.password=your_password
spring.jpa.hibernate.ddl-auto=update
spring.jpa.show-sql=true
```

3. Entity Class:
   Define an entity with JPA annotations:

```
import javax.persistence.*;
@Entity
@Table(name = "users")
public class User {
@Id
@GeneratedValue(strategy = GenerationType.IDENTITY)
```

```
private Long id;
@Column(name = "name")
private String name;
@Column(name = "email")
private String email;
// Getters and Setters
}
```

4. DAO Layer:
   Define a DAO interface and implementation.
   Interface:

```
import java.util.List;
public interface UserDao {
void save(User user);
User getById(Long id);
List<User>getAll();
void update(User user);
void delete(User user);
}
```

5. Service Layer:
   The service layer provides business logic and calls DAO methods.
6. Controller Layer:

   Test CRUD operations through expose REST APIs or through a controller.

### 5.5.2 Advantages of Spring + Hibernate integration

1. Hibernate configuration and dependencies: Spring takes care of Hibernate configuration.
2. Transaction management: Spring declarative transaction management simplifies the CRUD operations.
3. Abstraction: There is a clean abstraction of DAO and service layers.
4. Scalability: Supports the large-scale applications with relational databases. It is a clean and modular design that allows manipulating database operations with the power of Spring and Hibernate.

## 5.6 Life cycle of Hiberate Object-Relational Mapping using Create, Read, Update, and Delete operations

CRUD in Hibernate has several steps, including the generation of a session till the execution of transactions and entity state.

1. Create (Insert Operation):
   Lifecycle:
   a. Session Creation:
      i. A Session object is created using the SessionFactory.
      ii. The session represents a single unit of work with the database.
   b. Entity Creation:
      i. A new object of the entity class is instantiated (transient state).
   c. Entity Save:
      i. The save() or persist() method is called to save the entity.
      ii. The entity has entered the persistent state, and it is under the Hibernate session.
   d. Transaction Commit:
      i. Transaction.commit() is used to commit the transaction, and SQL INSERT statement is used.
      Entity States:
      i. Transient → Persistent

      Syntax:
```
Session session = sessionFactory.openSession();
Transaction transaction = session.beginTransaction();
User user = new User();
user.setName("usharani");
user.setEmail("usharani@example.com");
session.save(user);
transaction.commit();
session.close();
```
2. Read (Select Operation):
   Lifecycle:
   a. Session Creation:
      i. A Session object is opened.
   b. Entity Retrieval:
      i. The entity is retrieved using methods like get(), load(), or HQL queries.
   c. Transaction:
      i. If the session is in a transactional context, it ensures the retrieved data is consistent.
   d. Session Close:
      i. Once the entity is retrieved, the session is closed.
      Entity States:
      i. Persistent: The entity stays in the session till it is closed or directly detached.

      Syntax:
```
Session session = sessionFactory.openSession();
User user = session.get(User.class, 1 L); // Fetch user with ID 1
session.close();
```

3. Update (Modify Operation):
   Lifecycle:
   a. Session Creation:
      i. A Session object is created.
   b. Entity Retrieval:
      i. The entity to be updated is retrieved using get() or load().
   c. Entity Update:
      i. The entity is updated using setters, and the changes are tracked automatically if the entity is in a persistent state.
   d. Transaction Commit:
      i. The transaction.commit() executes the SQL UPDATE statement.
      Entity States:
      i. Detached → Persistent (updating)

      Syntax:
```
Session session = sessionFactory.openSession();
Transaction transaction = session.beginTransaction();
User user = session.get(User.class, 1 L); // Retrieve user
user.setEmail("new.email@example.com"); // Update email
session.update(user);
transaction.commit();
session.close();
```
4. Delete (Remove Operation):
   Lifecycle:
   a. Session Creation:
      i. A Session object is created.
   b. Entity Retrieval:
      i. The entity to be deleted is retrieved using get() or load().
   c. Entity Deletion:
      i. The delete() method is called, marking the entity for removal.
   d. Transaction Commit:
      i. The SQL DELETE statement is executed when the transaction is committed.
      Entity States:
      i. Persistent → Removed

   Syntax:
```
Session session = sessionFactory.openSession();
Transaction transaction = session.beginTransaction();
User user = session.get(User.class, 1 L); // Retrieve user
session.delete(user); // Delete user
transaction.commit();
session.close();
```

### 5.6.1 Lifecycle of an entity in Create, Read, Update, and Delete operations

1. Transient State:
   - The entity is created but not yet associated with a Hibernate session.
   - Example: new User();
2. Persistent State:
   - The entity is associated with a session and managed by Hibernate.
   - Example: session.save(user);
3. Detached State:
   - The entity is no longer associated with a session, typically after the session is closed.
   - Example: After session.close().
4. Removed State:
   - The entity is marked for deletion and will be removed from the database after the transaction commits.
   - Example: session.delete(user);

### 5.6.2 Transactions in Create, Read, Update, and Delete operations

1. Mandatory Transaction Management:
   i. Each CRUD operation in Hibernate is transactional to ensure data consistency.
2. Begin Transaction:
   ii. Use session.beginTransaction().
3. Commit Transaction:
   iii. Use transaction.commit() to finalize the operation and execute the SQL statements.
4. Rollback Transaction:
   iv. Use transaction.rollback() to undo changes in case of an exception.

### 5.6.3 Advantages of Hibernate in Create, Read, Update, and Delete lifecycles

1. Automatic State Management:
   - Hibernate tracks changes to entities in the persistent state.
2. Optimized SQL:
   - Hibernate generates SQL dynamically based on the entity's state and operation.
3. Lazy and Eager Fetching:
   - Hibernate manages how associated entities are loaded, reducing unnecessary database queries.
4. Caching:
   - Hibernate uses first-level and second-level caches to improve read performance.
5. Simplified Transactions:
   - Built-in transaction management simplifies the lifecycle of CRUD operations.

Hibernate provides efficient and consistent communications with the database by following the lifecycle of CRUD operations and also by hiding the complexity of SQL.

### 5.6.3.1 Components

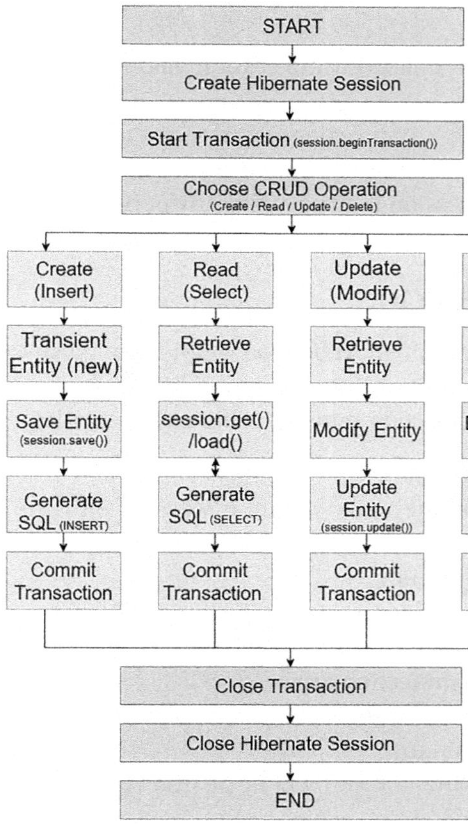


1. Session Creation:
   - The process begins by creating a Hibernate Session object from the SessionFactory.
2. Transaction Initialization:
   - Before any operation, a transaction must be started using session.beginTransaction().
3. CRUD Operation Decision:
   - Depending on the operation, choose one of the four paths: Create, Read, Update, or Delete.
4. Create:
   - A new transient entity is instantiated.
   - It is saved into the database with session.save(), transitioning the entity to the persistent state.

5. Read:
   - An existing entity is retrieved from the database using session.get() or session.load(), keeping it in the persistent state.
6. Update:
   - An entity is retrieved and modified. Changes are tracked by Hibernate if the entity is persistent or explicitly updated using session.update().
7. Delete:
   - An entity is retrieved and deleted using session.delete().
8. Transaction Finalization:
   - Each operation ends with a transaction commit or rollback to finalize the operation.
9. Session Close:
   - After the operation, the session is closed, and any persistent entities become detached.

## 5.7 Database connection

To establish a database connection in Hibernate ORM, you must configure the Hibernate configuration file (hibernate.cfg.xml) or the properties file (hibernate.properties). These configurations define the database connection settings, Hibernate properties, and mapping files.

1. hibernate.cfg.xml Configuration:
   The hibernate.cfg.xml file is the most common way to configure a Hibernate database connection.
2. hibernate.properties Configuration
   Alternatively, you can use a hibernate.properties file for database connection settings.
   **Key Components of the Configuration**
   a. Driver Class (hibernate.connection.driver_class):
      i. Specifies the JDBC driver for the database (e.g., com.mysql.cj.jdbc.Driver for MySQL).
   b. URL (hibernate.connection.url):
      ii. Specifies the JDBC URL for connecting to the database. Example: jdbc:mysql://localhost:3306/your_database_name.
   c. Username and Password:
      iii. Required to authenticate with the database.
   d. Dialect (hibernate.dialect):
      iv. Tells Hibernate how to generate SQL statements for the database.

Examples:
org.hibernate.dialect.MySQLDialect (for MySQL).
org.hibernate.dialect.PostgreSQLDialect (for PostgreSQL).
org.hibernate.dialect.Oracle10gDialect (for Oracle).
   a. Connection Pooling:
      i. Hibernate provides built-in connection pooling using C3P0 for managing database connections efficiently.

   b. SQL Logs (hibernate.show_sql and hibernate.format_sql):
      i. Logs the SQL statements executed by Hibernate.
   c. Mapping Resource:
      i. Defines the mapping file (.hbm.xml) or annotated entity classes.
3. Java Code to Load Configuration:
   Once the configuration is set, load it using Configuration and create a SessionFactory:

```
import org.hibernate.SessionFactory;
import org.hibernate.cfg.Configuration;
public class HibernateUtil {
private static SessionFactorysessionFactory;
static {
try {
// Load the configuration
sessionFactory = new Configuration().configure("hibernate.cfg.xml").buildSessionFactory
();
} catch (Exception e) {
e.printStackTrace();
throw new ExceptionInInitializerError("SessionFactory creation failed");
}
}
public static SessionFactorygetSessionFactory() {
returnsessionFactory;
}
}
```

4. Execution Flow:
   a. Configuration File: Hibernate reads the configuration (hibernate.cfg.xml or hibernate.properties) to connect to the database.
   b. SessionFactory: A SessionFactory is created for establishing sessions.
   c. Session: A Session is created to interact with the database for CRUD operations.
   d. Transaction: Transactions are started and committed/rolled back based on operations.
   e. This setup is essential for integrating Hibernate ORM with a database for seamless CRUD operations.

## 5.8 SQL dialect

Hibernate ORM defines the SQL dialect on which the specific database generated by Hibernate is based. The dialect assists Hibernate to convert its HQL or Criteria queries to SQL compatible with the target database because their respective databases havs their own SQL syntax and characteristics.

## 5.8.1 Why is SQL dialect needed in Hibernate?

1. Database-Specific Syntax: SQL syntax varies in different databases (e.g., SQL keyword differences, SQL functions, SQL limit clauses).
2. Automatic Query Generation: Hibernate is able to generate the correct SQL statements to use in CRUD operations, joins, and so on using the dialect.
3. Feature Support: Not all databases implement such advanced SQL features as LIMIT, OFFSET, or SEQUENCE. The dialect makes it compatible.

## 5.8.2 Common SQL dialects in Hibernate

### 5.8.2.1 How to configure SQL dialect in Hibernate

The SQL dialect is set at the hibernate.cfg.xml or hibernate.properties file.

1. Using hibernate.cfg.xml

```
<hibernate-configuration>
<session-factory>
<!– SQL Dialect Configuration –>
<property name="hibernate.dialect">org.hibernate.dialect.MySQL5Dialect</property>
</session-factory>
</hibernate-configuration>
```

2. Using hibernate.properties

```
hibernate.dialect=org.hibernate.dialect.MySQL5Dialect
```

### 5.8.2.2 How Hibernate uses SQL dialect

1. Query Translation:
   - In the query case of HQL (e.g., from Employee where id =:id), Hibernate converts the query into SQL depending on the dialect used.
   - Example:

```
HQL: from Employee where id =:id
MySQL SQL: SELECT * FROM Employee WHERE id =?
PostgreSQL SQL: SELECT * FROM "Employee" WHERE id =?
```

1. Keyword Differences:
   - MySQL has a LIMIT used to perform pagination, whereas pagination in Oracle uses ROWNUM. The dialect guarantees the use of the appropriate keyword.
2. Data Types:
   - Dialects convert Java data types into SQL data types of databases.

## 5.9 Entity in Hibernate Object-Relational Mapping

In Hibernate ORM, an entity represents a table in the database, and each entity instance corresponds to a row in that table. The @Entity annotation is used to declare a class as an entity.

Annotations

1. @Entity
   - Marks the class as a persistent Hibernate entity.
   - The class will be mapped to a table in the database.
2. @Table
   - (Optional) Used to specify the table name explicitly.
   - If not used, Hibernate assumes the table name is the same as the class name.
3. @Id
   - Specifies the primary key for the entity.
4. @Column
   - Maps a field to a column in the database.
   - Optional attributes include:
     - name: Specifies the column name.
     - nullable: Decides whether the column may be empty or not (true or false).
     - unique: This command is used to make sure that the column values are unique.
     - length: This is used to give the length of the column used in String fields.
5. @Id

   ```
   @GeneratedValue(strategy = GenerationType.IDENTITY) // Auto-generate primary key
   private Long id;
   ```

   **Relationships**:

   ```
   @OneToMany(mappedBy = "entityName")
   private List<OtherEntity>relatedEntities;
   ```

   - Many-to-One Example:

     ```
     import jakarta.persistence.ManyToOne;
     @ManyToOne
     private AnotherEntityanotherEntity;
     ```

   - One-to-One Example:

     ```
     import jakarta.persistence.OneToOne;
     @OneToOne
     private SomeEntitysomeEntity;
     ```

   - Many-to-Many Example:

   ```
   import jakarta.persistence.ManyToMany;

   @ManyToMany
   private List<AnotherEntity>anotherEntities;
   ```

These annotations provide the structure for mapping Java objects to relational database tables using Hibernate ORM.

## 5.10 Utilities Hibernate Object-Relational Mapping

Hibernate ORM also has a number of utilities to simplify the operations with databases and effectively manipulate the entities. These utilities have session management, transaction management, and configuration features, among others. Hibernate ORM major utilities include the following:

1. SessionFactory:
   - SessionFactory is a thread-safe object whereby we use it to create session objects. This is developed once in the application lifecycle, and it is utilized to create a database connection, cache configuration, and other properties of Hibernate ORM.
     SessionFactorysessionFactory = new Configuration().configure().buildSessionFactory();
   - Configuration().configure() loads the Hibernate configuration using hibernate.cfg.xml file.
   - buildSessionfactory: This is used to create the SessionFactory object upon which you can open up session instances.
2. Session:
   - The CRUD operations are carried out on the database by using session (e.g., saving, updating, deleting, and querying entities). It describes an individual work item (a database transaction).
     Session session = sessionFactory.openSession();
     Transaction transaction = session.beginTransaction();
   - openSession()opens a new session of the SessionFactory.
   - beginTransaction() begins opens up a new transaction to the session.
   - You are able to make use of the session to carry out operations such as save(), update (), delete() and query().
   - Always roll off or undo the transaction and close the session in the end.
3. Transaction:
   - Hibernate Transaction is used to control the transaction lifecycle. It makes sure that the processes such as saving or updating an entity are reflected in the database or reverted in case of any error.
     Transaction transaction = session.beginTransaction();
     transaction.commit(); // or transaction.rollback();
   - beginTransaction() initiates a new transaction.
   - commit()makes the transaction permanent and into the database.
   - rollback()reverses the changes that are in the ongoing transaction in case something goes wrong.
4. Query and Criteria API:

- Hibernate offers alternative forms of querying the database: HQL, Criteria API, and Native SQL. HQL is executed with Query, and Criteria is a more object-oriented means of querying.
- Query Syntax:
  Query query = session.createQuery("FROM Entity WHERE property=:value");
  query.setParameter("value", someValue);
  List<Entity> result = query.list();
- Criteria API Syntax:
  Criteria criteria = session.createCriteria(Entity.class);
  criteria.add(Restrictions.eq("property", someValue));
  List<Entity> result = criteria.list();
- createQuery() creates a query from HQL.
- createCriteria() creates a Criteria object to build more dynamic queries using method chaining.

**5.** TransactionManager:
- Hibernate also has a TransactionManager interface that is used to administer distributed transactions in more sophisticated applications. It is commonly applied in those environments that need a Java Transaction API (JTA) or multidatabase operations.
- You can set up the transaction manager in a JTA environment like Java EE or Spring for managing distributed transactions.

**6.** HibernateUtil (Utility Class):
- A utility class to simplify session management and Hibernate setup in an application.
- HibernateUtil is used to initialize and configure the Hibernate SessionFactory.
- The getSession() method can be used to retrieve the current session.

**7.** Transaction Management with Spring (if using Spring Framework):
- If you use Spring, Hibernate transactions can be managed with @Transactional annotations, reducing boilerplate code.

  Example:
  @Transactional
  public void saveEntity(Entity entity) {
  session.save(entity);
  }
- Spring's @Transactional annotation manages the transaction boundaries, and you don't need to manually start or commit the transaction.

**8.** Session.get() and Session.load():
- Both methods are used to retrieve an entity from the database.
- session.get(): Fetches an entity by its primary key. Returns null if the entity is not found.
- session.load(): Fetches an entity by its primary key. Throws an exception if the entity is not found.
  Entity entity1 = session.get(Entity.class, entityId);
  Entity entity2 = session.load(Entity.class, entityId);

- get() will return null if the entity is not found.
- load() will throw an exception (e.g., ObjectNotFoundException) if the entity does not exist.

9. Session.clear() and Session.evict():
   - These methods are used to manage the session's cache.
   - session.clear(): Clears the session cache. This is helpful when you want to free up memory and remove all cached entities.
   - session.evict(): Removes a specific entity from the session cache.
     session.clear(); // Clears all objects in session cache
     session.evict(entity); // Evicts specific entity from session cache
   - clear() clears the session's entire cache.
   - evict() removes a specific entity from the session's cache, which forces a fresh query the next time it's accessed.
10. SessionFactory.openSession()
    - Opens a new session with the database. This is needed to interact with the database and perform CRUD operations.
      Session session = sessionFactory.openSession();
    - openSession() creates a new session object from the session factory. Sessions are lightweight and should be closed after use to avoid memory leaks.

## 5.11 Data Access Object class

The DAO is a very important class of Hibernate ORM, and it determines how an application communicates with a database. It gets between the application and underlying database, and contains all the data access logic, and hides it under the business logic.

### 5.11.1 Need of Data Access Object class in Hibernate Object-Relational Mapping

1. Separation of Concerns:
   - The DAO class decouples the persistence logic (i.e., work concerning saving, retrieving, updating, and deleting data into the database) and the business logic. This ensures that there is clean and maintainable code, as there is only one place where the data access logic is stored, and it is not interwoven with the business logic.
2. Abstraction:
   - The DAO type is an abstraction layer, which conceals the details of direct Hibernate work. As an illustration, you do not need to work with raw SQL queries, session management, and other issues with transactions in your business logic. All of this is done automatically by the DAO.
3. Reusability:
   - Reuse of the same code anywhere that it is needed by placing database operations in the DAO layer. This removes the redundancy and eases the maintenance where

alterations to the data access logic are required (i.e., switching Hibernate to some other ORM).

4. Transaction Management:
   - Transactions with the DAO class tend to start, execute, or undo a transaction when making a CRUD operation. This makes operations implemented successfully or reversed in case of error, data consistency and integrity are maintained.
5. Error Handling:
   - The DAO class contains centralized database error handling. This enables the application to deal with database errors (connection failures, constraint violations, or invalid queries) uniformly and respond.
6. Encapsulation:
   - The DAO encompasses the logic of interacting with the database and can be changed to change the database schema or the underlying persistence technology without touching the rest of the application. Should you also change the ORM (e.g., change Hibernate to another, such as JPA), the DAO can be changed without touching the application logic.
7. Simplified Testing:
   - By encapsulating all database interactions in the DAO class, it becomes easier to mock or stub these interactions when testing other parts of the application. Unit tests can focus on business logic without needing to interact with a live database.
8. Flexibility and Maintainability:
   - The DAO design allows you to update or optimize data access logic independently. For example, if you need to change the query logic or optimize performance by adjusting SQL queries, you can do it in the DAO without touching the rest of the application.
9. Consistency:
   - With a DAO class in place, you can ensure consistent behavior across the application. All database-related actions follow the same pattern, making the application more predictable and easier to maintain.
10. Database Independence:
    - Hibernate itself abstracts away the database-specific details (e.g., SQL dialects), and using DAO, you can keep the business logic database-independent. If you want to switch to a different database in the future, you may only need to modify the DAO layer (e.g., changing database connection settings).

### 5.11.2 Benefits of Data Access Object class in Hibernate Object-Relational Mapping

1. Promotes clean code architecture by following the Single Responsibility Principle.
2. Improves testability by isolating the data access logic.
3. Reduces code duplication by centralizing common data access operations (CRUD).
4. Ensures easier future changes when modifying database interactions.

5. Provides better error management and transaction handling.

DAO in Hibernate ORM has assisted in ensuring that the application architecture is well managed, scalable, and flexible so that the database-related activities are not bound to the core business process of the application.

Hibernate ORM contains a DAO class that is a class that is in charge of all the communication with the database, which is an abstraction layer between the database operations and application logic. The DAO itself has CRUD operations, such as saving, retrieving, updating, and deleting objects in the database. To individual CRUD operations and display the result you have to do the following steps:

1. Create an instance of UserDao.
2. Use the appropriate methods (save, get, update, delete, getAll) from the UserDao class.
3. Display the results using standard Java output (System.out.println()).

# Bibliography

Hibernate. (2024). CRUD Operations. https://hibernate.org

IBM. (2024). Database Connectivity. https://www.ibm.com/docs

MongoDB. (2024). MongoDB Docs. https://www.mongodb.com/docs/

Oracle. (2024). MySQL JDBC Guide. https://dev.mysql.com/doc/

PostgreSQL. (2024). JDBC Docs. https://www.postgresql.org/docs/

Spring. (2024). Spring Data JPA Docs. https://docs.spring.io/spring-data/jpa/docs/current/reference/html/

# 6 Advanced Hibernate: inheritance, relationships, and performance tuning

## 6.1 Inheritance in Hibernate Object-Relational Mapping

In Hibernate Object-Relational Mapping (ORM), inheritance refers to the ability to map an object-oriented class hierarchy (i.e., parent and child classes) to a relational database schema. This is used when you want to model class hierarchies, where subclasses inherit attributes and behaviors from the superclass.

Categories of inheritance in Hibernate ORM

1. Single table inheritance (STI)
2. Joined table inheritance (JTI)
3. Table per class inheritance (TPC)

1. **Single Table Inheritance**

- All classes in the hierarchy are mapped to a single table. A discriminator column is used to distinguish between different subclasses.

```
@Entity
@Inheritance(strategy=InheritanceType.SINGLE_TABLE)
@DiscriminatorColumn(name="type", discriminatorType=DiscriminatorType.STRING)
public class SuperClass {
@Id
@GeneratedValue(strategy=GenerationType.IDENTITY)
private Long id;
private String name;
}
@Entity
@DiscriminatorValue("SubClassA")
public class SubClassA extends SuperClass {
private String fieldA;
}
@Entity
@DiscriminatorValue("SubClassB")
public class SubClassB extends SuperClass {
private String fieldB;
}
```

Mastering Java Full Stack Development. DOI: https://doi.org/10.1016/B978-0-443-51683-2.00006-0

**2. Joined Table Inheritance**

- Each class in the hierarchy is mapped to its own table, and a join is performed between them to retrieve the complete object.

```
@Entity
@Inheritance(strategy=InheritanceType.JOINED)
public class SuperClass {
@Id
@GeneratedValue(strategy=GenerationType.IDENTITY)
private Long id;
private String name;
}
@Entity
public class SubClassA extends SuperClass {
private String fieldA;
}
@Entity
public class SubClassB extends SuperClass {
private String fieldB;
}
```

**3. Table Per Class Inheritance**

- Each class in the hierarchy is mapped to its own table, which includes all the fields for both the superclass and subclass. No join is required.

```
@Entity
@Inheritance(strategy=InheritanceType.TABLE_PER_CLASS)
public class SuperClass {
@Id
@GeneratedValue(strategy=GenerationType.IDENTITY)
private Long id;
private String name;
}
@Entity
public class SubClassA extends SuperClass {
private String fieldA;
}
@Entity
public class SubClassB extends SuperClass {
private String fieldB;
}
```

## 6.2 Configurations in inheritance in Hibernate Object-Relational Mapping

**1. @Inheritance**

- Specifies the inheritance strategy for the entity class.

@Inheritance(strategy=InheritanceType.[STRATEGY_TYPE])

- Options for InheritanceType:
- SINGLE_TABLE
- JOINED
- TABLE_PER_CLASS

**2. @DiscriminatorColumn**

- Used to define a column for the discriminator in single table inheritance.

@DiscriminatorColumn(name="[COLUMN_NAME]", discriminatorType=DiscriminatorType.[DISCRIMINATOR_TYPE])

- Options for DiscriminatorType:
- STRING
- INTEGER

**3. @DiscriminatorValue**

- Specifies the value for the discriminator column in single table inheritance.

@DiscriminatorValue("[DISCRIMINATOR_VALUE]")

**4. @Entity**

- Marks the class as a persistent entity that will be mapped to a table in the database.

```
@Entity
public class [ClassName] {
// Fields and methods
}
```

**5. @Id**

- Specifies the primary key of the entity.

```
@Id
@GeneratedValue(strategy=GenerationType.[ID_GENERATION_STRATEGY])
private [DataType] [fieldName];
```

- Options for GenerationType:
- IDENTITY

- SEQUENCE
- AUTO

**6. @GeneratedValue**

- Defines the strategy for generating primary key values.

@GeneratedValue(strategy=GenerationType.[ID_GENERATION_STRATEGY])

- Options for GenerationType:
- IDENTITY
- SEQUENCE
- AUTO

**7. @Table**

- Specifies the name of the table to which the entity will be mapped.

@Table(name="[TABLE_NAME]")

**8. @Column**

- Defines the properties of a column that maps to an entity field.

@Column(name="[COLUMN_NAME]", [optional attributes like length, nullable, etc.])
private [DataType] [fieldName];

## 6.3 Polymorphism

In Hibernate ORM, polymorphism refers to the ability of a class to be treated as an instance of its superclass or subclass, allowing for dynamic method dispatch. It enables different subclasses to be stored in the same table or multiple tables depending on the inheritance strategy.

**Categories of polymorphism in Hibernate ORM:**

1. Single Table Inheritance

- All subclasses are stored in a single table. A discriminator column differentiates between different subclasses.

Syntax:
@Inheritance(strategy=InheritanceType.SINGLE_TABLE)
@DiscriminatorColumn(name="[discriminator_column_name]",
discriminatorType=DiscriminatorType.[DISCRIMINATOR_TYPE])

2. Joined Table Inheritance

- Each subclass is stored in its own table, and tables are joined when data is fetched. This method uses a foreign key relationship between the subclass and the superclass.

Syntax:
@Inheritance(strategy=InheritanceType.JOINED)

**3.** Table Per Class Inheritance

- Each class in the inheritance hierarchy has its own table, and no join operations are needed. Each table includes all fields of the class.

Syntax:
@Inheritance(strategy=InheritanceType.TABLE_PER_CLASS)

**Key annotations for polymorphism:**

- @Inheritance(strategy=InheritanceType.[STRATEGY]): Specifies the inheritance strategy.
- SINGLE_TABLE
- JOINED
- TABLE_PER_CLASS
- @DiscriminatorColumn(name="[column_name]", discriminatorType=DiscriminatorType.[type]): Used for Single Table Inheritance (STI) to specify the discriminator column.
- DiscriminatorType.STRING
- DiscriminatorType.INTEGER
- @DiscriminatorValue("[value]"): Defines the discriminator value in subclasses when using STI.

These annotations enable polymorphism in Hibernate ORM by allowing inheritance hierarchies to be mapped to database tables with specific strategies.

## 6.4 Relations in Hibernate Object-Relational Mapping

In Hibernate ORM, relationships refer to how entities are related to one another, and Hibernate uses annotations to map these relationships to the database.

**Types of relationships in Hibernate ORM:**

**1.** One-to-One Relationship

- A one-to-one relationship means that each record in one entity is associated with exactly one record in another entity.

Syntax:
@OneToOne
@JoinColumn(name="[column_name]")

**2.** One-to-Many Relationship

- A one-to-many relationship means that one record in an entity is associated with multiple records in another entity.

Syntax:

```
@OneToMany
@JoinColumn(name="[column_name]")
```

3. Many-to-One Relationship

- A many-to-one relationship means that many records in one entity are associated with a single record in another entity.

  Syntax:

```
@ManyToOne
@JoinColumn(name="[column_name]")
```

4. Many-to-Many Relationship

- A many-to-many relationship means that many records in one entity are associated with many records in another entity.

Syntax:

```
@ManyToMany
@JoinTable(
name="[join_table_name]",
joinColumns=@JoinColumn(name="[column_name_in_entity]"),
inverseJoinColumns=@JoinColumn(name="[column_name_in_other_entity]")
)
```

**Common annotations:**

- @OneToOne: Maps a one-to-one relationship.
- @OneToMany: Maps a one-to-many relationship.
- @ManyToOne: Maps a many-to-one relationship.
- @ManyToMany: Maps a many-to-many relationship.
- @JoinColumn: Specifies the column for joining tables in one-to-one, one-to-many, and many-to-one relationships.
- @JoinTable: Used for many-to-many relationships to specify the join table and its columns.
- mappedBy: Used in a one-to-many or many-to-one association to specify the owning side of the relationship. This is used in the inverse side of a relationship.

**Fetch types in associated relationships:**

- Lazy Fetching: Data is loaded only when it is accessed.

```
@OneToMany(fetch=FetchType.LAZY)
```

- Eager Fetching: Data is loaded immediately when the parent entity is loaded.

```
@OneToMany(fetch=FetchType.EAGER)
```

**Cascade types in associated relationships:**

- CascadeType.ALL: Applies all cascade operations.

@OneToMany(cascade=CascadeType.ALL)

- CascadeType.PERSIST: Propagates the persist() operation.
- CascadeType.MERGE: Propagates the merge() operation.
- CascadeType.REMOVE: Propagates the remove() operation.

These annotations help Hibernate manage relationships between entities and the corresponding foreign key relationships in the database. They define how entities are associated and how operations (like saving, updating, or deleting) are cascaded across related entities.

## 6.5 Cascade types in Hibernate Object-Relational Mapping

In Hibernate, cascade types refer to the set of operations that can be propagated from a parent entity to its related entities. This allows for automatic handling of operations like save, update, delete, etc., on associated entities when a certain operation is performed on the parent entity.

**Cascade types in Hibernate:**

1. **CascadeType.ALL**

- Propagates all operations (save, update, delete, etc.) to the associated entity.

Syntax:
@OneToMany(cascade=CascadeType.ALL)

2. **CascadeType.PERSIST**

- Propagates the persist() operation, meaning that if the parent entity is saved, the associated entities will be saved as well.

Syntax:
@OneToMany(cascade=CascadeType.PERSIST)

3. **CascadeType.MERGE**

- Propagates the merge() operation, meaning that if the parent entity is updated, the associated entities will be updated as well.

**Syntax:**
@OneToMany(cascade=CascadeType.MERGE)

4. **CascadeType.REMOVE**

- Propagates the remove() operation, meaning that if the parent entity is deleted, the associated entities will also be deleted.

Syntax:
@OneToMany(cascade=CascadeType.REMOVE)

**5. CascadeType.REFRESH**

- Propagates the refresh() operation, meaning that if the parent entity is refreshed (reloaded from the database), the associated entities will also be refreshed.

Syntax:
@OneToMany(cascade=CascadeType.REFRESH)

**6. CascadeType.DETACH**

- Propagates the detach() operation, meaning that if the parent entity is detached from the persistence context, the associated entities will also be detached.

Syntax:
@OneToMany(cascade=CascadeType.DETACH)

**Cascade types in action:**

- Multiple Cascade Types: You can specify more than one cascade type, separated by commas.

@OneToMany(cascade={CascadeType.PERSIST, CascadeType.MERGE})

- Default Cascade Behavior: If no cascade is specified, no cascading will occur by default, meaning associated entities will not be affected by operations on the parent entity unless explicitly specified.

**Example of using cascade types in a relationship:**

@OneToMany(cascade=CascadeType.ALL)
private Set<Book> books;
This means that all operations (save, update, delete, etc.) on the parent entity will be cascaded to the books collection.

## 6.6 Advanced relationship in Hibernate Object-Relational Mapping

In Hibernate ORM, advanced relationship operations refer to complex or custom actions that are performed when working with entity associations like OneToOne, OneToMany, ManyToOne, and ManyToMany. These operations allow you to manage how entities are related and how data is propagated across these relationships, including cascading operations, lazy loading, fetch strategies, and more.

1. Cascading Operations

Cascading allows operations (like persist, merge, remove, etc.) to propagate to related entities automatically. You can specify which operations should cascade to the related entities.

Syntax:

```
@OneToMany(cascade=CascadeType.ALL) // Cascades all operations (persist, merge, remove, refresh)
private Set<EntityName> relatedEntities;
```

Cascade Types include:

- CascadeType.PERSIST: Cascades save() operation.
- CascadeType.MERGE: Cascades update() operation.
- CascadeType.REMOVE: Cascades delete() operation.
- CascadeType.REFRESH: Cascades refresh() operation.
- CascadeType.DETACH: Cascades detach() operation.
- CascadeType.ALL: Cascades all the above operations.

**2.** Fetch Strategies (Lazy vs Eager Loading)

Fetching strategies determine how related entities are loaded. Lazy loading fetches related entities on-demand, while eager loading fetches them immediately.

Syntax for Lazy Loading:

```
@OneToMany(fetch=FetchType.LAZY) // Default fetch type for collections
private Set<EntityName> relatedEntities;
```

Syntax for Eager Loading:

```
@OneToMany(fetch=FetchType.EAGER) // Forces immediate fetching
private Set<EntityName> relatedEntities;
```

**3.** Join Fetching (Using HQL or Criteria API)

In some cases, it's useful to join related entities explicitly using HQL or the Criteria API to optimize fetching.

Syntax with HQL:

```
String hql="SELECT e FROM Entity e JOIN FETCH e.relatedEntities WHERE e.property=:value";
Query<Entity> query=session.createQuery(hql);
query.setParameter("value", value);
List<Entity> result=query.getResultList();
```

Syntax with Criteria API:

```
CriteriaBuilder cb=session.getCriteriaBuilder();
CriteriaQuery<Entity> cq=cb.createQuery(Entity.class);
Root<Entity> root=cq.from(Entity.class);
root.fetch("relatedEntities", JoinType.LEFT);
cq.select(root).where(cb.equal(root.get("property"), value));
Query<Entity> query=session.createQuery(cq);
List<Entity> results=query.getResultList();
```

**4.** Bidirectional Relationships

In bidirectional relationships, both entities can reference each other. You typically use the mappedBy attribute to avoid creating two foreign keys.

Syntax for OneToMany and ManyToOne:

```
@ManyToOne
@JoinColumn(name="entity_id")
private EntityName entity;
@OneToMany(mappedBy="entity") // 'entity' is the field in the other class
private Set<RelatedEntity> relatedEntities;
```

**5.** Many-to-Many Relationship

In a many-to-many relationship, both entities reference each other, and an intermediary join table is usually created automatically.

Syntax for ManyToMany:

```
@ManyToMany(cascade=CascadeType.ALL, fetch=FetchType.LAZY)
@JoinTable(
name="Entity_EntityName", // Join table name
joinColumns=@JoinColumn(name="entity_id"), // Foreign key in the join table
inverseJoinColumns=@JoinColumn(name="related_entity_id") // Foreign key to the other entity
)
private Set<RelatedEntity> relatedEntities;
```

**6.** Mapping with @JoinTable

In case of ManyToMany or custom join strategies, you can explicitly define the join table and columns using @JoinTable.

Syntax:

```
@ManyToMany
@JoinTable(
name="book_author", // Name of the join table
joinColumns=@JoinColumn(name="book_id"), // Foreign key in the current entity table
inverseJoinColumns=@JoinColumn(name="author_id") // Foreign key in the related entity table
)
private Set<Author> authors;
```

**7.** Optional Relationships

By default, relationships in Hibernate are required. If a relationship is optional, you can specify it using optional in the annotation.

Syntax for OneToOne Optional Relationship:

```
@OneToOne(optional=true)
@JoinColumn(name="profile_id")
private Profile profile;
```

**8.** Mapping the Relationship with Inheritance

When dealing with inheritance, you can use relationships between parent and child classes. Here, entities can inherit properties or relationships.

Syntax for Inheritance (with @OneToMany on Parent Class):

```
@OneToMany(cascade=CascadeType.ALL, fetch=FetchType.LAZY)
@JoinColumn(name="parent_id")
private Set<ChildEntity> childEntities;
```

**9.** Delete-orphan Cascade Type

In certain cases, orphaned entities (entities that are removed from a relationship) should be automatically deleted. This can be achieved by using the CascadeType.REMOVE along with the orphanRemoval flag.

Syntax:

```
@OneToMany(cascade=CascadeType.ALL, orphanRemoval=true)
private Set<EntityName> relatedEntities;
```

**10.** Composite Key in Relationships

In case of composite keys, relationships are mapped using @Embeddable and @EmbeddedId.

Syntax for EmbeddedId:

```
@EmbeddedId
private CompositeKey key;
@ManyToOne
@JoinColumn(name="foreign_key_column")
private EntityName relatedEntity;
```

**11.** Using @Fetch and @BatchSize for Optimized Fetching

You can control the batch size for fetching collections to reduce the number of SQL queries executed.

Syntax:

```
@OneToMany(fetch=FetchType.LAZY)
@Fetch(FetchMode.SUBSELECT)
@BatchSize(size=10) // Batch size for fetching related entities
private Set<EntityName> relatedEntities;
```

## 6.7 Unidirectional versus bidirectional relationship

In Hibernate ORM, relationships between entities can be classified as **unidirectional** or **bidirectional**. These terms refer to the direction in which the relationship is navigated. The key difference lies in how the relationship is represented on either side (or both sides) of the entities involved.

### 1. Unidirectional Relationship

A **unidirectional relationship** means that one entity references another, but the reverse is not true. This type of relationship is only navigable from one side (one entity class) to the other. The other entity does not have any reference to the first one.

**Syntax for Unidirectional Relationships**

**One-to-One Unidirectional:**

```
@OneToOne
@JoinColumn(name="entity_id") // Foreign key column in the table
private EntityName entity;
```

**One-to-Many Unidirectional:**

```
@OneToMany
@JoinColumn(name="entity_id") // Foreign key column in the related table
private Set<EntityName> relatedEntities;
```

**Many-to-One Unidirectional:**

```
@ManyToOne
@JoinColumn(name="related_entity_id") // Foreign key column
private EntityName entity;
```

**Many-to-Many Unidirectional:**

```
@ManyToMany
@JoinTable(
name="entity_related_entity", // Join table name
joinColumns=@JoinColumn(name="entity_id"), // Foreign key column for the current entity
inverseJoinColumns=@JoinColumn(name="related_entity_id") // Foreign key for related entity
)
private Set<RelatedEntity> relatedEntities;
```

Characteristics of Unidirectional Relationships:

- Only one entity knows about the other (either the source or the target entity).
- The target entity does not maintain a reference to the source entity, which can sometimes simplify the domain model but limit functionality (such as navigating the relationship from both sides).

### 2. Bidirectional Relationship

Bidirectional relationship implies that each entity knows about each other as well as there is a reference to one another. This gives the ability to navigate the relationship in both directions and in most cases, involves the delicate maintenance of the relationship to avoid complications such as circular dependencies or foreign key constraints.

**Syntax for Bidirectional Relationships**

**One-to-One Bidirectional:**

```
// In the parent entity
@OneToOne(mappedBy="parent") // 'parent' is the field in the child entity
```

```
private ChildEntity child;
// In the child entity
@OneToOne
@JoinColumn(name="parent_id") // Foreign key column in the child entity's table
private ParentEntity parent;
```

**One-to-Many Bidirectional:**

```
// In the parent entity
@OneToMany(mappedBy="parent") // 'parent' is the field in the child entity
private Set<ChildEntity> children;
// In the child entity
@ManyToOne
@JoinColumn(name="parent_id") // Foreign key column in the child entity's table
private ParentEntity parent;
```

**Many-to-One Bidirectional:**

```
// In the parent entity
@ManyToOne
@JoinColumn(name="related_entity_id")
private EntityName relatedEntity;
// In the related entity
@OneToMany(mappedBy="relatedEntity")
private Set<ParentEntity> parentEntities;
```

**Many-to-Many Bidirectional:**

```
// In the first entity
@ManyToMany(mappedBy="entities")
private Set<OtherEntity> otherEntities;
// In the second entity
@ManyToMany
@JoinTable(
name="entity_other_entity", // Join table name
joinColumns=@JoinColumn(name="entity_id"),
inverseJoinColumns=@JoinColumn(name="other_entity_id")
)
private Set<Entity> entities;
```

Characteristics of Bidirectional Relationships:

- Both entities have references to each other.
- Bidirectional relationships are typically more complex than unidirectional ones because both sides must be kept in sync to avoid inconsistent or invalid states.
- **MappedBy** attribute is used on the inverse side to avoid duplicate foreign key columns and allow Hibernate to manage the relationship correctly. For example, in a bidirectional OneToMany or ManyToMany relationship, the mappedBy attribute tells Hibernate that one side of the relationship owns the mapping, preventing unnecessary foreign key columns.

**Unidirectional versus Bidirectional**

| Feature | Unidirectional | Bidirectional |
|---|---|---|
| **Reference** | One entity refers to the other. | Both entities refer to each other. |
| **Relationship navigation** | Can be navigated in one direction only. | Can be navigated in both directions. |
| **Mapping complexity** | Simpler, no need for mappedBy. | More complex, uses mappedBy to prevent redundancy. |
| **Use case** | Suitable for simpler relationships. | Used for more complex relationships requiring mutual navigation. |
| **Foreign key ownership** | Foreign key exists only in one table. | Foreign keys may exist in both tables. |

## 6.8 Key entities in Hibernate Object-Relational Mapping

In Hibernate ORM, relationships between entities are managed using key entities. These entities are central to understanding how data is represented and how foreign key constraints and relationships are managed. The key entities in relationships are as follows:

### 1. Primary Key

Primary key is a special identifier of the given entity in the database. The primary key will be mapped in the Hibernate with the help of the annotation-@ID. It ensures that each record in a table can be uniquely identified. The primary key can be a single attribute or a combination of multiple attributes (composite key).

Syntax:

```
@Entity
public class EntityName {
@Id
@GeneratedValue(strategy=GenerationType.IDENTITY)
private Long id;
}
```

### 2. Foreign Key

A **foreign key** is a key that links one table to another. It references the primary key of another entity, establishing the relationship between two entities. In Hibernate, foreign keys are mapped using the @ManyToOne, @OneToMany, @ManyToMany, or @OneToOne annotations, depending on the type of relationship.

Syntax for Foreign Key in Various Relationships:

**One-to-Many:**

```
@OneToMany
@JoinColumn(name="foreign_key_column")
```

```
private Set<ChildEntity> children;
```

**Many-to-One:**

```
@ManyToOne
@JoinColumn(name="foreign_key_column")
private ParentEntity parent;
```

**Many-to-Many:**

```
@ManyToMany
@JoinTable(
name="entity_related_entity",
joinColumns=@JoinColumn(name="entity_id"),
inverseJoinColumns=@JoinColumn(name="related_entity_id")
)
private Set<RelatedEntity> relatedEntities;
```

### 3. Join Table

A **join table** is used in **Many-to-Many** relationships to store the associations between two entities. It contains foreign keys from both the entities involved in the relationship. In Hibernate, it is specified using the @JoinTable annotation.

Syntax for Join Table in Many-to-Many:

```
@ManyToMany
@JoinTable(
name="entity_related_entity", // Join table name
joinColumns=@JoinColumn(name="entity_id"), // Foreign key for the current entity
inverseJoinColumns=@JoinColumn(name="related_entity_id") // Foreign key for related entity
)
private Set<RelatedEntity> relatedEntities;
```

### 4. MappedBy

The mappedBy attribute is used in bidirectional relationships to define the ownership of the relationship. It indicates that the relationship is mapped on the other side and prevents the creation of redundant foreign key columns.

Syntax:

**One-to-Many (Bidirectional):**

```
@OneToMany(mappedBy="parent")
private Set<ChildEntity> children;
```

In the ChildEntity, the parent is the field that refers back to the ParentEntity. Hibernate will not create another foreign key column in the ParentEntity table because the relationship is owned by the ChildEntity.

### 5. Composite Key

A **composite key** is used when a combination of multiple fields is required to uniquely identify a record. In Hibernate, composite keys are represented using the @Embeddable and @EmbeddedId annotations.

Syntax:
**Composite Key using** @EmbeddedId:

```
@Embeddable
public class CompositeKey implements Serializable {
private Long idPart1;
private Long idPart2;
}
@Entity
public class Entity {
@EmbeddedId
private CompositeKey id;
}
```

### 6. Inverse Join Column

An **inverse join column** is used in bidirectional relationships where the owning side of the relationship defines the foreign key column in the database. It is defined using the inverseJoinColumns attribute in the @JoinTable annotation.

Syntax:

```
@ManyToMany
@JoinTable(
name="entity_related_entity",
joinColumns=@JoinColumn(name="entity_id"),
inverseJoinColumns=@JoinColumn(name="related_entity_id") // Inverse join column
)
private Set<RelatedEntity> relatedEntities;
```

Key entities in hibernate relationships:

| Key entity | Description | Hibernate annotation |
|---|---|---|
| **Primary key** | Uniquely identifies a record in the entity's table. | @Id, @GeneratedValue |
| **Foreign key** | References the primary key of another entity to establish relationships. | @ManyToOne, @OneToMany, @ManyToMany, @OneToOne, @JoinColumn |
| **Join table** | Used in many-to-many relationships to store foreign keys from both sides. | @JoinTable |
| **MappedBy** | Defines the owning side of the relationship in bidirectional relationships. | mappedBy (on the inverse side) |
| **Composite key** | A key made up of multiple fields to uniquely identify a record. | @EmbeddedId, @Embeddable |
| **Inverse join column** | Defines the column that represents the inverse foreign key in a bidirectional relationship. | inverseJoinColumns |

These key entities form the backbone of how relationships are structured and maintained in Hibernate ORM. Proper configuration and mapping of these key entities allow Hibernate to handle relationships, foreign keys, and cascading operations effectively.

## 6.9 Self-referencing

Self-referencing relationships are present with Hibernate ORM because a self-related entity exists. This normally comes in handy in situations when we have a hierarchical arrangement, such as when we have the bosses managing the employees, or where we have a category with the subcategories. The various forms of self-referencing relationships along with their explanations are provided below:

**1.** One-to-One Self-Referencing Relationship

Syntax:
```
@OneToOne
@JoinColumn(name="foreign_key_column")
private EntityClass entityReference;
```

**2.** One-to-Many Self-Referencing Relationship

Syntax:
```
@OneToMany(mappedBy="entityReference")
private Set<EntityClass> relatedEntities;
```

**3.** Many-to-Many Self-Referencing Relationship

Syntax:
```
@ManyToMany
@JoinTable(
name="join_table_name",
joinColumns=@JoinColumn(name="foreign_key_column"),
inverseJoinColumns=@JoinColumn(name="related_entity_foreign_key_column")
)
private Set<EntityClass> relatedEntities;
```

## Bibliography

Hibernate. (2024). Inheritance Mapping. https://hibernate.org.

IBM. (2024). ORM Relationships. https://www.ibm.com/docs.

Oracle. (2024). JPA Relationships. https://docs.oracle.com.

Red Hat. (2024). Hibernate Advanced Mapping. https://access.redhat.com.

Spring. (2024). Data Relationships Docs. https://docs.spring.io.

# 7

# Spring Model-View-Controller and building web applications

## 7.1 Model-View-Controller web architecture

1. Client Request
   - The client (browser, mobile app, etc.) makes an HTTP request to the server.
2. DispatcherServlet
   - The core of the Spring Web Model-View-Controller (MVC) framework. It intercepts all incoming requests and delegates the request handling to appropriate components like controllers and view resolvers.
   - It serves as a front controller, ensuring centralized control over the request–response process.
3. HandlerMapping
   - The DispatcherServlet consults the HandlerMapping to find the correct controller that should handle the incoming request.
   - Based on the URL pattern, HTTP method, and other criteria, it maps the request to an appropriate controller.
4. Controller
   - The controller processes the incoming request, executes business logic, and interacts with the model (database, service layer, etc.).
   - It then prepares a ModelAndView object, which contains the model (data) and the view name (the page to render).
5. ModelAndView
   - This object holds two pieces of information:
   - Model: Data to be displayed on the view (e.g., user information, order details).
   - View: The logical name of the view to render (e.g., JavaServer Pages [JSP], Thymeleaf template).
6. ViewResolver
   - The ViewResolver resolves the view name to an actual view (JSP, Thymeleaf, FreeMarker, etc.).
   - It maps the name of the logical view that is availed by the controller to a physical view (file) that will render the response.
7. View
   - The view is charged with the responsibility of rendering the model (data) in a friendly format (HTML, JSON, etc.).
   - It works with such technologies as JSP, Thymeleaf, etc., to dynamically create the view material.

Mastering Java Full Stack Development. DOI: https://doi.org/10.1016/B978-0-443-51683-2.00007-2

8. Response Sent to Client
    - The view it produces the last response, which is returned to the client.
    - The client takes the reply and presents the information on the user interface.

## 7.2 Working of web application

The Spring web application architecture is designed into a few layers, which deal with particular issues of the request–response life cycle. These layers allow a clear separation of concerns, and the application is easier to maintain, test, and scale. The major layers of the Spring web application architecture are as follows:

1. Presentation Layer (Client Layer)
    - This layer is the client side of the application, which is usually the web browser or a mobile client communicating with the server side. It is tasked with making the HTTP requests to the server and presenting the responses.
    - Responsibilities:
        - Making HTTP requests (GET, POST, PUT, DELETE) to the server.
        - The presentation of the responses in an easy-to-use format, that is, HTML, JSON, or XML.
        - Processing of user interactions and giving feedback to the server.
2. Web Layer (Controller Layer)
   This is the point at which the main Spring web MVC framework works. The primary constituent in this layer is the DispatcherServlet, which performs the role of the front controller in the Spring MVC structure. It accepts every received request and forwards the request processing to the correct controller.
    - Responsibilities:
        - Handling HTTP requests.
        - Sending requests to relevant controller procedures to be processed.
        - Belonging to the mediation layer between business logic layer and the view (UI).
        - Sending back the view and model information on completion of processing the request.
    - Key Components:
        - DispatcherServlet: It serves as the front controller, which redirects the requests to the right handlers.
        - HandlerMapping: Associates received requests to the appropriate controller method.
        - Controller: This holds the business logic and processes the request.
        - ModelAndView: This is a result of the controller that is a combination of the model (data) and view (template).
3. Service Layer (Business Logic Layer)
    - Business logic and services are stored in the core of the application in this layer. This layer is bounded to the controller layer and is used to implement the business logic.

It handles the computations and data validation as well as communicating with the persistence layer (database).

- Responsibilities:
  - Wrapping up business logic and business rules.
  - Communicating with the data access layer to access or update data.
  - Checking and processing of the data and sending it back to the controller.
- Key Components:
  - Services: Java classes annotated with an annotation of service that carry the business logic.
  - Transaction Management: This is to monitor that business operations are carried out within the framework of a transaction that data remains consistent.

**4.** Persistence Layer (Data Access Layer)

- This layer has the task of communicating with the database and the persistence of application data. It typically uses Object-Relational Mapping (ORM) systems such as Hibernate or JPA to perform database transactions. The persistence layer hides the details of the actual database access and offers a more convenient method of executing the Create, Read, Update, and Delete (CRUD) operations.
- Responsibilities:
  - Storing and accessing data to/from the database.
  - Entity relationship and query management.
  - Working with database connection and transaction handling.
- Key Components:
  - Data Access Object (DAO): The classes that interact with database (CRUD operations).
  - JPA/Hibernate: ORM systems that offer high-level abstraction in communication with databases.
  - Repositories: Spring Data repositories which make the usage of JPA/Hibernate easier.

**5.** Maintain View (Presentation) Layer

This view layer deals with creating the user interface and displaying the model data in a manner that is easy to be displayed to the user. This layer is usually based on such technologies as JSP, Thymeleaf, or FreeMarker in Spring.

- Responsibilities:
  - Extracting the user interface based on model data.
  - Transforming dynamic model data (lists of products, user information, etc.) into HTML, JSON, or XML.
  - Creating dynamic content with view technologies such as JSP or Thymeleaf.
- Key Components:
  - JSP: A view technology that generates HTML content in the server side.
  - Thymeleaf: Thymeleaf is a web application templating engine that is typically used to render HTML and XML.
  - ViewResolver: Maps view names to the real views, according to the configuration.

6. Spring Security Layer
   Security layer is in charge of dealing with authentication, authorization, and security in the application. It has to do with the security of certain resources or the procedure of certain operations that only authorized users may have access.
   - Responsibilities:
     - Authentication (user identity verifying).
     - Authorization (access control [user-based permissions]).
     - Securing against the typical threats in security such as CSRF, XSS, and session fixation.
   - Key Components:
     - Authentication Manager: Deals with the authentication.
     - Security Filters: Filters that protect the HTTP requests and responses.
     - Role-Based Access Control (RBAC): This ensures that the resources can be accessed by the authorized users.
7. Integration Layer
   The layer is expected to perform the communication between the Spring Web Application and the external systems (e.g., third-party APIs, messaging systems, RabbitMQ, Kafka, etc.). It enables Spring to be compatible with other applications and services.
   - Responsibilities:
     - Leveraging and creating messages or web services.
     - Connection to outside systems via REST or SOAP or message queues.
   - Key Components:
     - REST Controllers: Making API endpoints available so that other applications can use them.
     - Java Message Service: Supports communication involving messages with external systems.

All these layers interact with each other such that they maintain a clean and modular architecture, which makes the application easier to maintain, scale, and test. The separation of concerns allows the clear separation of user interface, business logic, and access to data, in favor of a more maintainable codebase.

## 7.3 Form elements

Form elements in Spring MVC bind the form data to Java objects (model objects) and play a vital role in communication with the backend. Below are the most commonly used Spring form elements, their purpose, and their syntax.

1. <form:form>
   - The main container for a form that binds the form data to a model object.

     Syntax:
     <form:form modelAttribute="user">

```
<!- Form elements go here ->
</form:form>
```

- The modelAttribute attribute specifies the Java object (model) to which the form data will be bound.

**2.** <form:input>
- Creates an input field (typically for text or numbers) and binds it to a model property.

Syntax:
```
<form:input path="name"/>
```

- The path attribute specifies which property of the model object will be bound to the input field.

**3.** <form:password>
- Creates a password input field.

Syntax:
```
<form:password path="password"/>
```

- The path attribute binds the password input to the property of the model object (password).

**4.** <form:textarea>
- Creates a multiline text input field (textarea) for larger input.

Syntax:
```
<form:textarea path="description"/>
```

- The path attribute binds the textarea field to the property (description) of the model object.

**5.** <form:select>
- Creates a dropdown (select box) for choosing one option from multiple.

Syntax:
```
<form:select path="gender">
<form:option value="male">Male</form:option>
<form:option value="female">Female</form:option>
</form:select>
```

- The path attribute binds the select field to the gender property. Each form:option element represents an option within the dropdown.

**6.** <form:option>
- Represents an individual option inside a form:select.

Syntax:
```
<form:option value="1">Option 1</form:option>
```

- The value attribute specifies the value that will be sent to the server when the option is selected.

**7.** <form:checkbox>
- Creates a checkbox for boolean values.

  Syntax:
  <form:checkbox path="accepted"/>

- The path attribute binds the checkbox to a boolean property (accepted). It returns true if checked, false if unchecked.

**8.** <form:radio>
- Creates a radio button for selecting one option from a set.

  Syntax:
  <form:radio path="status" value="active"/>
  <form:radio path="status" value="inactive"/>

- The path attribute binds the radio button group to the status property, and value specifies the value for each option.

**9.** <form:hidden>
- Creates a hidden input field.

  Syntax:
  <form:hidden path="userId"/>

- The path attribute binds the hidden input field to the userId property. The value is not visible but is submitted with the form.

**10.** <form:button>
- Creates a button inside a form.

  Syntax:
  <form:button>Submit</form:button>

- This element creates a standard HTML button inside the form.

**11.** <form:errors>
- Displays error messages for form fields that failed validation.

  Syntax:
  <form:errors path="name" cssClass="error"/>

- The path attribute specifies the form field to check for errors, and the cssClass attribute allows you to apply custom styling for error messages.

**12.** <form:label>
- Creates a label for a form element.

  Syntax:
  <form:label path="name">Name</form:label>

- The path attribute binds the label to a specific property of the model object (name), and the text inside the tag is the label text.

**13.** <form:inputCheckbox>

- An input tag specifically used for checkboxes (alternative to form:checkbox).

  Syntax:
  ```
  <form:inputCheckbox path="newsletterSubscription"/>
  ```

- The path attribute binds the checkbox input to a boolean property.

**14.** <form:selectItems>

- Allows you to dynamically populate a form:select dropdown from a collection.

  Syntax:
  ```
  <form:select path="gender">
  <form:selectItems items="${genderOptions}" />
  </form:select>
  ```

- This refers to a collection (like a list or array) that is used to populate the options in the select box.

**15.** <form:date>

- Creates a date input field.

  Syntax:
  ```
  <form:date path="birthDate" />
  ```

- The path binds the date field to a property (birthDate).

**16.** <form:datetime>

- Creates a datetime input field.

  Syntax:
  ```
  <form:datetime path="eventDate" />
  ```

- Binds the datetime input to a Java property (eventDate) representing a date and time.

**17.** <form:range>

- Creates a range input (slider).

  Syntax:
  ```
  <form:range path="age" min="18" max="100"/>
  ```

- The min and max attributes define the range of values, and path binds the range field to the age property.

**18.** <form:inputDate>

- Creates an input field for date entries.

  Syntax:
  ```
  <form:inputDate path="dateOfBirth"/>
  ```

- The path binds the input field to the dateOfBirth property.

**19.** <form:file>

- Creates a file upload field.

Syntax:

```
<form:file path="profilePic"/>
```

- The path binds the file input to the profilePic property.

**20.** <form:inputHidden>

- An alternative to <form:hidden>, it creates a hidden input field.

  Syntax:

  ```
  <form:inputHidden path="userSessionId"/>
  ```

- Binds the hidden input field to the userSessionId property.

## 7.4 Form validation controls

In Spring MVC, form validation is a crucial aspect of ensuring that the data entered by users is valid before being processed by the application. Spring provides several ways to implement form validations, such as using annotations, command objects, and validation frameworks like JSR-303/JSR-380.

### 7.4.1 Common form validation controls in Spring Model-View-Controller

**1.** @Valid Annotation

- This annotation is used to trigger validation on form objects in Spring MVC. It is usually placed on the command object in the controller method.

  Syntax:

  ```
  @PostMapping("/submitForm")
  public String submitForm(@Valid @ModelAttribute("form") User user, BindingResult
  result) {
  if (result.hasErrors()) {
  return "formPage"; // Return to form if validation fails
  }
  // Proceed with further processing if validation is successful
  return "successPage";
  }
  ```

**2.** @NotNull

- Ensures that the field is not null.

  Syntax:

  ```
  @NotNull(message = "Name cannot be null")
  private String name;
  ```

- If the field is null, a validation error message will be generated.

**3.** @NotEmpty

- Validates that the field is not empty (works for String and Collection types).

Syntax:

```
@NotEmpty(message = "Email cannot be empty")
private String email;
```

4. @Size
   - Validates the size of a string, collection, or array.

   Syntax:

```
@Size(min = 2, max = 10, message = "Username must be between 2 and 10 characters")
private String username;
```

   - Checks that the size of the string/array/collection is within the specified bounds.
5. @Pattern
   - Ensures that the value matches a specified regular expression pattern.

   Syntax:

```
@Pattern(regexp = "^\\d{10}$", message = "Phone number must be exactly 10 digits")
private String phoneNumber;
```

6. @Min and @Max
   - Validates that the value is within a specified range for numeric values.

   Syntax:

```
@Min(value = 18, message = "Age must be at least 18")
private int age;
@Max(value = 60, message = "Age must be less than or equal to 60")
private int age;
```

7. @Email
   - Validates that the field is a valid email address.

   Syntax:

```
@Email(message = "Please provide a valid email address")
private String email;
```

8. Custom Validator
   - Create custom validation logic for specific requirements.

   Syntax:

```
@Constraint(validatedBy = CustomValidator.class)
@Target({ElementType.METHOD, ElementType.FIELD,
ElementType.ANNOTATION_TYPE, ElementType.PARAMETER})
@Retention(RetentionPolicy.RUNTIME)
public @interface ValidPhoneNumber {
String message() default "Invalid phone number";
Class<?>[] groups() default {};
Class<? extends Payload>[] payload() default {};
}
```

```
CustomValidator.java:
public class CustomValidator implements ConstraintValidator<ValidPhoneNumber,
String> {
@Override
public void initialize(ValidPhoneNumber constraintAnnotation) {}
@Override
public boolean isValid(String value, ConstraintValidatorContext context) {
return value!=null && value.matches("^[0-9]{10}$");
}
}
```

- This custom validator checks if the phone number matches a specific pattern (e.g., 10 digits).

1. @Future and @Past
   - Validates that the date is in the future or past.

   Syntax:
   ```
   @Future(message = "Date must be in the future")
   private Date startDate;
   @Past(message = "Date must be in the past")
   private Date endDate;
   ```

2. @Validating Groups
   - Define different validation groups for different use cases.

   Syntax:
   ```
   public interface CreateGroup {}
   public interface UpdateGroup {}
   @NotNull(groups = CreateGroup.class)
   private String name;
   @Size(min = 10, max = 100, groups = UpdateGroup.class)
   private String address;
   ```

   - Group-based validation is used to apply specific validations during different phases (e.g., create or update).

### 7.4.2 Integrating form validation in Spring Model-View-Controller

Controller Setup:

```
@Controller
public class UserController {
@PostMapping("/submitForm")
public String submitForm(@Valid @ModelAttribute("user") User user, BindingResult
result) {
```

```
if (result.hasErrors()) {
return "userForm"; // Return to form if validation fails
}
return "success";
}
}
```

Form Page Setup (JSP/Thymeleaf):

```
<form:form modelAttribute="user">
<form:input path="name" />
<form:errors path="name" cssClass="error" />
<form:input path="email" />
<form:errors path="email" cssClass="error" />
</form:form>
```

## 7.5 Configurations

To run a Spring Web MVC application, several configurations need to be in place.

**1.** web.xml Configuration (DispatcherServlet and Mapping)
The web.xml is used to configure the DispatcherServlet, which acts as the front controller for the application, routing requests to appropriate controllers.

```
<servlet>
<servlet-name>dispatcher</servlet-name>
<servlet-class>org.springframework.web.servlet.DispatcherServlet</servlet-class>
<init-param>
<param-name>contextConfigLocation</param-name>
<param-value>path_to_spring_config_file</param-value>
</init-param>
<load-on-startup>1</load-on-startup>
</servlet>
<servlet-mapping>
<servlet-name>dispatcher</servlet-name>
<url-pattern>/</url-pattern>
</servlet-mapping>
```

- <servlet>: Configures the Spring DispatcherServlet.
- <init-param>: Specifies the location of the Spring configuration file (e.g., dispatcher-servlet.xml).
- <servlet-mapping>: Maps the DispatcherServlet to the / URL pattern, meaning it will handle all incoming requests.

2. Spring Configuration File (dispatcher-servlet.xml)
   The Spring configuration file (e.g., dispatcher-servlet.xml) holds the Spring beans, view resolvers, and other configurations.

```
<beans xmlns="http://www.springframework.org/schema/beans"
xmlns:xsi="http://www.w3.org/2001/XMLSchema-instance"
xsi:schemaLocation="http://www.springframework.org/schema/beans
http://www.springframework.org/schema/beans/spring-beans.xsd">
<bean
class="org.springframework.web.servlet.view.InternalResourceViewResolver">
<property name="prefix" value="view_prefix" />
<property name="suffix" value="view_suffix" />
</bean>
<context:component-scan base-package="com.example.controller" />
</beans>
```

   - <bean class="org.springframework.web.servlet.view.InternalResourceViewResolver">: Defines the ViewResolver bean to resolve views (JSPs).
   - <property name="prefix" value="view_prefix" />: Specifies the directory where views are stored.
   - <property name="suffix" value="view_suffix" />: Specifies the file extension of views (e.g., .jsp).
   - <context:component-scan base-package="com.example.controller" />: Scans the specified package for Spring-managed components (controllers).

3. Controller Configuration (with Annotations)
   The controller handles the HTTP requests and returns a view name to be rendered. Spring's @Controller annotation marks the class as a controller.

```
@Controller
public class YourController {
@RequestMapping("/yourPath")
public String handleRequest(Model model) {
// Add attributes to model
return "viewName"; // The name of the view to be rendered
}
}
```

   - @Controller: Marks the class as a Spring MVC controller.
   - @RequestMapping("/yourPath"): Maps HTTP requests to the handleRequest() method.
   - return "viewName": Returns the logical name of the view (JSP).

4. ViewResolver Configuration (JSP)
   The ViewResolver bean is used to resolve view names into actual view files (e.g., JSP files).

```
<bean
class="org.springframework.web.servlet.view.InternalResourceViewResolver">
```

```
<property name="prefix" value="/WEB-INF/views/" />
<property name="suffix" value=".jsp" />
</bean>
```

- <property name="prefix" value="/WEB-INF/views/" />: Specifies the folder where JSP files are located.
- <property name="suffix" value=".jsp" />: Specifies the extension of the JSP files.

5. DispatcherServlet Context Configuration in web.xml
In web.xml, we provide the location of the Spring configuration file.

```
<init-param>
<param-name>contextConfigLocation</param-name>
<param-value>/WEB-INF/dispatcher-servlet.xml</param-value>
</init-param>
```

- <init-param>: Specifies the location of the Spring configuration file (dispatcher-servlet.xml).

6. Spring Annotation Config for Controller Scanning
This configuration is used to scan for Spring beans in specific packages.

```
<context:component-scan base-package="com.example.controller" />
```

- <context:component-scan base-package="com.example.controller" />: Scans the specified package (com.example.controller) for annotated Spring beans such as controllers.

7. Spring Java Configuration (For Spring Boot or Java Config)
In modern Spring configurations, Java configuration (instead of XML) is often used for simplicity and flexibility.

```
@Configuration
@EnableWebMvc
@ComponentScan("com.example.controller")
public class WebConfig extends WebMvcConfigurerAdapter {
@Override
public void configureViewResolvers(ViewResolverRegistry registry) {
registry.jsp("/WEB-INF/views/", ".jsp");
}
}
```

- @Configuration: Marks the class as a configuration class.
- @EnableWebMvc: Enables Spring MVC functionality.
- @ComponentScan("com.example.controller"): Scans the specified package for Spring beans.
- configureViewResolvers(ViewResolverRegistry registry): Configures the ViewResolver using Java config.

# 7.6 How to run web application

To run a Spring web application, you need to perform several steps for configuring the project. Below are the key configurations and their syntaxes to run a Spring Web Application.

1. Set Up web.xml
   Configure the Spring DispatcherServlet, which handles incoming HTTP requests and forwards them to appropriate controllers.

```
<servlet>
<servlet-name>dispatcher</servlet-name>
<servlet-class>org.springframework.web.servlet.DispatcherServlet</servlet-class>
<init-param>
<param-name>contextConfigLocation</param-name>
<param-value>/WEB-INF/spring-servlet.xml</param-value>
</init-param>
<load-on-startup>1</load-on-startup>
</servlet>
<servlet-mapping>
<servlet-name>dispatcher</servlet-name>
<url-pattern>/</url-pattern>
</servlet-mapping>
```

   - <servlet-name>: Specifies the name of the DispatcherServlet.
   - <servlet-class>: Defines the class of the DispatcherServlet.
   - <init-param>: Defines initialization parameters. The contextConfigLocation specifies the location of Spring's configuration file.
   - <servlet-mapping>: Maps the DispatcherServlet to the / URL pattern.

2. Configure Spring Beans (spring-servlet.xml)
   This XML configuration file specifies Spring beans like ViewResolver, component scanning, etc.

```
<bean class="org.springframework.web.servlet.view.InternalResourceViewResolver">
<property name="prefix" value="/WEB-INF/views/" />
<property name="suffix" value=".jsp" />
</bean>
<context:component-scan base-package="com.example.controller" />
```

   - <bean>: Configures a Spring bean for ViewResolver to resolve views (JSP files).
   - <context:component-scan>: Enables component scanning for controllers in the specified package.

3. Controller Configuration
   Mark a class as a Spring controller and map methods to specific URLs.

```
@Controller
```

```
public class YourController {
@RequestMapping("/yourPath")
public String handleRequest(Model model) {
// Handle the request and add attributes to the model
return "viewName"; // Logical view name
}
}
```

- @Controller: Marks the class as a Spring MVC controller.
- @RequestMapping("/yourPath"): Maps HTTP requests to the handleRequest() method.

4. View Resolver Configuration
   Defines the location of JSP views and resolves logical view names to actual views.

```
<bean
class="org.springframework.web.servlet.view.InternalResourceViewResolver">
<property name="prefix" value="/WEB-INF/views/" />
<property name="suffix" value=".jsp" />
</bean>
```

- <property name="prefix" value="/WEB-INF/views/" />: Specifies the directory where JSP files are stored.
- <property name="suffix" value=".jsp" />: Specifies the file extension for JSP files.

5. Deploy to a Servlet Container (e.g., Tomcat)
   Deploy the application to a servlet container (e.g., Apache Tomcat) to run the application.
   - Build and Deploy: Package the application as a ⊡war file and deploy it to the servlet container (Tomcat, e.g.).
   - Example of deploying to Tomcat: Place the ⊡war file in the webapps folder of Tomcat and start the server.
6. Spring Java Configuration (Optional, for Spring Boot or Java Config)
   You can also configure the Spring MVC application using Java-based configuration.

```
@Configuration
@EnableWebMvc
@ComponentScan("com.example.controller")
public class WebConfig extends WebMvcConfigurerAdapter {
@Override
public void configureViewResolvers(ViewResolverRegistry registry) {
registry.jsp("/WEB-INF/views/", ".jsp");
}
}
```

- @Configuration: Marks the class as a configuration class.
- @EnableWebMvc: Enables Spring MVC functionality.

- @ComponentScan("com.example.controller"): Specifies the package to scan for controller classes.
- configureViewResolvers(ViewResolverRegistry registry): Configures the ViewResolver using Java-based configuration.

7. Start the Web Application
   Once the application is deployed to the server, access the application via a web browser.
   - URL: The application can be accessed by use of the following URL depending on the configuration and servlet container: http://localhost:8080/yourAppContext/yourPath.

## 7.7 Custom validation

A Spring web application has custom validation components that are defined in terms of application requirements. Custom validators are used to make sure that input data meets some constraints, which may not be enforced by some inbuilt validation annotations such as @NotNull, @Size, etc.

Custom validators in Spring web application: Custom validators enable you to specify custom validation logic that cannot be represented by the default annotations. These validators aid in imposing business regulations and making sure the data is validated per certain requirements.

Key Components for Custom Validators in Spring:

1. Creating a Custom Validator Class
2. Defining a Custom Annotation (Optional)
3. Registering the Validator
4. Handling Validation in Controllers
5. Customizing Error Messages

1. Developing a Custom Validator Class.
   You use the interface of Validator in Spring to develop your own validator. The validate method has the logic of validating an object.

   Syntactics (Custom Implementation):
   class CustomValidator is a public class, which implements Validator.
   @Override
   public boolean supports(Class clazz)
   return YourClass.class.equals(clazz); // Ensure that the class is suitable to this validator.
   }
   @Override
   public void validateObject target, Errors errors)
   YourClass yourClass = (YourClass) target;
   // Custom validation logic
   when (yourClass.getSomeField is a null or yourClass.getSomeField is empty)
   rejectValue (someField, fact, someField.empty);

```
}
}
}
```

- supports(Class<?> clazz): Specifies whether the validator supports a particular class.
- validate(Object target, Errors errors): Contains the logic for validation. If validation fails, add errors using errors.rejectValue().

2. Defining a Custom Annotation (Optional)
   You can define a custom annotation for your validation, which will make it easier to apply the validator on fields in your beans.

   Syntax (Custom Annotation):

```
@Target({ElementType.FIELD, ElementType.METHOD, ElementType.PARAMETER})
@Retention(RetentionPolicy.RUNTIME)
@Constraint(validatedBy = CustomValidator.class) // The validator class
public @interface ValidCustom {
String message() default "Invalid value"; // Default error message
Class<?>[] groups() default {}; // Groups for validation
Class<? extends Payload>[] payload() default {}; // For carrying additional data
}
```

- @Constraint: Specifies the custom validator class that handles validation for this annotation.
- message: Defines the default validation error message.

3. Registering the Validator
   Once you have created a custom validator, you need to register it in your Spring application. This is done either via XML configuration or Java-based configuration.

   Syntax (Java Configuration):

```
@Configuration
public class WebConfig implements WebMvcConfigurer {
@Override
public void addValidators(List<Validator> validators) {
validators.add(new CustomValidator()); // Register the custom validator
}
}
```

- addValidators(List<Validator> validators): Registers the custom validator with the Spring MVC framework.

4. Handling Validation in Controllers
   When handling form submission or binding a model object in Spring MVC, you can use the @Valid annotation to trigger the validation process.

   Syntax (Controller Method):

```
@Controller
```

```
public class YourController {
@RequestMapping("/submit")
public String handleSubmit(@ModelAttribute @Valid YourForm form, BindingResult
result) {
if (result.hasErrors()) {
return "formPage"; // Return the form page if validation fails
}
return "successPage"; // Proceed to the success page if validation succeeds
}
}
```

- @Valid: Initiates the validation for the model attribute (YourForm).
- BindingResult result: Stores the validation results. If there are errors, you can handle them appropriately.

5. Customizing Error Messages
   You can customize error messages in a properties file (messages.properties) to provide more user-friendly messages.

   Syntax (messages.properties):
   ```
   someField.empty=The field cannot be empty. Please provide a value.
   ```

   - someField.empty: The message associated with the validation failure for the someField field.

The key components and steps to implement custom validation in a Spring web application are as follows:

1. Custom Validator Interface
   To create custom validation logic, you need to implement the Validator interface in Spring.

   Syntax:
   ```
   public class CustomValidator implements Validator {
   @Override
   public boolean supports(Class<?> clazz) {
   // Check if the class is a type that can be validated by this validator
   return YourClass.class.equals(clazz);
   }
   @Override
   public void validate(Object target, Errors errors) {
   // Implement custom validation logic
   YourClass yourClass = (YourClass) target;
   if (yourClass.getSomeField() == null || yourClass.getSomeField().isEmpty()) {
   errors.rejectValue("someField", "someField.empty", "Field cannot be empty");
   }
   ```

```
}
}
```

- supports(Class<?> clazz): Determines if this validator supports the given class type.
- validate(Object target, Errors errors): Contains the logic to validate the object. If validation fails, add error messages using errors.rejectValue().

2. Register the Custom Validator in Spring Configuration
   You need to configure Spring to use your custom validator. This can be done either via XML configuration or Java-based configuration.

   Syntax (Java-based Configuration):

```
@Configuration
public class WebConfig implements WebMvcConfigurer {
@Override
public void addValidators(List<Validator> validators) {
validators.add(new CustomValidator());
}
}
```

- addValidators(List<Validator> validators): Registers your custom validator with the Spring application context.

3. Custom Validation Annotations (Optional)
   You can also create custom annotations for validation, which gives you more flexibility and is useful for declarative validation in Spring MVC forms.

   Define Custom Annotation:

```
@Target({ElementType.FIELD, ElementType.METHOD, ElementType.PARAMETER,
ElementType.ANNOTATION_TYPE})
@Retention(RetentionPolicy.RUNTIME)
@Constraint(validatedBy = CustomValidator.class)
public @interface ValidCustom {
String message() default "Invalid value";
Class<?>[] groups() default {};
Class<? extends Payload>[] payload() default {};
}
```

- @Constraint: Specifies the validator class for this annotation.
- @ValidCustom: Custom annotation definition.

  Validator for the Custom Annotation:

```
public class CustomValidator implements ConstraintValidator<ValidCustom, String> {
@Override
public void initialize(ValidCustom constraintAnnotation) {
// Initialize if necessary
}
```

```
@Override
public boolean isValid(String value, ConstraintValidatorContext context) {
if (value == null || value.isEmpty()) {
return false; // Invalid if empty
}
return true;
}
}
```

4. Use Custom Validation in Form or Data Transfer Object
   Once the custom validator or annotation is created, it can be used in your forms or Data Transfer Objects (DTOs) for validation.

   Syntax (DTO):
```
public class YourForm {
@ValidCustom
private String someField;
// Getters and Setters
}
```

   - @ValidCustom: Apply the custom annotation to the field you want to validate.

5. Handling Validation Errors in Controller
   Validation errors can be handled in the controller using BindingResult. If validation fails, it will populate the BindingResult object with error details.

   Syntax (Controller):
```
@Controller
public class YourController {
@RequestMapping("/submit")
public String handleSubmit(@ModelAttribute @Valid YourForm form, BindingResult
result) {
if (result.hasErrors()) {
// Handle validation errors
return "formPage"; // Return to form page with errors
}
// Proceed with normal flow
return "successPage";
}
}
```

   - @Valid: Trigger validation on the model.
   - BindingResult: Stores the validation errors.

6. Custom Validation Messages
   You can also define custom validation messages for your custom validators in the

messages.properties file.

Syntax (messages.properties):
someField.empty=This field cannot be empty

- someField.empty: Custom message associated with a validation failure.

## 7.8 Regular expressions

In Spring web applications, Regular Expression (RegEx) validation is often used to ensure that user input matches a specified pattern. This is typically done using annotations like @Pattern in combination with Spring's validation framework. The @Pattern annotation allows you to specify a regular expression to validate a field.

**Key components for regular expression validation**:

1. @Pattern Annotation:
   - This annotation is used to apply regular expression validation to a field.
   - It checks if the value of a field matches the pattern defined by the regular expression.

   Syntax for Regular Expression Validation in Spring:
2. Using @Pattern Annotation for Field Validation:

   The @Pattern annotation is used directly on a field, providing a regular expression pattern and an optional error message.

```
import javax.validation.constraints.Pattern;
public class User {
@Pattern(regexp = "^[a-zA-Z0-9]{5,15}$", message = "Username must be between 5 and 15
characters and contain only alphanumeric characters.")
private String username;
// Getters and Setters
}
```

   - regexp: This is the regular expression pattern. In this case, the pattern "^[a-zA-Z0-9]{5,15}$" ensures the username is between 5 and 15 characters long and contains only alphanumeric characters (letters and numbers).
   - message: The error message that will be displayed if the input doesn't match the regular expression.
3. Using @Valid Annotation in Controller:

   In Spring MVC, you can use the @Valid annotation to trigger validation on the model object, which includes the @Pattern annotation.

```
@Controller
public class UserController {
@RequestMapping(value = "/register", method = RequestMethod.POST)
public String registerUser(@ModelAttribute @Valid User user, BindingResult result) {
if (result.hasErrors()) {
```

```
return "registerForm"; // Return to the form page if there are errors
}
return "successPage"; // Proceed to the success page if validation passes
}
}
```

- @ModelAttribute @Valid: The @Valid annotation triggers validation of the User object before the controller method is executed.
- BindingResult result: Holds the validation errors. You can check if there are errors and handle them accordingly.

4. Custom Regular Expressions for Different Validations:
   You can define different regular expressions for various kinds of validations, such as validating email addresses, phone numbers, zip codes, etc.

   - Email Validation:

   ```
   @Pattern(regexp = "^[a-zA-Z0-9_+&*-]+(?:\\.[a-zA-Z0-9_+&*-]+)*@(?:[a-zA-Z0-9-]+\\.)
   +[a-zA-Z]{2,7}$", message = "Invalid email address")
   private String email;
   Phone Number Validation:
   @Pattern(regexp = "^\\+?[0-9]{10,15}$", message = "Phone number must be between
   10 to 15 digits")
   private String phoneNumber;
   ```

   - Zip Code Validation:

   ```
   @Pattern(regexp = "^[0-9]{5}-[0-9]{4}$", message = "Invalid ZIP code format")
   private String zipCode;
   ```

5. Customizing Error Messages:
   You can define the error messages in the properties file (messages.properties) to make them more user-friendly and localized.

   ```
   # messages.properties
   username.invalid=Username must be between 5 and 15 characters and contain only
   alphanumeric characters.
   email.invalid=Please enter a valid email address.
   phone.invalid=Phone number must be between 10 to 15 digits.
   zip.invalid=Invalid ZIP code format.
   ```

## 7.9 Display data from the form

In Spring MVC, capturing and displaying data from a registration form involves multiple steps, including creating the form, binding it to a model object, performing validation, and displaying the results. The following is a summary of the implementation of this in a Spring MVC web application, including the relevant settings and syntax.

1. Insert Maven Dependencies (pom.xml)
   Ensure that your pom.xml contains the necessary dependencies of Spring MVC and validation. In the case of Maven, the following dependencies must be added:

```
<dependencies>
<!- Spring Web MVC ->
<dependency>
<groupId>org.springframework</groupId>
<artifactId>spring-webmvc</artifactId>
<version>5.3.8</version>
</dependency>
<!- Spring Context ->
<dependency>
<groupId>org.springframework</groupId>
<artifactId>spring-context</artifactId>
<version>5.3.8</version>
</dependency>
<!- Hibernate Validator for Validation ->
<dependency>
<groupId>org.hibernate</groupId>
<artifactId>hibernate-validator</artifactId>
<version>6.1.0.Final</version>
</dependency>
<!- JSP Support ->
<dependency>
<groupId>javax.servlet.jsp</groupId>
<artifactId>javax.servlet.jsp-api</artifactId>
<version>2.3.3</version>
<scope>provided</scope>
</dependency>
<!- JSTL ->
<dependency>
<groupId>javax.servlet</groupId>
<artifactId>javax.servlet-api</artifactId>
<version>4.0.1</version>
<scope>provided</scope>
</dependency>
</dependencies>
```

2. Configure Spring Dispatcher Servlet (web.xml)
   The servlet container (such as Tomcat) configuration file is the web.xml file. Add the following setup:

```
<web-app xmlns="http://java.sun.com/xml/ns/javaee"
xmlns:xsi="http://www.w3.org/2001/XMLSchema-instance"
xsi:schemaLocation="http://java.sun.com/xml/ns/javaee
http://java.sun.com/xml/ns/javaee/web-app_4_0.xsd"
version="4.0">
<!- Spring Dispatcher Servlet ->
<servlet>
<servlet-name>dispatcher</servlet-name>
<servlet-class>org.springframework.web.servlet.DispatcherServlet</servlet-class>
<load-on-startup>1</load-on-startup>
</servlet>
<servlet-mapping>
<servlet-name>dispatcher</servlet-name>
<url-pattern>/</url-pattern>
</servlet-mapping>
<!- Spring Context Configuration ->
<context-param>
<param-name>contextConfigLocation</param-name>
<param-value>/WEB-INF/applicationContext.xml</param-value>
</context-param>
</web-app>
```

This setup establishes the DispatcherServlet and the Spring context location.

**3.** spring-mvc-servlet.xml Spring MVC Configuration
Set up of the Spring MVC framework in spring-mvc-servlet.xml in WEB-INF. It will configure the component scanning and view resolver and Spring annotations:

```
<beans xmlns="http://www.springframework.org/schema/beans"
xmlns:xsi="http://www.w3.org/2001/XMLSchema-instance"
xsi:schemaLocation="http://www.springframework.org/schema/beans
http://www.springframework.org/schema/beans/spring-beans-4.3.xsd">
<!- Allow configuration via annotation -
<mvc:annotation-driven/>
<!- Setting View Resolver of JSP pages -
bean id= viewResolver class = org.springframework.web.servlet.view. InternalResource
ViewResolver.
prefix value set to/WEB-INF/views/
suffix. name property = suffix. value =.jsp.
</bean>
</beans>
```

**4.** Create the Model (User.java)
The User class is just a plain JavaBean with validation annotations to make sure that the user inputs are checked up.

```
import javax.validation.constraints.NotEmpty;
import javax.validation.constraints.Email;
import javax.validation.constraints.Size;
public class User {
NotEmpty(message="Name is required to be filled not empty)
private String name;
NotEmpty( message = email cannot be empty)
Email(text = $"Wrong email format)
private String email;
Size (min=6, max=20, message= password should have between 6 and 20 characters)
private String password;
// Getters and Setters
public String getName() {
return name;
}
public void setName(String name) {
this.name = name;
}
public String getEmail() {
return email;
}
public void setEmail(String email) {
this.email = email;
}
public String getPassword() {
return password;
}
public void setPassword(String password) {
this.password = password;
}
}
```

5. **Create Controller** (RegistrationController.java)
   This controller handles both displaying the form and processing the form submission.

```
import org.springframework.stereotype.Controller;
import org.springframework.validation.BindingResult;
import org.springframework.web.bind.annotation.GetMapping;
import org.springframework.web.bind.annotation.PostMapping;
import org.springframework.web.bind.annotation.ModelAttribute;
import javax.validation.Valid;
@Controller
public class RegistrationController {
```

```
@GetMapping("/register")
public String showForm(@ModelAttribute("user") User user) {
return "registrationForm";
}
@PostMapping("/register")
public String submitForm(@Valid @ModelAttribute("user") User user, BindingResult
result) {
if (result.hasErrors()) {
return "registrationForm";
}
return "registrationSuccess";
}
}
```

6. **Create JSP Views** (registrationForm.jsp **&** registrationSuccess.jsp)
   registrationForm.jsp:

```
<!DOCTYPE html>
<html>
<head>
<title>Registration Form</title>
</head>
<body>
<h2>Registration Form</h2>
<form:form modelAttribute="user" action="/register" method="POST">
<label for="name">Name:</label>
<form:input path="name"/>
<form:errors path="name" cssClass="error"/><br/>
<label for="email">Email:</label>
<form:input path="email"/>
<form:errors path="email" cssClass="error"/><br/>
<label for="password">Password:</label>
<form:password path="password"/>
<form:errors path="password" cssClass="error"/><br/>
<button type="submit">Register</button>
</form:form>
</body>
</html>
```

registrationSuccess.jsp:

```
<!DOCTYPE html>
<html>
<head>
<title>Registration Successful</title>
```

```
</head>
<body>
<h2>Registration Successful</h2>
<p>Name: ${user.name}</p>
<p>Email: ${user.email}</p>
</body>
</html>
```

7. Run the Application
   a. **Build the Project:** If using Maven, run mvn clean install to build the application.
   b. **Deploy to Server:** Deploy your application (e.g., to Apache Tomcat).
      i. If using Eclipse or IntelliJ IDEA, you can directly run the application by configuring the server.
   c. **Access the Form:** Open a browser and navigate to http://localhost:8080/register. You should see the registration form.
   d. **Submit the Form:** Fill out the form and submit it. If validation is successful, you will be redirected to the success page showing the entered data.

## 7.10 What is pom.xml?

pom.xml is an abbreviation of Project Object Model XML, and this is a very important configuration file in Java projects that are based on Maven. It includes all the project details including metadata, dependencies, build settings, and plugins among others that are needed to effectively administer the project. Maven uses this file in order to develop and maintain the project lifecycle.

pom.xml file is very essential in the lifecycle management of a Maven project. It is employed in defining the metadata of the project, its dependencies, and the build process and also in providing it with the ability to be automated using Maven plugsins. The components inside pom.xml help standardize the build and packaging process, ensuring consistent results across different environments.

Key Components of pom.xml

Here are the key components found in the pom.xml file:

<modelVersion>: Specifies the version of the POM model being used. For most projects, it will be 4.0.0.

```
<modelVersion>4.0.0</modelVersion>
```

<groupId>: This uniquely identifies the group or organization that owns the project. It is typically the reverse of your domain name.

```
<groupId>com.example</groupId>
```

<artifactId>: This specifies the name of the project or module (artifact) that Maven will create. It is unique within the group.

```
<artifactId>my-project</artifactId>
```

<version>: Defines the version of the project artifact.

```
<version>1.0-SNAPSHOT</version>
```

<packaging>: Specifies the type of artifact (e.g., jar, war, ear). For web applications, this is typically war.

```
<packaging>war</packaging>
```

<dependencies>: Contains all the external libraries or dependencies your project needs. These dependencies can be libraries, frameworks, or other projects that your project relies on.

```
<dependencies>
<dependency>
<groupId>org.springframework</groupId>
<artifactId>spring-webmvc</artifactId>
<version>5.3.8</version>
</dependency>
</dependencies>
```

<repositories>: Defines external repositories from which Maven will download dependencies if they are not available in the local repository.

```
<repositories>
<repository>
<id>central</id>
<url>https://repo.maven.apache.org/maven2</url>
</repository>
</repositories>
```

<build>: Contains configurations related to the build process, such as plugins used for compiling, packaging, and other tasks like running tests.

```
<build>
<plugins>
<plugin>
<groupId>org.apache.maven.plugins</groupId>
<artifactId>maven-compiler-plugin</artifactId>
<version>3.8.1</version>
<configuration>
<source>1.8</source>
<target>1.8</target>
</configuration>
</plugin>
</plugins>
</build>
```

<properties>: This section is used to define reusable properties that can be referenced throughout the pom.xml. For example, defining the version of Java to use.

```
<properties>
<maven.compiler.source>1.8</maven.compiler.source>
<maven.compiler.target>1.8</maven.compiler.target>
```

</properties>

<profiles>: Defines different build configurations (e.g., development, production) that can be activated depending on the environment.

<profiles>
<profile>
<id>development</id>
<properties>
<devMode>true</devMode>
</properties>
</profile>
</profiles>

<dependenciesManagement>: Allows you to manage the version of dependencies used in submodules. It avoids conflicts between dependency versions.

<dependencyManagement>
<dependencies>
<dependency>
<groupId>org.springframework</groupId>
<artifactId>spring-core</artifactId>
<version>5.3.8</version>
</dependency>
</dependencies>
</dependencyManagement>

## 7.11 What is web.xml?

web.xml is the deployment descriptor for Java web applications that conform to the Servlet API. It is an essential part of a web application's configuration and resides in the WEB-INF folder of the application. This file contains information about how the web application behaves, including servlet mappings, filters, listeners, and other configuration settings needed by the application to function properly within a servlet container (e.g., Apache Tomcat).

In Spring-based web applications, web.xml is often used to configure the DispatcherServlet and other configurations like filters and listeners, especially when not using Spring Boot.

web.xml is a key configuration file for Java web applications, particularly for servlet-based frameworks like Spring MVC. It serves as the central place to configure servlets, filters, listeners, error handling, and other web-related settings. While newer Spring applications, particularly those using Spring Boot, often do not require web.xml due to auto-configuration, traditional Spring MVC applications still rely on it for web configuration.

Key Components of web.xml

Here are the key elements commonly used in web.xml:

1. <web-app>: The root element of the web.xml file. It specifies the web application version and any necessary configurations.

```
<web-app xmlns="http://java.sun.com/xml/ns/javaee"
xmlns:xsi="http://www.w3.org/2001/XMLSchema-instance"
xsi:schemaLocation="http://java.sun.com/xml/ns/javaee
http://java.sun.com/xml/ns/javaee/web-app_3_0.xsd"
version="3.0">
</web-app>
```

2. <servlet>: This defines a servlet in the application. A servlet is a Java class that processes HTTP requests and generates responses.

```
<servlet>
<servlet-name>dispatcher</servlet-name>
<servlet-class>org.springframework.web.servlet.DispatcherServlet</servlet-class>
<load-on-startup>1</load-on-startup>
</servlet>
```

3. <servlet-mapping>: This maps a URL pattern to a servlet. When the servlet container receives a request that matches the URL pattern, the corresponding servlet is invoked.

```
<servlet-mapping>
<servlet-name>dispatcher</servlet-name>
<url-pattern>/</url-pattern>
</servlet-mapping>
```

4. <filter>: This defines a filter that can intercept requests before they reach the servlet and/or manipulate responses before they are sent to the client.

```
<filter>
<filter-name>encodingFilter</filter-name>
<filter-class>org.springframework.web.filter.CharacterEncodingFilter</filter-class>
<init-param>
<param-name>encoding</param-name>
<param-value>UTF-8</param-value>
</init-param>
</filter>
```

5. <filter-mapping>: This specifies which filters apply to which servlet or URL pattern.

```
<filter-mapping>
<filter-name>encodingFilter</filter-name>
<url-pattern>/*</url-pattern>
</filter-mapping>
```

6. <listener>: This defines an event listener class that listens for specific events such as application startup, shutdown, and session creation or destruction.

```
<listener>
<listener-class>org.springframework.web.context.ContextLoaderListener</listener-class>
</listener>
```

7. <error-page>: This defines custom error pages for handling specific error codes or exceptions.

```
<error-page>
<error-code>404</error-code>
<location>/error/404.jsp</location>
</error-page>
```

8. <welcome-file-list>: This specifies the default page to show when the user accesses the root of the web application.

```
<welcome-file-list>
<welcome-file>index.jsp</welcome-file>
</welcome-file-list>
```

**Usage of web.xml for Spring MVC**
Here is a general overview to configure a Spring MVC application using web.xml:

1. Define the DispatcherServlet:
   - You will configure the DispatcherServlet in web.xml, which is the main controller for handling HTTP requests in a Spring MVC web application.
   - The DispatcherServlet should be mapped to the root URL (/), ensuring that all requests are handled by Spring's dispatcher.
2. Character Encoding Filter:
   - You may configure a filter to ensure that the encoding of HTTP requests and responses is set correctly (e.g., UTF-8).
3. ContextLoaderListener:
   - The ContextLoaderListener is responsible for initializing the Spring application context and managing the lifecycle of beans for the application.

## 7.12 What is spring-mvc-servlet.xml?

1. The Spring configuration file that is generally utilized in a Spring MVC application is spring-mvc-servlet.xml that is used to define the components in the application, including controllers, view resolvers, message converters, and other Spring beans. The DispatcherServlet (the front controller of Spring MVC) uses this XML file to initialize and set the Spring application context to process the HTTP requests.
2. The spring-mvc-servlet.xml is a core configuration file of a typical spring MVC application. It outlines some of the important parts like view resolvers, controller mappings, interceptors, and handling of a statical resource. It allows configuring Spring MVC

elements in an elastic and declarative manner, which allows a pure separation of concerns and simplifies the control of the behavior of the application.

3. Normally, in a standard Spring MVC application, the file is configured in the web.xml in which the Spring settings are loaded and the mapping of the HTTP requests to controllers and views is done.

***spring-mvc-servlet.xml purpose***:

1. Configuration of Controllers: It determines Spring bean of controllers.
2. View Resolver: Sets the View Resolver to solve views to render the response.
3. Handler Mapping: Defines the mappings between the HTTP requests and the corresponding controllers.
   - Message Converters: Configures the components for data binding and transformation (e.g., JSON or XML).
   - Other Beans: It can also define various beans that are required by the application, such as service layer beans, DAO beans, and utility beans.

**Key components of spring-mvc-servlet.xml**

Below are the key components and configuration options you would typically find in a spring-mvc-servlet.xml file:

1. Component Scan: Enables component scanning to automatically detect Spring beans (like controllers, services, and repositories).

```
<context:component-scan base-package="com.example.controller"/>
```

2. View Resolver: Configures a view resolver to map logical view names (like "home") to actual view files (e.g., JSP files).

```
<bean
class="org.springframework.web.servlet.view.InternalResourceViewResolver">
<property name="prefix" value="/WEB-INF/views/"/>
<property name="suffix" value=".jsp"/>
</bean>
```

3. Handler Mapping: Specifies how Spring MVC will map HTTP requests to handler methods in controllers. By default, Dispatcher Servlet automatically maps HTTP requests to methods based on the @RequestMapping annotation, but custom mappings can be configured here.

```
<bean class="org.springframework.web.servlet.handler.BeanNameUrlHandlerMapping"/>
```

4. Message Converters: Configures the message converters for handling different types of requests and responses (e.g., JSON, XML).

```
<bean class="org.springframework.http.converter.json.MappingJackson2HttpMessage
Converter"/>
```

5. Locale Resolver: Defines how the application handles locale settings (such as internationalization).

```
<bean class="org.springframework.web.servlet.i18n.SessionLocaleResolver"/>
```

6. Custom Filters and Interceptors: Spring MVC allows you to configure custom filters and interceptors that can perform tasks like logging, authentication, or preprocessing HTTP requests.

```
<mvc:interceptors>
<bean class="com.example.interceptor.CustomInterceptor"/>
</mvc:interceptors>
```

7. Static Resource Handling: Configures handling for static resources like CSS, JavaScript, and images.

```
<mvc:resources mapping="/resources/**" location="/WEB-INF/resources/"/>
```

8. DispatcherServlet Configuration: In Spring, DispatcherServlet is responsible for dispatching requests to the appropriate controllers. You would configure this in web.xml, but spring-mvc-servlet.xml contains other important settings related to how requests are handled.

**Example of a basic spring-mvc-servlet.xml configuration**

Here's a basic example of how a typical spring-mvc-servlet.xml file might look:

```
<?xml version="1.0" encoding="UTF-8"?>
<beans xmlns="http://www.springframework.org/schema/beans"
xmlns:xsi="http://www.w3.org/2001/XMLSchema-instance"
xmlns:mvc="http://www.springframework.org/schema/mvc"
xsi:schemaLocation="http://www.springframework.org/schema/beans
http://www.springframework.org/schema/beans/spring-beans-3.0.xsd
http://www.springframework.org/schema/mvc
http://www.springframework.org/schema/mvc/spring-mvc-3.0.xsd">
<!- Enable annotation-based configuration (for @Controller, @RequestMapping, etc.) ->
<context:component-scan base-package="com.example.controller"/>
<!- Configure the View Resolver ->
<bean
class="org.springframework.web.servlet.view.InternalResourceViewResolver">
<property name="prefix" value="/WEB-INF/views/"/>
<property name="suffix" value=".jsp"/>
</bean>
<!- Configure static resource handling ->
<mvc:resources mapping="/resources/**" location="/WEB-INF/resources/"/>
<!- Enable Spring MVC annotations like @RequestMapping ->
<mvc:annotation-driven/>
<!- Configure custom interceptors ->
<mvc:interceptors>
<bean class="com.example.interceptor.CustomInterceptor"/>
</mvc:interceptors>
</beans>
```

## 7.13 Spring Model-View-Controller

Spring MVC can be used in both web and nonweb environments, but typically, Spring MVC is web-focused. But the given example below is a Spring MVC in a nonweb environment (like a standalone Java application):

**Steps to run a Spring MVC program (in Nonweb application context):**

1. Add Spring MVC Dependencies
   - You need to add Spring's core and MVC dependencies to your project for Spring to manage your beans and handle controller logic.

   Example pom.xml (for Maven-based projects):

```
<dependencies>
<!- Spring Core ->
<dependency>
<groupId>org.springframework</groupId>
<artifactId>spring-core</artifactId>
<version>5.3.x</version>
</dependency>
<!- Spring Web MVC ->
<dependency>
<groupId>org.springframework</groupId>
<artifactId>spring-webmvc</artifactId>
<version>5.3.x</version>
</dependency>
<!- Spring Beans for DI ->
<dependency>
<groupId>org.springframework</groupId>
<artifactId>spring-beans</artifactId>
<version>5.3.x</version>
</dependency>
</dependencies>
```

2. Set Up ApplicationContext for Spring MVC: Spring MVC usually requires a DispatcherServlet, but for a nonweb application, you don't need an actual web container. Instead, you can use a Spring ApplicationContext (e.g., AnnotationConfigApplicationContext) to initialize Spring beans.

   Example configuration class:

```
@Configuration
@ComponentScan(basePackages = "com.example") // Scan for components
public class AppConfig {
}
```

3. Controller Creation: Create a controller that handles the logic or requests. In a web application, this would typically be an HTTP request, but in a standalone application, you

can trigger the controller method directly.

Example Controller:

```
@Controller
public class MyController {
@RequestMapping("/greet")
public String greet() {
System.out.println("Hello from Spring MVC Controller!");
return "Greeted!";
}
}
```

4. Set Up Application in a Main Method: In a typical Spring MVC web application, the DispatcherServlet is set up in web.xml. For a standalone application, we directly initialize Spring's ApplicationContext in the main method.

Example Main Application Class:

```
public class MainApp {
public static void main(String[] args) {
// Load Spring context configuration
AnnotationConfigApplicationContext context = new AnnotationConfigApplicationContext
(AppConfig.class);
// Retrieve the controller (as if handling a request)
MyController controller = context.getBean(MyController.class);
String response = controller.greet(); // This simulates the request handling in a web
environment.
System.out.println("Response: " + response);
context.close();
}
}
```

# 7.14 HTTP Request and HTTP Response

In a Spring web application, HttpRequest and HttpResponse objects play a critical role in handling client requests and sending back responses. These are standard objects in the Servlet API, but Spring MVC provides a more flexible way to work with them through controllers and Handler Mappings.

Flow of HTTP Request and HTTP Response in Spring MVC

1. **Client Sends HTTP Request**:
   - A client (browser or any other HTTP client) sends an HTTP request to a Spring application. The request typically includes:
   - The URL (for routing).

- HTTP method (GET, POST, etc.).
- Headers (to specify content types, authentication, etc.).
- Body (in case of POST, PUT requests containing data).

2. **DispatcherServlet**:
   - The DispatcherServlet is the front controller in the Spring MVC architecture. It is mapped to handle all incoming requests (configured in web.xml or Spring Boot auto-configures it for you).
   - The DispatcherServlet intercepts the HTTP request and forwards it to the appropriate HandlerMapping based on the request's URL.
3. **HandlerMapping**:
   - HandlerMapping is responsible for determining which controller should handle the request.
   - It maps the incoming HTTP request to a Controller or Handler method based on the URL and HTTP method.
4. **Controller**:
   - The controller method is invoked by Spring MVC. The HttpServletRequest and HttpServletResponse objects can be accessed directly as method arguments in the controller.

```
@RequestMapping("/greet")
public String greet(HttpServletRequest request, HttpServletResponse response) {
// You can manipulate request or response objects here
String name = request.getParameter("name");
response.setStatus(HttpServletResponse.SC_OK);
return "greetView";
}
```

   - HttpServletRequest provides access to request parameters, headers, attributes, etc.
   - HttpServletResponse is used to set response codes, headers, cookies, and content.
5. **View Resolver**:
   - After the controller method executes, Spring MVC resolves the view to be used to render the response. It can either be a JSP, HTML, Thymeleaf, etc., depending on the configuration and return type of the controller.
   - The view is rendered, and the HTTP response body is populated with the data (e.g., HTML content, JSON).
6. **HTTP Response Sent to Client**:

   Once the view is rendered, the HttpServletResponse object is populated with the appropriate data. Spring then sends the response back to the client.
   - Response status (e.g., 200 OK, 404 Not Found).
   - Response headers (e.g., Content-Type, Cache-Control).
   - Response body (e.g., rendered HTML, JSON data).

Spring MVC provides an easy-to-use mechanism for handling HttpRequest and HttpResponse in a web application. The DispatcherServlet intercepts incoming requests, determines which controller should handle them, and processes the response accordingly.

The flow is highly configurable, enabling customization of how requests and responses are handled, and it is all built on top of the underlying Servlet API.

For a nonweb application using Spring (such as a Spring-based desktop application or a console application), the flow is slightly different because there is no web layer involved. However, the concepts of Dependency Injection (DI) and Inversion of Control (IoC) still apply, and Spring manages beans and their lifecycle.

For a command-line application, the flow starts from the main method where Spring is initialized, beans are injected, business logic is executed, and the results are printed to the console.

## Bibliography

IBM. (2024). Web Applications. https://www.ibm.com/docs.

MDN. (2024). HTML Forms. https://developer.mozilla.org.

Oracle. (2024) Java Regex. https://docs.oracle.com/javase/tutorial/essential/regex/.

Spring. (2024). Spring MVC Forms. https://docs.spring.io.

# 8

# Representational State Transfer web services with Spring Boot

## 8.1 Representational State Transfer services

Representational State Transfer (RESTful or REST) services are web services that are based on the principles and constraints of REST. REST is a type of system architecture that uses distributed system communication based on stateless communication using standard HTTP methods (such as GET, POST, PUT, and DELETE). The services based on REST can be used to enable communication between various software systems via the web in a lightweight and scalable form, typically transferring information in the form of the JSON or XML format.

Why RESTful services?

1. Ease of use: RESTful services are easy to operate and comprehend because they are based on HTTP, which is a well-known protocol.
2. Scalability: REST is stateless, that is, each request made by a client to the server has to include all the information that is required to be included and will ease the workload on the server, and the server is easier to scale.
3. Performance: RESTful services may use the capabilities of HTTP such as caching and compression to enhance performance.
4. Loose Coupling: RESTful services are not tied to the client or the server. That is, the client and the server can evolve without violating the architecture of REST.
5. Flexibility: REST is able to work with multiple formats (JSON, XML, and HTML) and can be easily incorporated in web-based applications.

Elements of RESTful services are as follows:

1. Resources:
   - Resources represent entities (like users, orders, and products) in the system and are typically identified by Uniform Resource Identifiers (URIs).
   - Each resource has a specific Uniform Resource Locator (URL) and can be acted upon using standard HTTP methods.
2. HTTP Methods:
   - GET: Retrieve data from the server (fetching a resource).
   - POST: Submit data to be processed to a server (creating a new resource).
   - PUT: Update an existing resource on the server.
   - DELETE: Remove a resource from the server.

Mastering Java Full Stack Development. DOI: https://doi.org/10.1016/B978-0-443-51683-2.00016-3

3. Statelessness:
   - Each request from the client to the server must contain all the information necessary to understand and process the request. The server does not store any session information about the client.
4. Uniform Interface:
   - RESTful services follow a consistent set of conventions and constraints, making it easy for clients to interact with various RESTful APIs without needing to learn different interfaces for each one.
5. Client–Server Architecture:
   - The client and server are separate entities that communicate over a network. The client requests resources, and the server processes and returns the appropriate response.
6. Cacheability:
   - Responses from the server can be explicitly marked as cacheable or noncacheable. Caching helps reduce server load and improve performance by storing responses on the client or intermediary servers.
7. Layered System:
   - A RESTful architecture can have multiple layers of servers, which allows for load balancing, shared caches, and security layers. The client cannot ordinarily tell whether it is connected directly to the end server or an intermediary.

These components together enable efficient, scalable, and easy-to-use web services based on RESTful principles.

## 8.2 Architecture

The architecture of RESTful services is built on a set of constraints that define how components (such as clients, servers, and resources) should interact with each other. It is based on the following six guiding principles:

1. Client–Server Architecture:
   - The system is split into two main components: the client and the server.
   - The client is responsible for the user interface and user experience, while the server manages the data storage and processing.
   - The client–server communication occurs on HTTP.
2. Statelessness:
   - Any request sent by the client to the server should also be complete with all the information needed by the server to comprehend the request and implement it.
   - The server does not maintain any session data concerning the client between requests.
   - This results in scalability whereby servers do not have to handle client state across requests.
3. Cacheability:
   - Server responses may contain an explicit mark as either a cacheable or a noncacheable response.

- In case the responses are cacheable, the response can be stored by the client or intermediary servers (such as proxies) and can be reused, so it does not need to be reprocessed in the server, which enhances performance.

4. Uniform Interface:
   - The RESTful services have to follow a standard, uniform interface that enables the client to communicate with the server without understanding the details of how the implementation is done.
   - This is generally done by standard HTTP (GET, POST, PUT, and DELETE), by conventions of uniform URLs, and by standard data formats (usually JSON or XML).
5. Layered System:
   - It is possible to use several layers (load balancers, proxies, and caching servers) between the server and the client using the RESTful architecture.
   - This allows the ability to scale horizontally as well as flexibility to handle requests without the client knowing whether it is communicating to the end server or going through layers.
6. Code on Demand (Optional):
   - This prevents the server from requiring executable code (more often JavaScript) to be sent to the client, and allows it to be used to enhance the functionality of the client.

Working of RESTful services is as follows:

1. Client Request:
   - The client makes an HTTP request to the server by specifying a URL that identifies the resource.
   - The request contains an HTTP method (GET, POST, PUT, and DELETE) that reflects the action that the client wishes to perform.
2. Server Processing:
   - The HTTP request is received by the server and processed. It will decode the URL in order to find out what resource is requested and what to do (according to the HTTP method).
   - The server can communicate with a database or any other systems to get, add, update, or erase data.
3. Resource Representation:
   - The server gives a representation of the resource which is usually in the form of either JSON or XML. This expression consists of the data and any important metadata.
   - For example, if a client requests information about a product, the server might respond with a JSON object containing the product details.
4. Stateless Communication:
   - Each request is independent, meaning the server does not store any state about previous requests. For each request, the client must send all necessary data.
   - For example, if a client wants to access the details of a product, it would send the product's ID in the request, and the server responds with the relevant product details.

5. Response to Client:
    - The server sends the response to the client, which contains the resource data (in the form of a representation) and a status code.
    - Common status codes include:
    - 200 OK: The request was successful, and the server returns the requested data.
    - 201 Created: The resource was successfully created (typically used for POST requests).
    - 204 No Content: The request was successful, but there is no content to return (commonly used with DELETE requests).
    - 400 Bad Request: The server cannot process the request due to a client error (e.g., malformed data).
    - 404 Not Found: The requested resource could not be found.
    - 500 Internal Server Error: There was an error processing the request on the server.
6. Statelessness in Practice:
    - Because RESTful services are stateless, every request from the client must be self-contained and independent. For instance, the client might include authentication tokens or session data in every request to ensure that the server can validate the request properly.
7. Caching (Optional):
    - The response from the server may include cache headers that allow the client or an intermediary to store the response for later use.
    - For example, if a client requests product details and the server responds with cacheable data, the client might store that response for a set period to avoid making repeated requests to the server.
8. Client Uses Data:
    - Once the client receives the response, it can use the data in the desired way, such as displaying it in the user interface or processing it further.

Example of RESTful interaction:
Let us take an example of a RESTful service for managing user information in a system:

- Request: A client sends a GET request to fetch details of a specific user from the server:
- GET /users/12345

The server processes this request, retrieves the user information from its database, and responds with the following:

```
HTTP/1.1 200 OK
Content-Type: application/json
{
"id": 12345,
"name": "John Doe",
"email": "johndoe@example.com"
}
```

• Create Request: When a client wants to add a new user, he/she makes a POST request:
POST /users
Content-Type: application/json
{
"name": "Jane Doe",
"email": "janedoe@example.com"
}

The server would reply with a 201 (Created) status, and the body would consist of the ID of the newly created user.

Following these principles and communication flow, RESTful services provide a consistent, scalable, and flexible system of constructing distributed applications.

This is a basic flowchart illustrating the in-text version:

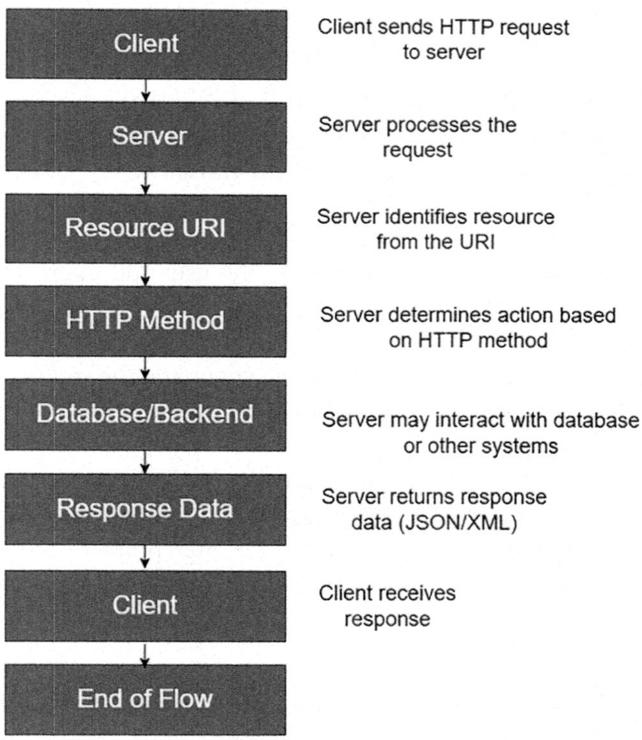


## 8.3 Layers

When designing a scalable and efficient architecture in the RESTful services, most commonly, five layers can be employed. There are specific roles that each layer plays, and they are as follows:

Layers in RESTful services are as follows:

1. Client Layer
2. Client-Side Proxy Layer (Optional)
3. Server Layer
4. Data Layer (Backend)
5. Caching Layer (Optional)

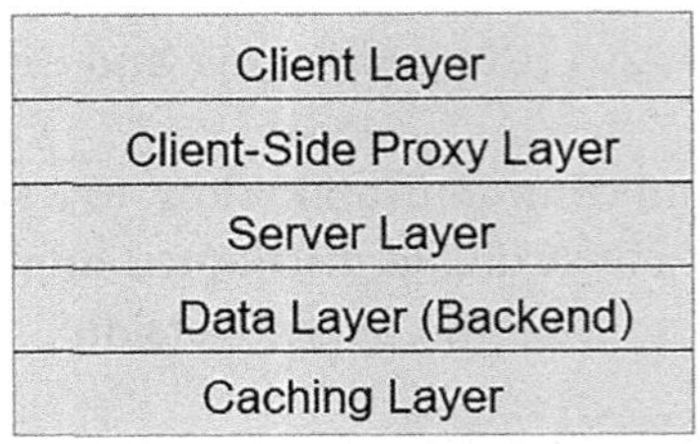


1. Client Layer:
   - Client layer is the application or device that makes requests to the server. The client may be any web browser, mobile application, or any other web service consumer. The client usually encodes HTTP requests, which consist of the URIs of the resource and any other information or data that is necessary to create, read, update, or delete resources.
   - It takes care of delivering the information to the user and interpreting the reply of the server.
2. Client-Side Proxy Layer (Optional):
   - Client-side proxy layer is the one that pits the client and the server together, though it is not common. Some of the tasks that a proxy can perform include request routing, load balancing, or caching.
   - To illustrate, a proxy may be used to address requests by forwarding them to the right server in a distributed system or keeping commonly requested resources in cache so that the server does not get overloaded. The encryption of SSL/TLS and improved security can also be done by the use of a client-side proxy.
3. Server Layer:
   - The server layer is responsible for processing the incoming HTTP requests from the client. When the server receives a request, it identifies the requested resource via the URI, determines which action to perform based on the HTTP method (GET, POST, PUT, and DELETE), and manages any necessary business logic to handle the request.
   - The server does not typically store session information, as RESTful services are stateless, meaning each request must be independent and self-contained. The server can return data or process an operation, such as creating, updating, or deleting a resource, and send back a response.

4. Data Layer (Backend):
   - The data layer refers to the system responsible for managing the actual data associated with the resources. This typically involves a database, but it could also be any other data storage mechanism (e.g., file storage, cloud storage, etc.).
   - The server interacts with this layer when the requested resource data is stored, retrieved, or modified. This is where the persistent data lives. When a client requests information (such as a user profile), the server queries the data layer and returns the appropriate data in the response.
   - This layer is important because it is where data integrity, security, and storage-related tasks are handled.
5. Caching Layer (Optional):
   - The caching layer is used to store frequently accessed resources temporarily to improve the performance of RESTful services. Caching can be implemented at various levels: client-side (in the client browser or mobile device), server-side (within the server), or through intermediary caches (such as content delivery networks, proxies, or reverse proxies).

With caching, the response to the request will be stored, and the next request to the same resource will be delivered straight off the cache without communicating with the server or the data layer. This minimizes the latency, enhances responsiveness, and minimizes server load, particularly in operations that are read-intensive.

Caching can also be effective with data that is not frequently changed like in the case of static data, like images or user profile information.

All these layers assist in attaining the fundamental guidelines of RESTful services, such as stateless communication, scalability, and loose-coupling between the client and the server. The optional caching and client-side proxy layers help in optimizing the performance, whereas data layer is used to ensure that the resources are managed efficiently and the data is stored properly.

## 8.4 Request and response flow

The RESTful services have a fixed process flow of request-response that defines communication between the client and server. This flow starts with a request made by a client and stops with a response made by the server. This flow has been explained in detail as follows:

1. Client Sends Request: It is an HTTP request the client, which is a web browser, mobile application, or any other user interface, makes out to the server. This request consists of an HTTP method (GET, POST, PUT, and DELETE), a resource identifier (URI) in the form of a resource, and any required headers or body content (in the case of such processes as POST or PUT).
   - GET: The client requests information about a resource.
   - POST: The client submits data to the server to create a resource.
   - PUT: The client updates an existing resource with new data.
   - DELETE: The client requests the deletion of a resource.

2. Server Processes Request: Upon receiving the request, the server examines it. The server checks the HTTP method and the URI on receiving the request, and what needs to be done. The server has the task of determining the resource, which is the match to the URI, and performing the proper action. To give an example, when there is a request in the form of a GET, then it will retrieve the requested information on the server; in the case of a POST request, there is a possibility that a new resource will be created.
   The server is governed by the principles of the REST meaning that the server is stateless and has no session information between the requests. All the requests should be autonomous and contain all the information needed to be processed.
3. Server Communicates with Data Layer (when necessary): The server will interoperate with the data layer in case the request is about the retrieval or manipulation of data. The actual data of the resource (in a database or other backend systems) is stored in the data layer. In case of the GET request, the server requests the database and retrieves the requested resource. In a POST or PUT request, the server will write new information or make changes to an existing record.
   The communication with the data layer can be performed as querying, inserting, updating, or deleting records, depending on the character of the HTTP method.
4. Response Prepares Response: Once the request has been processed by the server (it may also communicate with the data layer), the server constructs a response. The server encodes the information with a standard format, typically JSON or XML, and establishes the correct status code of the HTTP.
   - When the GET requests are successful, a status code such as a 200 OK is sent with the resource data.
   - In successful POST requests, the 201 Created status may be returned with a location header that points to the new resource.
   - In case of an error, the server will respond with a suitable status code, for example,. 400 Bad Request or 404 Not Found, and an error message.
5. Client Receives Response: This is the point at which the server is responding and the client is receiving it. This response can subsequently be processed by the client, and the user interface can be updated. The client might display the retrieved data or show an error message, depending on the status code and the data received.
6. End of the Process: This concludes the request–response cycle for a RESTful service. The client may initiate another request to the server, or the process may terminate if no further interaction is needed.

## 8.5 Running Representational State Transfer program

1. Spring Boot Application Class (@SpringBootApplication)

```
@SpringBootApplication
public class Application {
public static void main(String[] args) {
```

```
SpringApplication.run(Application.class, args);
}
}
```

2. Entity Class (@Entity)

```
@Entity
public class Resource {
@Id
private Long id;
private String name;
private String description;
// Getters and Setters
}
```

3. Repository Interface (JpaRepository)

```
public interface ResourceRepository extends JpaRepository<Resource, Long> {
// Custom query methods can be defined here if needed
}
```

4. Controller Class (@RestController)

```
@RestController
@RequestMapping("/api/resources")
public class ResourceController {
@Autowired
private ResourceRepository resourceRepository;
@GetMapping("/{id}")
public ResponseEntity<Resource> getResource(@PathVariable Long id) {
Optional<Resource> resource = resourceRepository.findById(id);
return resource.map(ResponseEntity::ok).orElseGet(() -> ResponseEntity.notFound().build
());
}
@PostMapping
public ResponseEntity<Resource> createResource(@RequestBody Resource resource) {
Resource savedResource = resourceRepository.save(resource);
return ResponseEntity.ok(savedResource);
}
// More methods for PUT, DELETE.
}
```

5. Application Configuration (application.properties)

```
server.port=8080
spring.datasource.url=jdbc:h2:mem:testdb
spring.datasource.driverClassName=org.h2.Driver
```

```
spring.datasource.username=sa
spring.datasource.password=password
spring.jpa.database-platform=org.hibernate.dialect.H2Dialect
```

6. Maven Dependency Configuration (pom.xml)

```
<dependency>
<groupId>org.springframework.boot</groupId>
<artifactId>spring-boot-starter-web</artifactId>
</dependency>
<dependency>
<groupId>org.springframework.boot</groupId>
<artifactId>spring-boot-starter-data-jpa</artifactId>
</dependency>
<dependency>
<groupId>com.h2database</groupId>
<artifactId>h2</artifactId>
<scope>runtime</scope>
</dependency>
```

7. HTTP Request/Response Handling (GET, POST, PUT, DELETE)

GET Request:

```
@GetMapping("/{id}")
public ResponseEntity<Resource> getResource(@PathVariable Long id) {
// Logic to fetch resource
}
```

POST Request:

```
@PostMapping
public ResponseEntity<Resource> createResource(@RequestBody Resource resource) {
// Logic to create a new resource
}
```

PUT Request:

```
@PutMapping("/{id}")
public ResponseEntity<Resource> updateResource(@PathVariable Long id, @RequestBody
Resource resource) {
// Logic to update an existing resource
}
```

DELETE Request:

```
@DeleteMapping("/{id}")
public ResponseEntity<Void> deleteResource(@PathVariable Long id) {
// Logic to delete a resource
}
```

## 8.6 Methods in Representational State Transfer web services

**1.** GET Method

The GET method is used to retrieve data from the server. It is a safe operation, meaning it does not change the resource, and idempotent, meaning multiple identical GET requests will result in the same response. This makes GET the ideal choice for fetching data without causing any side effects on the server. To get data or information from the server. For example, retrieving a list of users, articles, or any other resource.

Syntax:

```
@GetMapping("/{id}")
public ResponseEntity<Resource> getResource(@PathVariable Long id) {
// Logic to retrieve the resource by ID
return ResponseEntity.ok(resourceService.findById(id));
}
```

**2.** POST Method

The POST method is used to send data to the server to create a new resource. Unlike GET, it can include a body in the request to send data. The POST method is not idempotent, meaning repeated requests can result in multiple resource creations. To submit data that creates a new resource or triggers an action (such as submitting a form or adding a new user).

Syntax:

```
@PostMapping
public ResponseEntity<Resource> createResource(@RequestBody Resource resource) {
// Logic to save the resource
return ResponseEntity.status(HttpStatus.CREATED).body(resourceService.save(resource));
}
```

**3.** PUT Method

The PUT method is used to update an existing resource or replace it entirely. It is idempotent, meaning calling the same request multiple times will not result in additional changes or side effects. Typically, the complete resource is sent in the request body to replace the current version. To replace or update an entire resource. If a resource already exists, PUT will overwrite it with the new data provided in the request body.

Syntax:

```
@PutMapping("/{id}")
public ResponseEntity<Resource> updateResource(@PathVariable Long id, @RequestBody
Resource resource) {
// Logic to update the resource by ID
return ResponseEntity.ok(resourceService.update(id, resource));
}
```

4. DELETE Method

The DELETE method is used to delete a resource identified by the given URL. It is idempotent, meaning that deleting the same resource multiple times will have the same result, that is, the resource will be deleted once and further requests won't affect the server. To remove a resource from the server, such as deleting a user or a product from a system.

Syntax:

```
@DeleteMapping("/{id}")
public ResponseEntity<Void> deleteResource(@PathVariable Long id) {
// Logic to delete the resource by ID
resourceService.delete(id);
return ResponseEntity.noContent().build();
}
```

5. PATCH Method

The PATCH method is used for partially updating an existing resource. Unlike PUT, which replaces the entire resource, PATCH only updates the fields specified in the request. It is useful when you need to update a subset of a resource. To make partial updates to a resource when you don't need to send the entire data. It helps to reduce the amount of data sent over the network.

Syntax:

```
@PatchMapping("/{id}")
public ResponseEntity<Resource> partialUpdateResource(@PathVariable Long id, @
RequestBody Resource resource) {
// Logic to partially update the resource by ID
return ResponseEntity.ok(resourceService.partialUpdate(id, resource));
}
```

6. HEAD Method

The HEAD method is similar to GET but does not return the body of the resource. It only retrieves the headers, which can be useful to check if a resource exists or to gather metadata without downloading the entire content. To check the status or existence of a resource (e.g., checking if a resource is available or if it has been modified) without retrieving its body.

Syntax:

```
@RequestMapping(value = "/resource/{id}", method = RequestMethod.HEAD)
public ResponseEntity<Void> checkResourceExists(@PathVariable Long id) {
// Logic to check if resource exists
return ResponseEntity.ok().build();
}
```

7. OPTIONS Method

The OPTIONS method is used to retrieve the allowed methods for a resource (e.g., GET, POST, PUT, and DELETE). This is typically used for CORS (Cross-Origin Resource Sharing) requests, allowing the client to know which methods are supported by the server. To understand what actions can be performed on a resource. It is particularly useful for browsers to determine allowed HTTP methods before sending requests.

Syntax:

```
@RequestMapping(value = "/resource/{id}", method = RequestMethod.OPTIONS)
public ResponseEntity<Void> checkAllowedMethods(@PathVariable Long id) {
// Logic to return allowed HTTP methods for the resource
return ResponseEntity.ok().allow(HttpMethod.GET, HttpMethod.POST, HttpMethod.
PUT).build();
}
```

The methods of the HTTP are used to interface with resources in RESTful services to help ensure that your web service architecture remains clean and separated.

## 8.7 Representational State Transfer web program

**Step 1:** Add Dependencies in pom.xml (Maven)

```
<dependency>
<groupId>org.springframework.boot</groupId>
<artifactId>spring-boot-starter-web</artifactId>
</dependency>
<dependency>
<groupId>org.springframework.boot</groupId>
<artifactId>spring-boot-starter-data-jpa</artifactId>
</dependency>
<dependency>
<groupId>com.h2database</groupId>
<artifactId>h2</artifactId>
<scope>runtime</scope>
</dependency>
```

**Step 2:** Define Model Class (User.java)

```
@Entity
public class User {
@Id
private Long id;
private String name;
private String email;
// Getters and Setters
}
```

**Step 3**: Repository Interface (UserRepository.java) definition.
public interface UserRepository is the JpaRepository of type User, Long.

```
// Custom queries if necessary
}
```

**Step 4:** Define Service Class (UserService.java)

```
@Service
public class UserService {
@Autowired
private UserRepository userRepository;
public List<User> getAllUsers() {
return userRepository.findAll();
}
public Optional<User> getUserById(Long id) {
return userRepository.findById(id);
}
public User createUser(User user) {
return userRepository.save(user);
}
public User updateUser(Long id, User user) {
user.setId(id);
return userRepository.save(user);
}
public void deleteUser(Long id) {
userRepository.deleteById(id);
}
}
```

**Step 5:** Define Controller Class (UserController.java)

```
@RestController
@RequestMapping("/api/users")
public class UserController {
@Autowired
private UserService userService;
@GetMapping
public List<User> getAllUsers() {
return userService.getAllUsers();
}
@GetMapping("/{id}")
public Optional<User> getUserById(@PathVariable Long id) {
return userService.getUserById(id);
}
@PostMapping
public User createUser(@RequestBody User user) {
```

```
return userService.createUser(user);
}
@PutMapping("/{id}")
public User updateUser(@PathVariable Long id, @RequestBody User user) {
return userService.updateUser(id, user);
}
@DeleteMapping("/{id}")
public void deleteUser(@PathVariable Long id) {
userService.deleteUser(id);
}
}
```

**Step 6:** Run the Application (Application.java)

```
@SpringBootApplication
public class Application {
public static void main(String[] args) {
SpringApplication.run(Application.class, args);
}
}
```

## 8.8 Validators in Representational State Transfer web services

For validating data in RESTful web services, several approaches can be used to ensure that the incoming data is valid, consistent, and secure. Below are some common validation techniques that can be implemented in a Spring Boot RESTful service.

1. Validation Annotations (Using Java Bean Validation—JSR 303/JSR 380)
   You can use annotations from the javax.validation.constraints package to validate the fields in your model. These annotations are processed during request handling.

   Syntax:
   ```
   import javax.validation.constraints.NotNull;
   import javax.validation.constraints.Size;
   import javax.validation.constraints.Email;
   import javax.validation.constraints.Min;
   public class User {
   @NotNull(message = "ID cannot be null")
   private Long id;
   @NotNull(message = "Name cannot be null")
   @Size(min = 2, max = 50, message = "Name must be between 2 and 50 characters")
   private String name;
   @Email(message = "Email should be valid")
   ```

```
@NotNull(message = "Email cannot be null")
private String email;
@Min(value = 18, message = "Age must be greater than or equal to 18")
private int age;
// Getters and Setters
}
```

2. @Valid Annotation for Controller Method Arguments
   In your controller, use the @Valid annotation to enable validation of incoming request bodies.

   Syntax:

```
import org.springframework.web.bind.annotation.*;
import javax.validation.Valid;
@RestController
@RequestMapping("/api/users")
public class UserController {
@PostMapping
public ResponseEntity<User> createUser(@Valid @RequestBody User user) {
// The 'user' object will be validated before it reaches here.
// If validation fails, it will return a 400 Bad Request with validation messages.
return ResponseEntity.status(HttpStatus.CREATED).body(user);
}
}
```

3. Global Exception Handling with @ControllerAdvice
   To handle validation errors globally and send meaningful responses, use @ControllerAdvice to catch validation exceptions and provide a customized error message.

   Syntax:

```
import org.springframework.http.HttpStatus;
import org.springframework.http.ResponseEntity;
import org.springframework.validation.BindingResult;
import org.springframework.web.bind.annotation.ControllerAdvice;
import org.springframework.web.bind.annotation.ExceptionHandler;
import org.springframework.web.bind.MethodArgumentNotValidException;
import org.springframework.validation.FieldError;
import java.util.List;
@ControllerAdvice
public class GlobalExceptionHandler {
@ExceptionHandler(MethodArgumentNotValidException.class)
public ResponseEntity<Object> handleValidationExceptions
(MethodArgumentNotValidException ex) {
List<FieldError> errors = ex.getBindingResult().getFieldErrors();
```

```
StringBuilder errorMessage = new StringBuilder();
for (FieldError error : errors) {
errorMessage.append(error.getField())
.append(": ")
.append(error.getDefaultMessage())
.append(" ");
}
return new ResponseEntity<>(errorMessage.toString(), HttpStatus.BAD_REQUEST);
}
}
```

4. Custom Validations

   You can create custom validation annotations if the existing ones don't meet your needs. This requires implementing ConstraintValidator.

   Syntax (Custom Validator):

   1. Create the custom annotation:

```
import javax.validation.Constraint;
import javax.validation.Payload;
import java.lang.annotation.ElementType;
import java.lang.annotation.Retention;
import java.lang.annotation.RetentionPolicy;
import java.lang.annotation.Target;
@Constraint(validatedBy = EmailValidator.class)
@Target({ ElementType.FIELD, ElementType.METHOD })
@Retention(RetentionPolicy.RUNTIME)
public @interface ValidEmail {
String message() default "Invalid email format";
Class<?>[] groups() default {};
Class<? extends Payload>[] payload() default {};
}
```

   2. Create the custom validator:

```
import javax.validation.ConstraintValidator;
import javax.validation.ConstraintValidatorContext;
import java.util.regex.Pattern;
public class EmailValidator implements ConstraintValidator<ValidEmail, String> {
private static final String EMAIL_PATTERN = "^[A-Za-z0-9+_.-]+@(.+)$";
@Override
public void initialize(ValidEmail constraintAnnotation) {}
@Override
public boolean isValid(String value, ConstraintValidatorContext context) {
if (value == null || value.isEmpty()) {
```

```
return true;
}
return Pattern.matches(EMAIL_PATTERN, value);
}
}
```

3. Use the custom annotation:

```
public class User {
@ValidEmail
private String email;
// Getters and Setters
}
```

4. Handling Validation Errors in Responses
Spring provides detailed error messages for invalid inputs. When validation fails, it automatically returns a 400 Bad Request response with the validation error details.
Response Example:

```
{
"timestamp": "2025-01-17T12:00:00",
"status": 400,
"errors": [
"Name must be between 2 and 50 characters",
"Email should be valid"
]
}
```

5. Client-Side Validation
Though Spring Boot supports server-side validation, it is always recommended to also validate input on the client side (e.g., using JavaScript) to improve user experience and reduce unnecessary API calls.

## 8.9 Rest controllers

In Spring Boot, REST controllers are used to build RESTful web services by handling HTTP requests. The @RestController annotation is a combination of @Controller and @ ResponseBody, meaning it is a controller where every method returns a response body, and you do not need to use @ResponseBody explicitly.

REST controller features:

- Handles HTTP requests: Maps HTTP requests to Java methods.
- Automatic response serialization: Returns data (like JSON or XML) directly in the response body.

- HTTP method mapping: Supports various HTTP methods (GET, POST, PUT, and DELETE).

1. @RestController Annotation
   The @RestController annotation is used to define a RESTful web service controller. It marks a class as a Spring MVC controller, where methods will return response bodies directly.

   Syntax:
```
import org.springframework.web.bind.annotation.RestController;
import org.springframework.web.bind.annotation.RequestMapping;
@RestController
@RequestMapping("/api")
public class UserController {
// Methods will be here
}
```

2. @GetMapping, @PostMapping, @PutMapping, @DeleteMapping
   These annotations are used to map HTTP GET, POST, PUT, and DELETE requests to methods in the controller.

   Syntax:
```
import org.springframework.web.bind.annotation.GetMapping;
import org.springframework.web.bind.annotation.PostMapping;
import org.springframework.web.bind.annotation.PutMapping;
import org.springframework.web.bind.annotation.DeleteMapping;
import org.springframework.web.bind.annotation.RequestParam;
import org.springframework.web.bind.annotation.RequestBody;
@RestController
@RequestMapping("/api/users")
public class UserController {
@GetMapping("/{id}")
public User getUser(@PathVariable Long id) {
// Fetch user by ID
}
@PostMapping
public User createUser(@RequestBody User user) {
// Create new user
}
@PutMapping("/{id}")
public User updateUser(@PathVariable Long id, @RequestBody User user) {
// Update user information
}
@DeleteMapping("/{id}")
public void deleteUser(@PathVariable Long id) {
```

```
// Delete user by ID
}
}
```

3. Path Variables and Request Parameters
REST controllers often handle dynamic values in URLs using path variables and query parameters.

Path Variables:
Used to capture values directly from the URL path.

```
@GetMapping("/{id}")
public User getUserById(@PathVariable Long id) {
// Use 'id' captured from the URL to get user details
}
```

Request Parameters
Used to pass data in the URL, typically in the form of query strings.

```
@GetMapping
public List<User> getUsers(@RequestParam String name) {
// Use the 'name' parameter in the query string to filter users
}
```

4. @RequestBody and @ResponseBody
   - @RequestBody: Binds the incoming HTTP request body to a method parameter. This is typically used for POST and PUT requests to map the request body to Java objects.
   - @ResponseBody: Automatically serializes the return value to the HTTP response body (this is done by default in @RestController).

   Syntax:

   ```
   @PostMapping
   public User createUser(@RequestBody User user) {
   // 'user' will be populated with JSON data from the request body
   return userService.createUser(user);
   }
   ```

5. Handling Responses
You can customize HTTP responses by using ResponseEntity, which allows you to specify HTTP status codes, headers, and body.

Syntax:

```
import org.springframework.http.ResponseEntity;
import org.springframework.http.HttpStatus;
@GetMapping("/{id}")
public ResponseEntity<User> getUserById(@PathVariable Long id) {
Optional<User> user = userService.findById(id);
```

```
return user.isPresent()
? ResponseEntity.ok(user.get()) // 200 OK
: ResponseEntity.status(HttpStatus.NOT_FOUND).build(); // 404 Not Found
}
```

**6.** Exception Handling in REST Controllers
You can handle exceptions globally across all controllers using @ControllerAdvice or locally using @ExceptionHandler.

Syntax (Local Exception Handler):

```
@ExceptionHandler(UserNotFoundException.class)
public ResponseEntity<String> handleUserNotFound(UserNotFoundException ex) {
return ResponseEntity.status(HttpStatus.NOT_FOUND).body(ex.getMessage());
}
```

# Bibliography

Spring. (2024). REST Docs. https://docs.spring.io/spring-framework/reference/web/webmvc-rest/.

MDN. (2024). HTTP Methods. https://developer.mozilla.org.

IBM. (2024). REST APIs. https://www.ibm.com/docs.

Microsoft. (2024). REST API Design. https://learn.microsoft.com.

Red Hat. (2024). REST Overview. https://www.redhat.com.

# 9

# Securing the application: Spring Security and JSON Web Tokens

## 9.1 Introduction

The main aspect of modern web applications is vigorous security. The Spring Security is a third-party framework that is very customizable and has a wide range of securing offers to the application of Java. It is a stateless authentication system that is implemented with JSON Web Tokens (JWT) and can be scaled in accordance with the requirements when implemented in an application. The chapter explores the design of the Spring Security, the application of the Spring web applications, uses of security filters and security providers, and security administration of roles and privileges. Besides, we are going to talk about custom security validators and JWT implementation to protect RESTful services.

## 9.2 Spring Security Architecture

Spring Security is an adaptable as well as a robust authentication and access control framework of Java applications that is largely used in the security of Spring-based applications. It provides a combination of options that are quite broad in the manner of authentication, authorization, and other security concerns, such as protection against attacks such as Cross-Site Request Forgery (CSRF), cross-site scripting (XSS), and the fixation of the session.

The system that makes up Spring Security Architecture is a layered system that comprises many components such as filters, authentication managers, security context, and authorization decision makers. It is highly customizable and allows you to secure web apps and the Representational State Transfer (REST) Application Programming Interfaces (APIs) using different authentication mechanisms, such as form authentication, OAuth2, JWT, and basic authentication.

The major elements of Spring Security Architecture are as follows:

1. Security Filter Chain:
   - The core of Spring Security is its filter chain, which is a series of filters that process an HTTP request. These filters are applied in sequence, where each filter handles a specific aspect of security (authentication, authorization, CSRF protection, etc.).
   - FilterChainProxy is the main component that manages the entire security filter chain.
2. Authentication Filters:
   - UsernamePasswordAuthenticationFilter: This is the most common authentication filter, which handles form-based login (or basic authentication) by extracting the

**Mastering Java Full Stack Development. DOI: https://doi.org/10.1016/B978-0-443-51683-2.00004-7**

username and password from the HTTP request and passing them to the authentication manager.
- BasicAuthenticationFilter: This is used for HTTP basic authentication, extracting credentials from HTTP headers.
- BearerTokenAuthenticationFilter: This is used for JWT authentication, extracting a token from the HTTP request's Authorization header.

3. AuthenticationManager:
   - AuthenticationManager is responsible for validating the authentication request. It contains a series of AuthenticationProvider beans that perform the actual validation (e.g., checking user credentials against a database).
   - DaoAuthenticationProvider is a commonly used provider that checks credentials from a data source (like a database) using a user service.
4. SecurityContext:
   - Spring Security uses the SecurityContext to store information about the current user's authentication details. The SecurityContextHolder is used to retrieve and store the authentication object, which contains details like the username, roles, and authorities.
   - Authentication object is formed after authentication has been successful, and it is stored in the SecurityContext.
5. Authorization:
   - Once authenticated, the Spring Security will make authorization checks depending on the roles or permissions of the user.
   - AccessDecisionManager: This is in charge of making decisions concerning the eligibility of a user to access a specific resource.
   - AccessDecisionVoter: This is an element that votes on the access of the user to a resource.
   - Method Security: Spring Security also supports method-level security annotations like @PreAuthorize, @Secured, and @RolesAllowed.
6. Security Filters:
   - A series of security filters is used to intercept requests and apply various security measures.
   - SecurityContextPersistenceFilter: This is responsible for loading and saving the SecurityContext between HTTP requests and sessions.
   - CsrfFilter: This provides protection against CSRF attacks.
   - ExceptionTranslationFilter: This handles security-related exceptions by translating them into appropriate HTTP responses (like 403 Forbidden or 401 Unauthorized).
   - FilterSecurityInterceptor: This is responsible for performing access control checks and enforcing authorization.
7. Authentication Provider:
   - An AuthenticationProvider is responsible for authenticating a user. It checks the credentials (such as username and password) provided during authentication against some form of storage (database, LDAP, etc.).

- JdbcDaoImpl: This is a common implementation that authenticates against a relational database using JDBC.

8. UserDetailsService:
    - The UserDetailsService is used by Spring Security to load user-specific data (like username, password, roles) from a data source.
    - JdbcUserDetailsManager or InMemoryUserDetailsManager can be used to provide users' details from a database or in-memory data store.
9. Login and Logout Mechanism:
    - Spring Security provides built-in support for login and logout functionality.
    - Form Login: A login form is provided for user authentication, where a user submits credentials (username/password).
    - Basic Authentication: Used for browser-based or API-based authentication using the Authorization header.
    - Single Sign-On (SSO): Spring Security integrates with SSO services like OAuth2, OpenID, or CAS for centralized authentication.
    - Logout: Provides logout functionality to invalidate the session, clear authentication, and redirect the user to a logout page or another URL.
10. Session Management:
    - Session Fixation Protection: Spring Security protects against session fixation attacks by creating a new session after authentication.
    - Session Timeout and Concurrency Control: Configures session timeout and controls concurrent sessions for each user.
11. OAuth2 and OpenID Connect Support:
    - There is also deep integration with OAuth2 and OpenID Connect (OIDC) in which Spring Security could be used to authenticate against third-party identity vendors (such as Google, Facebook, and so on).
    - OAuth2Login: This is a OAuth2-based logging in mechanism.
    - OAuth2ResourceServer: This provides security of the REST APIs through OAuth2 tokens.
12. Security Configurations:
    - Spring Security is very customizable through Java or XML. Security configurations are used to define the roles, authentication procedures, authorization policies, and other security-related configurations.
    - HttpSecurity: It is used to set the security of HTTP, which can include CSRF protection, login, and access control policy.

Request and response of Spring Security flow are as follows:

1. Client Request:
    - The request made by the client (browser, mobile app, etc.) to the server. It contains necessary information, such as headers, body, and potentially authentication tokens.
2. Security Filter Chain:
    - A sequence of filters that intercept and process the HTTP request. Each filter handles a specific security concern, such as authentication, CSRF protection, etc.

3. Authentication Filters:
   - These filters check the incoming request to see if it contains valid credentials (e.g., form login, basic authentication, or token). If valid, they authenticate the user.
4. Authentication Manager:
   - This component is responsible for validating the credentials provided in the request (like username and password). It delegates this task to an AuthenticationProvider for the actual validation.
5. Authorization Filters:
   - These filters check whether the authenticated user has the necessary permissions (roles/authorities) to access the requested resource. If authorized, the request is allowed to proceed.
6. Access Decision Manager:
   - Based on the user's roles/permissions, this component makes the decision whether the user can access the requested resource or not.
7. Security Context:
   - After successful authentication, the user's details (e.g., username and roles) are stored in the SecurityContext for subsequent requests. The SecurityContextHolder is used to manage this context.
8. Authentication Success:
   - If authentication and authorization are successful, the response will be processed and returned to the client.

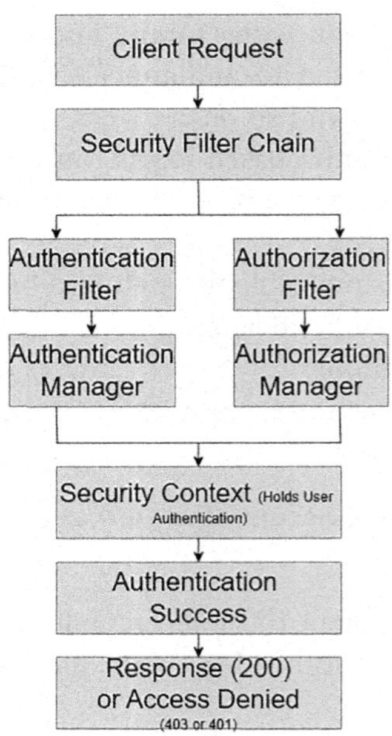


**FIGURE 9–1** Client request and server response in Spring Security.

9. Response:
   - Based on the outcome (successful authentication and authorization), the server sends a response:
   - If the user is authenticated and authorized, the requested resource is returned (HTTP 200).
   - If the user is not authorized, an HTTP 403 (Forbidden) response is returned.
   - In case of authentication failure, the response is an HTTP 401 (Unauthorized).

This flow will provide a request to be authenticated and authorized appropriately, after which they can gain access to the requested resources (Fig. 9–1):

## 9.3 Security in a Spring Web Application

Security in a Spring Web Application refers to the measures, settings, and practices that are undertaken in safeguarding the application against all sorts of security threats and to maintain control over access of particular resources or functions to only those people who are supposed to have access to those resources. It presents various stages such as authentication, authorization, and encryption among other security best practices to protect the application and application users.

A Spring Web Application has security that protects the application and data stored in the application against hacking and other attacks. This has been done with the help of authentication, authorization, secure communication, and data protection strategies, which have been woven together with the Spring Security.

Important points about security in a spring Web Application are as follows:

1. Authentication:
   - Authentication is the establishment quality of an identity of a user or a system. This can be done in a Spring Web Application with the help of Spring Security that is compatible with several authentication approaches, such as form-based login, HTTP Basic Authentication, JWT tokens, OAuth2, LDAP, and others.
   - Example: The application may need users to sign in by means of a username and password in order to gain access to the encrypted materials.
2. Authorization:
   - Authorization is used to specify what a user who is authenticated can or cannot do. An example will be some users are allowed to access administration features, and other users can only access general user feature.
   - Example: In a Spring Web Application, roles and permissions can be defined using Spring Security, allowing only users with specific roles (e.g., "ADMIN", "USER") to access specific endpoints.
3. Cross-Site Scripting Protection:
   - XSS prevents attackers from injecting malicious scripts into web pages viewed by other users. Spring Security includes mechanisms like output encoding and content security policies to mitigate such risks.

4. Cross-Site Request Forgery Protection:
   - CSRF attacks trick the user into performing unwanted actions on a website in which they are authenticated. Spring Security provides built-in CSRF protection, which requires that every state-changing request (like POST, PUT, DELETE) must include a CSRF token.
5. Secure Communication (HTTPS/SSL/TLS):
   - This ensures that communication between the client and server is encrypted. This protects data from being intercepted or altered during transmission. Spring Security can be configured to enforce HTTPS for certain endpoints or the entire application.
6. Session Management:
   - This manages user sessions securely by preventing session fixation (where an attacker forces a user to use a specific session ID) and session hijacking. Spring Security helps manage sessions effectively by tracking login attempts, limiting session concurrency, and automatically logging users out after a period of inactivity.
7. Password Storage:
   - Secure storage of passwords is essential to prevent unauthorized access if the application's database is compromised. Spring Security supports password encryption with algorithms like BCrypt, Argon2, or PBKDF2 to securely store hashed passwords in the database.
8. Access Control:
   - Spring Security provides granular access control mechanisms through annotations (e.g., @PreAuthorize, @Secured) or XML configurations. This enables access to resources based on roles, permissions, and security contexts.
9. OAuth2 and OpenID Connect Integration:
   - Spring Security supports third-party authentication and authorization mechanisms, like OAuth2 and OIDC, allowing the application to integrate with identity providers (Google, Facebook, etc.) for SSO capabilities.
10. Logging and Monitoring:
    - To track security-related events, Spring Security can integrate with logging frameworks to log important security actions (like failed login attempts, authorization denials, etc.). This allows for auditing and monitoring to detect suspicious activities.
11. Security Headers:
    - Spring Security can automatically add various HTTP security headers (e.g., Content-Security-Policy, X-Content-Type-Options, Strict-Transport-Security) to mitigate common web application vulnerabilities.

## 9.3.1 Why is security important for Spring Web Application?

- Protect Sensitive Data: Applications often handle sensitive user data (such as personal details, passwords, and financial data) that need to be protected from malicious actors.
- Prevent Unauthorized Access: It is also a kind of security that is enforced to protect the controlled access of specific information to users that are allowed to view or update it.

- Compliance: Many industries (including GDPR, HIPAA, and PCI-DSS) pose numerous regulatory demands, and the security of the application is required to protect the privacy and data.
- Keep Trust: Customers want to have a secure experience of dealing with applications. The application of effective security measures can assist in creating the trust and defending the image of the organization.

Security in a Spring Web Application is primarily provided by Spring Security, a comprehensive and customizable framework that addresses the most common security concerns, including authentication, authorization, and protection against various types of attacks. The way how security is typically provided in a Spring Web application is as follows:

1. Authentication:
   Authentication is the process of verifying the identity of the user or client. Spring Security supports several ways to authenticate users:
   - Form-Based Authentication:
     A user submits a form with credentials (username and password). Spring Security authenticates the credentials and sets up a session or token if the credentials are valid.
   - HTTP Basic Authentication:
     This involves sending the username and password in the Authorization header of the HTTP request.
   - JSON Web Token Authentication (Token-Based Authentication):
     Spring Security can integrate with JWT tokens to authenticate users. The server issues a token upon successful login, and the client sends this token in subsequent requests for authentication.
   - Lightweight Directory Access Protocol Authentication:
     Spring Security can authenticate users via an Lightweight Directory Access Protocol (LDAP) server.
   - OAuth2/OpenID Connect Authentication:
     Spring Security supports third-party authentication providers such as Google, Facebook, or corporate SSO systems using OAuth2 or OIDC for SSO.
2. Authorization:
   Authorization controls what authenticated users can and cannot do. Spring Security provides fine-grained control over user permissions:
   - Role-Based Access Control: Users are assigned roles, and each role has different access rights.
   - Method-Level Security: Security annotations such as @PreAuthorize, @Secured, and @RolesAllowed can be used to protect individual methods.
   - Access-Control Lists: For more granular access control, Spring Security supports Access-Control Lists, where permissions can be assigned to individual objects or resources.
3. Cross-Site Request Forgery Protection:
   CSRF attacks occur when a malicious user tricks an authenticated user into performing unwanted actions on a web application. Spring Security includes the built-in protection

against CSRF attacks by enabling CSRF token generation and CSRF token validation on a request-by-request basis.

CSRF all state-changing HTTP requests (POST, PUT, DELETE) will be provided with protection by default by Spring Security.

4. Session Management:

   The session management makes sure the user sessions are tracked and managed appropriately. Spring Security offers the means of avoiding session fixation, session expiry, and concurrent session cap.

   - Session Fixation Protection: Spring Security has the ability to avoid attackers to configure the user session to a predefined value (session fixation).
   - Session Timeout: It is a setting where the session is configured to expire after a specific time of not being used.
   - Session concurrency control: These are defined as the number of concurrent sessions that can be operated by a user.

5. HTTPS/SSL Configuration:

   In order to secure data transmission, one should make sure that all the sensitive traffic between client and server will be encrypted with the help of using SSL/TLS (i.e., HTTPS) all the time. Spring Security can be configured to redirect HTTP requests to HTTPS for security.

   Example:

```
@Override
protected void configure(HttpSecurity http) throws Exception {
http.requiresChannel()
.anyRequest().requiresSecure(); // Forces all requests to be redirected to HTTPS
}
```

6. Password Encryption:

   Storing passwords securely is crucial to prevent data breaches. Spring Security provides password encoders (e.g., BCrypt and PBKDF2) to securely hash and store passwords in the database.

   Example:

```
@Bean
public PasswordEncoderpasswordEncoder() {
return new BCryptPasswordEncoder(); // BCrypt is widely used for hashing passwords
}
```

7. Security Headers:

   Security headers are used to protect the application from various types of attacks, such as Clickjacking, MIME sniffing, and XSS. Spring Security can automatically add these headers to HTTP responses.

   - Content-Security-Policy: Helps prevent XSS attacks.
   - Strict-Transport-Security (HSTS): Enforces the use of HTTPS.

- X-Content-Type-Options: Prevents browsers from interpreting files as something they are not.

8. Cross-Origin Resource Sharing:
   Cross-Origin Resource Sharing (CORS) is a security feature implemented in browsers to prevent web applications from making requests to a different domain than the one that served the web page. Spring Security can be configured to enable or restrict CORS for your API endpoints.
9. Custom Security Filters:
   Spring Security defines custom filters that can handle specific security concerns, such as authentication tokens or logging requests.

## 9.4 Spring Security filters

Spring Security uses a chain of filters to handle authentication, authorization, and other security concerns. Each filter in the chain processes the incoming request and either passes it to the next filter or terminates the chain based on the logic.

The key filters provided by Spring Security are as follows:

1. SecurityContextPersistenceFilter
   - Restores the SecurityContext (user authentication details) from storage (e.g., session) for each request.
   - Ensures the SecurityContext is available throughout the request lifecycle.
2. UsernamePasswordAuthenticationFilter
   - Handles authentication for form-based login.
   - Processes the username and password submitted in a login form.
   - Delegates the credentials to the AuthenticationManager for validation.
3. BasicAuthenticationFilter
   - Processes HTTP Basic Authentication headers.
   - Extracts the username and password from the Authorization header of the request.
   - Delegates authentication to the AuthenticationManager.
4. BearerTokenAuthenticationFilter
   - Handles authentication for requests containing OAuth2 Bearer Tokens.
   - Typically used in securing REST APIs with token-based authentication.
5. OAuth2AuthorizationRequestRedirectFilter
   - Redirects users to the authorization server for OAuth2 login.
   - Starts the OAuth2 authorization flow.
6. OAuth2LoginAuthenticationFilter
   - Handles the callback from an OAuth2 authorization server.
   - Retrieves the access token and user details after successful authentication.
7. SessionManagementFilter
   - Manages session-related security tasks.

- Prevents session fixation attacks.
- Enforces session concurrency rules (e.g., one session per user).

8. CsrfFilter
   - Protects against CSRF attacks.
   - Validates the CSRF token sent with state-changing requests (e.g., POST, PUT, DELETE).
9. LogoutFilter
   - Handles user logout requests.
   - Clears the SecurityContext and invalidates the session.
   - Redirects the user to a specified logout success URL.
10. ExceptionTranslationFilter
    - Intercepts security-related exceptions (e.g., AccessDeniedException or AuthenticationException).
    - Redirects unauthenticated users to the login page.
    - For authenticated users, it forwards them to an access-denied handler.
11. FilterSecurityInterceptor
    - Handles access control (authorization) for protected resources.
    - Makes decisions based on:
    - URL patterns.
    - Role-based permissions.
    - Configured access control rules.
12. AnonymousAuthenticationFilter
    - Assigns an anonymous authentication token for unauthenticated users.
    - Ensures proper handling of users who have not logged in.
13. RememberMeAuthenticationFilter
    - Provides "Remember Me" functionality.
    - Automatically logs in users based on a persistent cookie stored in their browser.
14. AuthorizationFilter
    - Applies fine-grained access control for each request.
    - Enforces security rules defined in HttpSecurity.
15. CorsFilter
    - Handles CORS configurations.
    - Ensures only allowed domains can make requests to the server.
16. RequestCacheAwareFilter
    - Saves the original request before redirecting to the login page.
    - Restores the original request after successful authentication.
17. JwtAuthenticationFilter (Custom Implementation)
    - Often used in modern applications to handle JWT-based authentication.
    - Parses and authenticates the JWT of Authorization header.
    - Filter chain execution

- The filters are also executed in a sequence, and their execution is supervised by the FilterChainProxy. This order is essential so as to apply security in the right way. Filter chain is configured with the help of the Spring Security HttpSecurity.

## 9.5 Security providers

- Authentication providers are important elements of Spring Security which handle authentication of users. Each provider adheres to the AuthenticationProviderinterface and carries out certain authentication logic, which can be validation of user credentials, user detail retrieval, or token verification.

1. DaoAuthentication Provider
   - Provides the most extensively applied authentication in Spring Security.
   - Validates username and password against a user store.
   - Relies on:
   - A UserDetailsService to load user information.
   - A PasswordEncoder to validate passwords securely.
   - Customization:
   - Implements custom UserDetailsService to load user details from databases, LDAP, or other sources.
2. LdapAuthenticationProvider
   - Used for authentication against LDAP servers.
   - Relies on an LdapAuthoritiesPopulator for loading user roles and authorities.
   - Often used in enterprise applications where LDAP is the central user store.
   Key Features:
   - Supports both direct and delegated authentication to the LDAP server.
   - Customizable to match specific LDAP schema.

   Example Configuration:

```
@Bean
public AuthenticationManagerldapAuthenticationManager
(BaseLdapPathContextSourcecontextSource) {
return new ProviderManager
(
new LdapAuthenticationProvider
(
new BindAuthenticator(contextSource),
new DefaultLdapAuthoritiesPopulator(contextSource, "ou=groups")
)
);
}
```

3. PreAuthenticatedAuthenticationProvider
   - Used when authentication is performed externally, and Spring Security needs to process already authenticated users.
   - Typically used in scenarios like SSO or integration with an external authentication system.
   - Verifies the preauthenticated principal and grants appropriate authorities.
   Example Use Case:
   - A custom RequestHeaderAuthenticationFilter to extract preauthenticated details from HTTP headers.
4. JwtAuthenticationProvider (Custom)
   - A common custom implementation for modern applications that use JWT for stateless authentication.
   - Validates the JWT and extracts user details and authorities.
   - Used in REST APIs.

   Example Configuration:
   ```
   @Bean
   public AuthenticationProviderjwtAuthenticationProvider() {
   return new JwtAuthenticationProvider(jwtTokenService());
   }
   ```
5. OAuth2AuthenticationProvider
   - Used for OAuth2 and OIDC authentication flows.
   - Responsible for validating authorization codes, tokens, or user details retrieved from an OAuth2 provider (e.g., Google and Facebook).
   - Works with OAuth2UserService to load user information.

   Example Configuration:
   ```
   http.oauth2Login()
   .userInfoEndpoint()
   .userService(customOAuth2UserService());
   ```
6. AnonymousAuthenticationProvider
   - Provides anonymous authentication for unauthenticated users.
   - Ensures anonymous users can access specific resources without being logged in.
   - Used in conjunction with the AnonymousAuthenticationFilter.

   Example Configuration:
   ```
   http.authorizeRequests()
   .antMatchers("/public/**").permitAll()
   .anyRequest().authenticated();
   ```
7. RememberMeAuthenticationProvider
   - Supports the "Remember Me" feature.
   - Validates the persistent token (stored as a cookie in the user's browser) for automatic login.

- Cooperates with the RememberMeAuthentication filter.

  Example Configuration:

  ```
  http.rememberMe()
  .key("uniqueAndSecretKey")
  .rememberMeCookieName("remember-me-token");
  ```

8. OpenIDAuthenticationProvider (Deprecated)
   - Formerly used in the OpenID authentication.
   - Replaced by OAuth2AuthenticationProvider for modern OIDC flows.

   Custom Authentication Providers
   - Create custom providers by implementing the AuthenticationProvider interface.
   - Useful to integrate with third-party systems, APIs, or custom logic.

   Multiple Authentication Providers
   - Spring Security supports chaining multiple authentication providers.
   - Each provider is tried in sequence until one successfully authenticates or the chain fails.

   Example Configuration:

   ```
   @Bean
   public AuthenticationManagerauthenticationManager() {
   List<AuthenticationProvider> providers=List.of(
   new DaoAuthenticationProvider(),
   new LdapAuthenticationProvider(),
   new CustomAuthenticationProvider()
   );
   return new ProviderManager(providers);
   }
   ```

9. Benefits of Using Authentication Providers
   - Modularity: You can plug in multiple providers for different authentication mechanisms.
   - Customizability: Easily extend and implement your own logic.
   - Flexibility: Integrates seamlessly with modern and legacy authentication systems.
   - By combining these providers, Spring Security offers a robust framework for building secure and flexible authentication systems.

## 9.6 Spring Security—roles and privileges

In Spring Security, **roles** and **privileges** are essential for implementing fine-grained access control. They are used to define who can access which resources and perform specific actions.

1. **Roles**
   - A **role** represents a high-level grouping of permissions or privileges.

- For example, ROLE_ADMIN might include all privileges like creating, editing, and deleting resources, while ROLE_USER may only allow viewing resources.

  **Characteristics:**
- Prefixed by default with ROLE_ (configurable).
- Used to define broad access rights.
- Checked during authorization using hasRole().

**2. Privileges**
- A **privilege** (or authority) is a more granular permission, often representing specific actions a user can perform.
- For example:
- CREATE_USER
- EDIT_USER
- DELETE_USER
- VIEW_USER

  **Characteristics:**
- Represented as GrantedAuthority objects in Spring Security.
- Checked using hasAuthority() or hasAnyAuthority().

Table 9-1.

## 9.6.1 Role and privilege hierarchy

- Roles can include a set of privileges.
- For example:
- ROLE_ADMIN → CREATE_USER, DELETE_USER, VIEW_USER
- ROLE_USER → VIEW_USER

This allows **role-based access control** to be built on top of granular privileges.

## 9.6.2 Storing roles and privileges

### *9.6.2.1 Database schema example*

- **Tables:**
- users—Stores user credentials.
- roles—Stores roles (e.g., ROLE_ADMIN, ROLE_USER).
- privileges—Stores privileges (e.g., CREATE_USER, DELETE_USER).

**Table 9–1** Roles and privileges.

| Aspect | Roles | Privileges |
|---|---|---|
| Granularity | High-level | Fine-grained |
| Representation | ROLE_ADMIN | CREATE_USER, DELETE_USER |
| Used In | Broad access policies | Specific action checks |

- Join tables to map users to roles and roles to privileges.
  - Users Table
    CREATE TABLE users (id BIGINT PRIMARY KEY, username VARCHAR(255), password VARCHAR(255));
  - Roles Table
    CREATE TABLE roles (id BIGINT PRIMARY KEY, name VARCHAR(255));
  - Privileges Table
    CREATE TABLE privileges (id BIGINT PRIMARY KEY, name VARCHAR(255));
  - User-Role Mapping
    CREATE TABLE user_roles (user_id BIGINT,role_id BIGINT,FOREIGN KEY (user_id) REFERENCES users(id),FOREIGN KEY (role_id) REFERENCES roles(id));
  - Role-Privilege Mapping
    CREATE TABLE role_privileges (role_id BIGINT,privilege_id BIGINT, FOREIGN KEY (role_id) REFERENCES roles(id),FOREIGN KEY (privilege_id) REFERENCES privileges(id));

## 9.6.3 Spring Security configuration

1. **Define roles and privileges in code**
   Define roles and privileges directly in the application.

```
@Override
protected void configure(HttpSecurity http) throws Exception {
http
.authorizeRequests()
.antMatchers("/admin/**").hasRole("ADMIN") // Check for role
.antMatchers("/user/**").hasAnyRole("USER", "ADMIN") // Multiple roles
.antMatchers("/public/**").permitAll()
.antMatchers("/edit/**").hasAuthority("EDIT_USER") // Check for privilege
.anyRequest().authenticated()
.and()
.formLogin()
.and()
.logout();
}
```

2. **Implement role-privilege hierarchy**
   Create a role-privilege hierarchy by extending UserDetailsService and customizing roles.

```
@Service
public class CustomUserDetailsService implements UserDetailsService {
@Autowired
private UserRepositoryuserRepository;
@Override
```

```
public UserDetailsloadUserByUsername(String username) throws
UsernameNotFoundException {
User user=userRepository.findByUsername(username)
.orElseThrow(() -> new UsernameNotFoundException("User not found"));
List<GrantedAuthority> authorities=getAuthorities(user.getRoles());
return new org.springframework.security.core.userdetails.User(
user.getUsername(),
user.getPassword(),
authorities
);
}
private List<GrantedAuthority>getAuthorities(Set<Role> roles) {
Set<GrantedAuthority> authorities=new HashSet<>();
for (Role role: roles) {
authorities.add(new SimpleGrantedAuthority(role.getName()));
role.getPrivileges().forEach(privilege ->
authorities.add(new SimpleGrantedAuthority(privilege.getName())));
}
return new ArrayList<>(authorities);
}
}
```

## 9.6.4 Annotations for role and privilege-based access

- **@PreAuthorize:** Allows method-level access control.
- **@Secured:** Restricts access to specific roles.

**Example:**

```
@Service
public class UserService {
@PreAuthorize("hasRole('ADMIN')")
public void createUser(User user) {
// Only ADMIN can create users
}
@PreAuthorize("hasAuthority('VIEW_USER')")
public User getUser(Long id) {
// Anyone with VIEW_USER privilege can access this method
return userRepository.findById(id).orElse(null);
}
}
```

### 9.6.5 Customizing role prefix

By default, Spring Security adds a ROLE_ prefix to roles. To remove or change this:

```
@Bean
public GrantedAuthorityDefaultsgrantedAuthorityDefaults() {
return new GrantedAuthorityDefaults(""); // Remove ROLE_ prefix
}
```

## 9.7 Security custom validators

1. Custom Authentication Provider

```
public class CustomAuthenticationProvider implements AuthenticationProvider {
@Override
public Authentication authenticate(Authentication authentication) throws
AuthenticationException {
String username=authentication.getName(); // Extract username
String password=authentication.getCredentials().toString(); // Extract password
// Example custom validation logic
if ("user".equals(username) && "password".equals(password)) {
// Return authenticated token with roles
return new UsernamePasswordAuthenticationToken(username, password, List.of(new
SimpleGrantedAuthority("ROLE_USER")));
} else {
throw new BadCredentialsException("Invalid username or password"); // If invalid
}
}
@Override
public boolean supports(Class<?>authentication) {
// Specify the type of Authentication token this provider supports
return UsernamePasswordAuthenticationToken.class.isAssignableFrom(authentication);
}
}
```

Why It's Needed:

- AuthenticationProvider**:** Interface that enables custom authentication logic.
- authenticate(): Performs the actual authentication, verifying credentials and returning an authenticated token.
- supports(): Ensures this provider handles the specified token type (e.g., UsernamePasswordAuthenticationToken).

2. Custom Authentication Token (Optional)

```
public class CustomAuthenticationToken extends
UsernamePasswordAuthenticationToken {
```

```
public CustomAuthenticationToken(Object principal, Object credentials) {
super(principal, credentials);
}
public CustomAuthenticationToken(Object principal, Object credentials, Collection<?
extends GrantedAuthority>authorities) {
super(principal, credentials, authorities);
}
}
```

Why It's Needed:

- Custom Token: Useful if you need to extend UsernamePasswordAuthenticationToken to include additional properties, such as user-specific attributes.

3. Register Custom Provider

```
@Bean
public AuthenticationProvidercustomAuthenticationProvider() {
return new CustomAuthenticationProvider(); // Register the custom provider
}
@Bean
public AuthenticationManagerauthenticationManager() {
return new ProviderManager(List.of(customAuthenticationProvider())); // Add to
AuthenticationManager
}
```

Why It's Needed:

- Custom Provider Registration: Spring Security uses this provider during authentication.
- Authentication Manager: Manages the providers and decides which one to use for each request.

4. Security Filter Chain

```
@Bean
public SecurityFilterChainsecurityFilterChain(HttpSecurity http) throws Exception {
http
.authorizeHttpRequests(authz ->authz
.anyRequest().authenticated() // Protect all endpoints
)
.httpBasic(); // Enable Basic Authentication
return http.build();
}
```

Why It's Needed:

- SecurityFilterChain: Configures security rules for requests.
- Basic Authentication: Uses Authorization headers with username/password for authentication.

**5.** Integrate with External System (Optional)

If integrating with an external system (e.g., REST API, and LDAP), modify the authenticate () method.

```
@Override
public Authentication authenticate(Authentication authentication) throws
AuthenticationException {
String username=authentication.getName();
String password=authentication.getCredentials().toString();
// Example: Call an external API
if (externalAuthService.validate(username, password)) {
return new UsernamePasswordAuthenticationToken(username, password, List.of(new
SimpleGrantedAuthority("ROLE_USER")));
} else {
throw new BadCredentialsException("External system authentication failed");
}
}
```

Why It's Needed:

- Extends the custom provider to authenticate using nondatabase sources, providing flexibility for complex scenarios.

# 9.8 Security validators

## 9.8.1 Purpose of validators in Spring Security

Validators are used to ensure that user inputs (e.g., username, password, and email) meet specific criteria before proceeding with authentication or other security-related processes. This may involve authentication of form information on registration, login, or custom security processes.

Validators in Spring Security can be categorized as follows:

- Built-in Constraints (e.g., @NotBlank, @Email, and @Size).
- Custom Validation Logic for specific rules (e.g., password strength and username uniqueness).
- Support of custom authentication validations with Spring Security Filters.

**A.** Bean Validation (Hibernate Validator)

Standard Bean Validation is a means to force constraints on input fields within DTOs or models. It uses annotations on the declarative validation.

```
import jakarta.validation.constraints.*;
public class UserInputDto {
@NotBlank(message="Username is required")
private String username;
```

```
@Size(min=8, message="Password must be at least 8 characters")
private String password;
@Email(message="Invalid email format")
private String email;
}
```

- @NotBlank: Ensures the field is not null or empty.
- @Size: Validates the length of a string.
- @Email: Validates email format.

**B.** Custom Validators

When built-in constraints are insufficient, custom annotations and validators can be created.

- Create a Custom Annotation

```
import jakarta.validation.Constraint;
import java.lang.annotation.*;
@Documented
@Constraint(validatedBy=MyCustomValidator.class)
@Target({ElementType.FIELD})
@Retention(RetentionPolicy.RUNTIME)
public @interface CustomValidation {
String message() default "Default validation message";
Class<?>[] groups() default {};
Class<? extends Payload>[] payload() default {};
}
```

- Implement the Validation Logic

```
import jakarta.validation.ConstraintValidator;
import jakarta.validation.ConstraintValidatorContext;
public class MyCustomValidator implements ConstraintValidator<CustomValidation,
String> {
@Override
public booleanisValid(String value, ConstraintValidatorContext context) {
// Custom validation logic
return value!=null &&value.matches("^[A-Za-z0-9]+$");
}
}
```

@Constraint: Links the custom annotation to the validator class.
isValid(): Implements the validation logic.

**C.** Using Validators in Controllers

In Spring Security applications, controllers validate user input before processing it further.

```
import org.springframework.validation.annotation.Validated;
import org.springframework.web.bind.annotation.*;
```

```
@RestController
@RequestMapping("/register")
public class RegistrationController {
@PostMapping
public String registerUser(@Validated @RequestBody UserInputDtoinput) {
// Registration logic
return "Success";
}
}
```

- @Validated: Triggers validation on the annotated object.
- @RequestBody: Maps incoming JSON to a Java object.

**D.** Validation in Authentication Filters

Custom validators can be integrated into Spring Security filters to validate credentials during authentication.

```
public class CustomAuthenticationFilter extends UsernamePasswordAuthenticationFilter {
@Override
public Authentication attemptAuthentication(HttpServletRequest request,
HttpServletResponseresponse) {
String username=obtainUsername(request);
String password=obtainPassword(request);
// Add custom validation
if (!isValidInput(username, password)) {
throw new BadCredentialsException("Validation failed");
}
return super.attemptAuthentication(request, response);
}
}
```

### 9.8.2 Why validators are needed

- Security: Prevent invalid or malicious input during authentication or registration.
- User Experience: Provide feedback for incorrectly formatted inputs.
- Compliance: Enforce specific rules for sensitive data (e.g., passwords or emails).
- Flexibility: Allow custom business rule.

## 9.9 Spring Security with JSON Web Tokens

Under a Spring Security based on JWT-based authentication architecture, the process can be initiated when a client tries to submit a request to the server by inputting his/her username and password. When this request is received, a server authenticates the user based on the AuthenticationManager of the Spring Security that authenticates using the credentials. When the credentials are verified, the server issues a JWT, which contains crucial user details about the user, for example, the username and the roles, and forwards this token to the client.

The client transmits the JWT token in the Authorization header of each request, which is in the format Bearer <token> in the subsequent interactions. A server, when each request is sent to the server via it, uses its own JWT filter that intercepts the request, retrieves the token, and authenticates it. Validation process verifies the signature of the token to determine whether it has not been altered and also verifies the expiration time to ensure that it is still valid. When the token is valid, the server reads the user information of the claims in the token, which include the username and role, and sets up security context of the request. In case of an invalid or expired token, the server replies with an HTTP 401 Unauthorized request.

After the token has been verified, the roles or authorities stored with the token are then utilized by Spring Security to carry out authorization checks and either allow access or deny access to secured resources. This access control helps to limit access of the endpoints or resources to a user with the correct permission. JWT-based authentication is stateless; therefore there is no session data that the server is holding, and so this is very scalable to the distributed systems or microservices architecture.

The JWT token is signed with claims, such as identity of the user and user roles, and provides a signature to ensure integrity. The server will sign the JWT using a secret key or a pair of a public and a private key to confirm that it has not been spoilt. The token also expires, and hence a user must reauthenticate to get another token. This architecture offers a secure, scalable, and stateless way of dealing with authentication and authorization of a contemporary web app and APIs (Fig. 9–2).

1. Client Request (Login): The client sends a login request with the user's credentials (username and password).
2. Authentication: The server authenticates the credentials using AuthenticationManager from Spring Security.
3. JWT Token Generation: If authentication is successful, the server generates a JWT token, signs it with a secret key, and sends it back to the client.
4. Client Stores JWT: The client stores the JWT token, typically in localStorage, cookies, or session storage.
5. Client Sends Requests: For subsequent requests, the client sends the JWT token in the Authorization header as Bearer <token>.
6. JWT Filter: The server validates the JWT token using a custom JWT filter, extracting user details like roles and username from the token.
7. Security Context: According to the extracted information, the Spring Security establishes the authentication context; thus the server can authenticate the user.
8. Authorization: The system deems the roles or authorities of the token to grant the client access to secured resources.

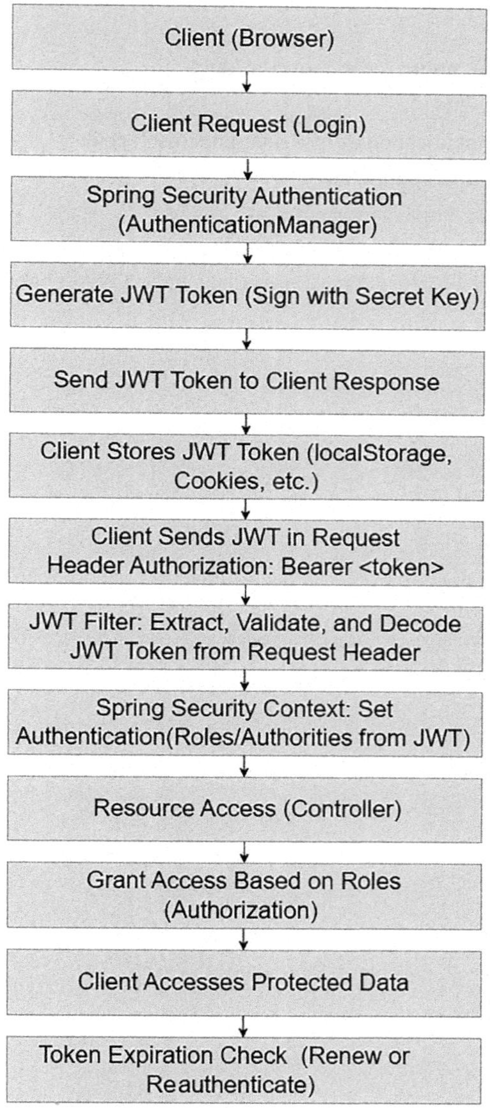


**FIGURE 9–2** Client request and response in JWT token.

9. Protected Data: The accessing client gets access to the requested information or resource depending on the assigned roles.
10. Token Expiration: The system verifies the presence of token expiration. In case the token has expired, a client should reauthenticate or obtain a new token.

## Bibliography

IBM. (2024). Security Concepts. https://www.ibm.com/docs.

JWT. (2024). JWT Docs. https://jwt.io.

Microsoft. (2024). Security Authentication. https://learn.microsoft.com.

OAuth. (2024). OAuth Docs. https://oauth.net.

OWASP. (2024). Security Guide. https://owasp.org.

Spring Security. (2024). Documentation. https://docs.spring.io/spring-security/reference/.

# 10

# Pagination, sorting, and filtering in Spring Model-View-Controller

## 10.1 Introduction

Paging (or pagination) in Spring Model-View-Controller (MVC) is the way of dividing a large data into small and manageable blocks, or pages, so that only a part of the data is loaded at any moment. This can be particularly handy when one has to display a list of items or records in a database or when the data is large. Instead of loading the whole dataset into memory, which may be inefficient and slow, paging means that the system loads only a given set of the data, the set usually being specified by the page number and the size of each page.

### 10.1.1 Architecture of paging in Spring Model-View-Controller

Paging plays an important role in the Spring MVC in efficiently working with mass data, ensuring only a part of the records is obtained at once. It enhances performance and cost optimization and enhances a better user experience.

Spring Data Paging:

- Spring Data provides built-in support for paging using Pageable and Page.
- Pageable: Represents the pagination parameters (page number and page size).
- Page: An instance of a page of results including data and pagination information such as the number of total pages.

Syntax Example:

```
public Page<Product>findByCategory(String category, Pageable pageable);
```

Here, findByCategory gets all the products in a certain category, but the response is paginated with Pageable to get a limited number of records.

## 10.2 Paging working procedure

The client requests come in with two important parameters, namely the page number (which specifies the page number of results to be retrieved) and the page size (which specifies the number of items to be displayed on a single page). Here is an example of a request: /items?page=2&size=10, requesting the second page of 10 items.

After the request is sent to the server, it is directed to the DispatcherServlet (front controller in a Spring MVC application), which then sends it to the right controller. The

Mastering Java Full Stack Development. DOI: https://doi.org/10.1016/B978-0-443-51683-2.00013-8

controller takes out the page number and the page size of the request and forwards the parameters to the service layer that contains the business logic of the application. The service layer communicates with the data access layer (usually Data Access Objects [DAO] or a repository) to get the paginated information.

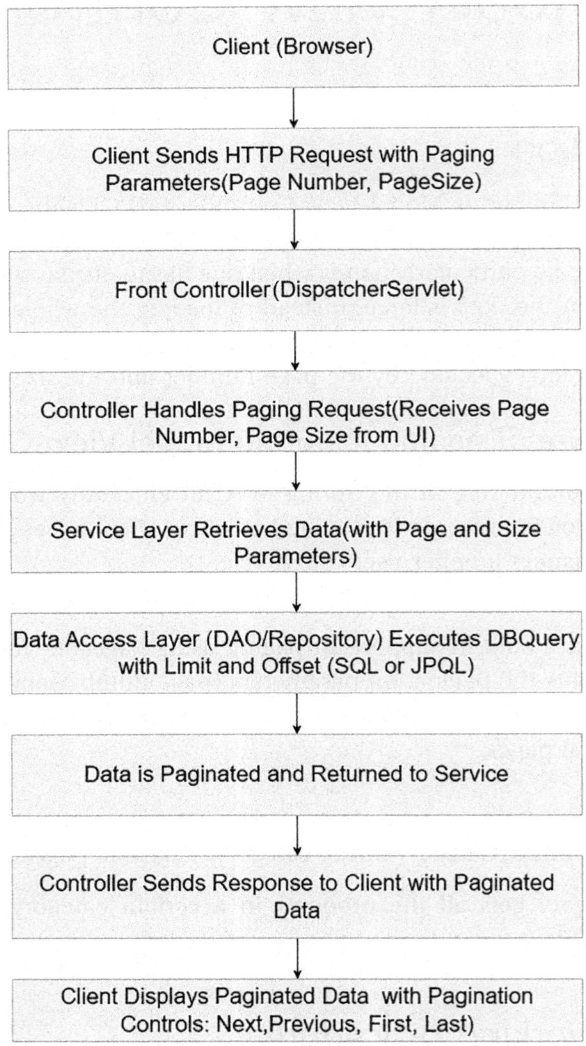


The data access layer, either Spring Data JPA or custom SQL queries, is used to apply pagination logic to retrieve the requested portion of data. This is usually done by SQL query using LIMIT and OFFSET or by calling upon the Pageable interface of Spring Data, which makes it easy to query paginated data. The data access layer gives the data in the form of a Page object that includes not only the requested records but also information about the metadata, such as the total number of records, the total number of pages, the current page, and the availability of the next or previous page.

This result is processed by one service layer and returned to the controller, which prepares the response and sends it to the client. The paginated data and the required metadata are provided to the client, and they can show the current page of results as well as give pagination controls like Next, previous, first, and last so that the user can browse the data effectively.

The ultimate product is a page of data, which is the one desired by the user together with pertinent pagination information (i.e., the total number of pages, the current page, etc.) such that the user can go through the data in bits, without overloading the system or the user interface with all the data at once.

The pagination architecture of Spring MVC application is as below in text form:

1. Client (Browser or Mobile Application):
   The client makes the request with a URL sent to the server containing the pagination parameters, the page number, and page size. An example would be such a request as /products?page=2&size=10 to access the second page of 10 products.
2. Front Controller: DispatcherServlet:
   The Spring MVC framework has the DispatcherServlet as the entry point. It accepts the request by the client and forwards it to the relevant controller, where it is processed.
3. Controller:
   The HTTP request supplies the pagination request (page number and page size) to the controller, which then forwards them to the service layer. It is used as an intermediary between the service layer and the client, and it interprets a request and responds.
4. Service Layer:
   The service layer is used to deal with business logic and communicates with the data access layer (DAO/Repository). It takes the pagination parameters as input in the controller and applies them on the data access layer to select the correct set of data (data on the page that was requested).
5. Data Access Objects (DAO/Repository):

DAO or repository layer deals with the database in order to retrieve the data. It implements pagination logic to allow retrieval of a subset of data with the page number and page size, using Spring Data JPA or custom SQL queries commonly with the use of LIMIT and OFFSET to specify the records to retrieve to the current page.

The repository delivers the data as a Page object, which includes the data of the current page and pagination metadata information, including the total records, the total pages, the current page, and the existence of the additional pages.

1. **Service Layer (Continued):**
   The service layer processes the paginated data received from the repository and includes pagination metadata (like total records, total pages, and current page) to be sent back to the controller.

1. **Controller(Continued)**: The controller prepares the response, packaging the data and pagination metadata. It sends this response back to the client.
2. **Client(Continued)**: The client receives the paginated data and the pagination metadata (such as total pages, current page, etc.). It uses this information to display the results and offer pagination controls (such as "Next," "Previous," "First," and "Last") for the user to navigate through the data.

The **final output** is a page of data, along with the necessary pagination information, sent back to the client. The client can use the metadata to allow the user to navigate through different pages of the dataset without overwhelming the user interface or the server.

## 10.3 Pagniation program procedure

1. Build the Project:
   First, ensure that the project is built using Maven or Gradle.
   For Maven:
   mvn clean install
   For Gradle:
   gradle build
2. Run the Spring Boot Application:
   After building the project, run the Spring Boot application. The main class should be annotated with @SpringBootApplication.
   For Maven:
   mvnspring-boot:run
   For Gradle:
   gradlebootRun
3. Controller Layer:
   The Controller layer is responsible for handling the HTTP request and invoking the service layer to retrieve paginated data.

```
@GetMapping("/items")
public String getPaginatedItems(@RequestParam("page") int page, @RequestParam
("size") int size, Model model) {
Pageable pageable = PageRequest.of(page, size);
Page<Item>itemsPage = itemService.getPaginatedItems(pageable);
model.addAttribute("items", itemsPage.getContent());
model.addAttribute("totalPages", itemsPage.getTotalPages());
model.addAttribute("currentPage", itemsPage.getNumber());
return "items"; // JSP or Thymeleaf template
}
```

4. Service Layer:
   The Service layer handles the logic of fetching the data and passing the Pageable object to

the repository for pagination.

```
@Service
public class ItemService {
@Autowired
private ItemRepositoryitemRepository;
public Page<Item>getPaginatedItems(Pageable pageable) {
return itemRepository.findAll(pageable);
}
}
```

5. Repository Layer:
The Repository layer extends JpaRepository to interact with the database and supports pagination by accepting a Pageable object.

```
@Repository
public interface ItemRepository extends JpaRepository<Item, Long> {
}
```

6. Entity Class (Item):
This is the entity class that represents the items in the database.

```
@Entity
public class Item {
@Id
@GeneratedValue(strategy = GenerationType.IDENTITY)
private Long id;
private String name;
// other fields, getters, setters
}
```

7. HTML (JSP or Thymeleaf):
The HTML template will display the paginated items and the pagination controls (Next, Previous, First, and Last).

```
<div>
<ul>
<li th:each="item : ${items}">
<span th:text="${item.name}"></span>
</li>
</ul>
<div>
<a href="/items?page=0&size=10" th:if="${currentPage> 0}">First</a>
<a href="/items?page=${currentPage - 1}&size=10" th:if="${currentPage> 0}">Previous</a>
<span th:text="${currentPage + 1}"></span>
<a href="/items?page=${currentPage + 1}&size=10" th:if="${currentPage<totalPages -
```

```
1}">Next</a>
<a href="/items?page=${totalPages - 1}&size=10" th:if="${currentPage<totalPages -
1}">Last</a>
</div>
</div>
```

8. Access the Application:
   Once the application starts, you can open your browser and access the paginated endpoint by specifying the page and size in the URL:
   http://localhost:8080/items?page=0&size=10
9. Testing:

Test pagination functionality by changing the page and size parameters in the URL or use a REST client like Postman to test various pages.

## 10.4 Sorting working procedure

In a Spring application, sorting allows you to retrieve data in a specific order, such as sorting records by date, name, or any other attribute. The sorting process works by using the Sort object from the Spring Data framework, which is passed to repository methods to define the sorting criteria.

First, the client submits a request to the controller, where the client indicates the sorting criteria, including the attribute that the data is to be sorted by (a name, a date, etc.) and the sorting order (up or down).

Pagination is frequently used together with sorting, which lets users navigate the large datasets and at the same time represent them in a predetermined order.

1. Client (Browser or API Consumer): The client sends out a request to retrieve data in order of priority. The request normally contains query parameters of the sorting field and sort direction, that is, ?sort=name, asc or ?sort=date, desc.
2. Controller: This is the controller that gets the incoming HTTP request. It retrieves the sorting parameters (e.g., sorting field and direction) of the request and forwards them to the service layer.

```
@GetMapping("/items")
public String getSortedItems(@RequestParam("sort") String sortField, @RequestParam
("direction") String direction, Model model) {
Sort sort = Sort.by(Sort.Order.by(sortField).with(Sort.Direction.fromString(direction)));
List<Item>sortedItems = itemService.getSortedItems(sort);
model.addAttribute("items", sortedItems);
return "items";
}
```

1. Service Layer: The service layer handles business logic and interacts with the repository layer. It receives the Sort object, which contains sorting criteria (field and direction), and passes it to the repository layer to retrieve sorted data. This layer may further process the data (such as filtering, formatting, etc.) before returning it to the controller.

```
@Service
public class ItemService {
@Autowired
private ItemRepositoryitemRepository;
public List<Item>getSortedItems(Sort sort) {
return itemRepository.findAll(sort);
}
}
```

2. Repository Layer: The repository layer extends JpaRepository or any Spring Data repository interface. It accepts the Sort object, which is used to build the correct query to fetch data in the desired sorted order. This is handled by Spring Data JPA, which automatically generates the query with ORDER BY clauses based on the sorting parameters.

```
@Repository
public interface ItemRepository extends JpaRepository<Item, Long> {
}
```

3. Database: The database (e.g., MySQL, PostgreSQL) executes the generated query with sorting instructions. The query results are returned in the order specified by the Sort object (ascending or descending), based on the field chosen for sorting.
4. Service Layer (Return Data): The service layer receives the sorted data from the repository and may perform further processing if needed (e.g., additional filtering, aggregation).
5. Controller (Return to Client): Finally, the controller sends the sorted data back to the client (browser or API consumer). This data is normally sent to a view in a web application (e.g., JSP, Thymeleaf) to be rendered. The response body in an API is a sorted list, usually in the form of JSON.

## 10.5 Filtering

Filtering process is a normal operation in a Spring application where several layers are utilized to access and deliver data with certain criteria. The filtering process works in the following way:

1. **Client Request:** This starts off with the client (browser or API consumer) making a request that contains filter criteria, for example, a field value or a range.
2. **Controller Layer:** The controller layer accepts the coming request and derives the filter parameters that have been entered in the URL, query parameters, or request body. It then transfers these parameters to the service layer.

```
@GetMapping("/items")

public String getFilteredItems(@RequestParam("minPrice") double minPrice, Model
model) {
    List<Item>filteredItems = itemService.getFilteredItems(minPrice);
    model.addAttribute("items", filteredItems);
    return "items"; // JSP or Thymeleaf template
    }
```

3. **Service Layer**: The service layer receives the filtering criteria from the controller. The service layer then passes the filter parameters to the repository layer to fetch the data that matches the specified conditions.

```
@Service

public class ItemService {
@Autowired
private ItemRepositoryitemRepository;
public List<Item>getFilteredItems(double minPrice) {
return itemRepository.findByPriceGreaterThan(minPrice);
}
}
```

4. **Repository Layer**: The repository layer, which extends JpaRepository or another Spring Data interface, uses the filtering parameters to construct the appropriate query. Spring Data JPA automatically translates method names like findByPriceGreaterThan into a corresponding SQL query that filters the data at the database level. The repository then returns the filtered data to the service layer.

```
@Repository

public interface ItemRepository extends JpaRepository<Item, Long> {
List<Item>findByPriceGreaterThan(double price);
}
```

5. **Database:** The database executes the query with the necessary conditions (e.g., filtering based on price). It retrieves only the records that match the filtering criteria and returns them to the repository.
6. **Service Layer (Return Data):** Once the service layer receives the filtered data from the repository, it may perform further processing, such as transforming or aggregating the results. It then returns the data to the controller.

7. **Controller (Return to Client):** Finally, the controller sends the filtered data back to the client. In a web application, this data is usually passed to a view (e.g., JSP, Thymeleaf) for rendering. In an API, the filtered data is returned as a JSON response, ready for consumption by the client.
8. **Client (Browser or API Consumer):** The client is the recipient of the filtered information. When it is a web application, the filtered list will be displayed on the page, and when it is an API, the response data will be delivered in the form of JSON. This data can then be used or shown according to the need of the client.

With this, Spring applications are able to quickly filter big data, meaning they use database-level filtering to reduce the volume of transferred and processed data.

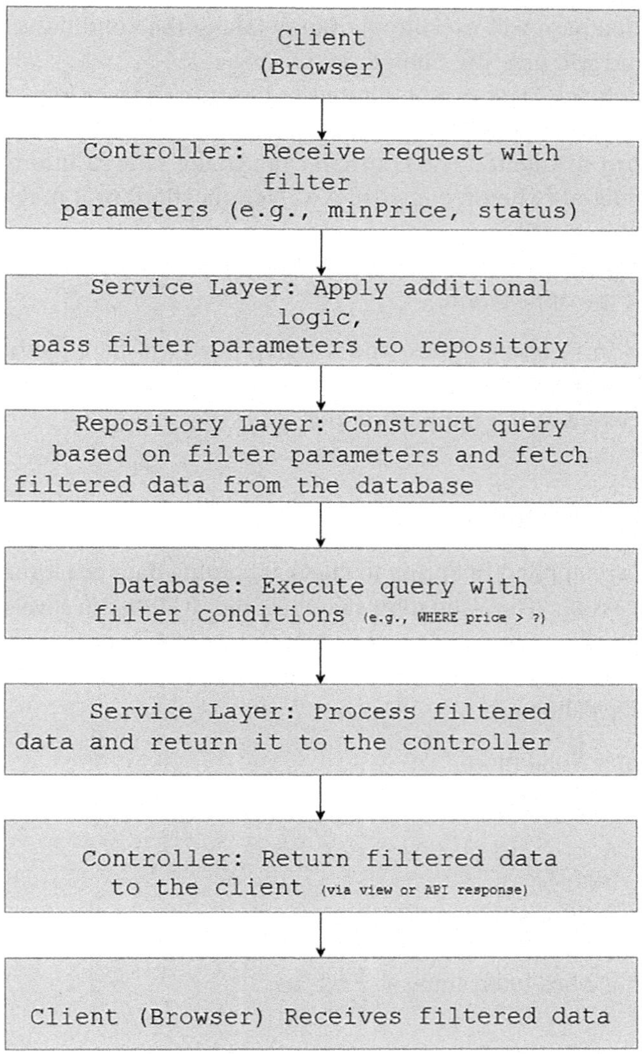

Flow of filtering approach.

1. Client (Browser): A request is made by the client with filtering criteria (e.g., price, category) as query parameters.
2. Controller: Controller takes the request and removes the filtering parameters and forwards them to the service layer to be processed.
3. Service Layer: This is the service layer that serves with business logic and does any further logic or validation on the filters. The filter criteria are then sent to the repository by it.
4. Repository Layer: The repository builds a database query with the filtering parameters (e.g., based on calls in the Spring Data JPA, such as findByPriceGreaterThan) and accepts the filtered data out of the database.
5. Database: The database will execute the query taking the conditions that will be used to filter the data and will give the filtered data.
6. Service Layer (Return): Data can be filtered in the service layer (e.g., sorting, transformations), then sent back to the controller.
7. Controller (Return to Client): The controller relays the filtered information to the client. This may be rendered (when it comes to a web application) or it may be a JSON response (when it comes to an API).
8. Client: The client is given the filtered data, which it consumes as required, either on a web page or through the application.

This design aids in isolating issues, and filtering logic will be effectively compiled at the repository tier (i.e., the database), which enhances performance by limiting the volume of data read and processed at the application tier.

## 10.6 Filtering validators

Filtering validators are applied in Spring to check incoming data or requests to apply to some criteria before processing. The validation may be used at different levels, including filtering invalid input in controllers, services, or request payloads. Below are common types of filtering validators and how they can be implemented in Spring.

Types of Filtering Validators

1. Request Parameter Validation
   Validate query parameters sent in HTTP requests using annotations.

   Example:
   ```
   @GetMapping("/items")
   public ResponseEntity<List<Item>>getItems(
   @RequestParam @Min(0) Integer minPrice,
   @RequestParam @Max(1000) Integer maxPrice
   ) {
   // Validation ensures minPrice and maxPrice are within range
   ```

```
return ResponseEntity.ok(itemService.findByPriceRange(minPrice, maxPrice));
}
```

Annotations Used:

- @Min
- @Max
- @Size
- @NotNull
- @NotEmpty

2. Request Body Validation
   Validate the incoming JSON payload for filtering, using annotations in the DTO.

   Example:

```
@PostMapping("/filter-items")
public ResponseEntity<List<Item>>filterItems(
@Valid @RequestBody ItemFilterDTOfilterDTO
) {
// Proceed only if filterDTO passes validation
return ResponseEntity.ok(itemService.filterItems(filterDTO));
}
```

   DTO Example:

```
public class ItemFilterDTO {
@NotEmpty(message = "Category must not be empty")
private String category;
@Min(value = 1, message = "Minimum price must be greater than 0")
private int minPrice;
@Max(value = 1000, message = "Maximum price must not exceed 1000")
private int maxPrice;
// Getters and Setters
}
```

3. Custom Validation
   Use a custom validator for more complex validation logic.

   Example:

```
@Component
public class ItemFilterValidator implements ConstraintValidator<ValidItemFilter,
ItemFilterDTO> {
@Override
public booleanisValid(ItemFilterDTO filter, ConstraintValidatorContext context) {
if (filter.getMinPrice() >filter.getMaxPrice()) {
context.buildConstraintViolationWithTemplate("Min price cannot be greater than max
price")
.addConstraintViolation();
```

```
return false;
}
return true;
}
}
```

Annotate the DTO:

```
@ValidItemFilter
public class ItemFilterDTO {
private int minPrice;
private int maxPrice;
// Getters and Setters
}
```

4. Method-Level Validation

   Validate inputs at the service or repository layer.

   Example:

```
@Service
public class ItemService {
public List<Item>findItems(@NotNull @Size(min = 3) String name) {
// Service logic here
}
}
```

   Enable validation at the method level in the Spring configuration:

```
@Configuration
@EnableMethodValidation
public class ValidationConfig {
}
```

5. Filter-Specific Validation Logic

   Validate filters dynamically based on specifications.

   Example:

```
public Specification<Item>validateAndBuildSpecification(ItemFilterDTO filter) {
if (filter.getMinPrice() >filter.getMaxPrice()) {
throw new IllegalArgumentException("Min price cannot be greater than max price");
}
return ItemSpecifications.createSpecification(filter);
}
```

   Common Annotations for Validation

- @Valid: Triggers validation of request body or parameters.
- @NotNull: Ensures a value is not null.

- @NotEmpty: Ensures a string is not empty.
- @NotBlank: Ensures a string is not blank (ignores whitespace).
- @Size: Ensures a string or collection is within a specific size range.
- @Pattern: Ensures a string matches a regex pattern.
- @Min: Ensures a value is not less than the minimum.
- @Max: Ensures a value is not greater than the maximum.
- @Email: Validates an email format.
- @AssertTrue/@AssertFalse: Ensures a boolean field is true/false.

Global Exception Handling for Validation

Use a @RestControllerAdvice class to handle validation errors globally.

Example:

```
@RestControllerAdvice
public class ValidationExceptionHandler {
@ExceptionHandler(MethodArgumentNotValidException.class)
public ResponseEntity<Map<String, String>>handleValidationExceptions(MethodArgument
NotValidException ex) {
Map<String, String> errors = new HashMap<>();
ex.getBindingResult().getFieldErrors().forEach(error ->
errors.put(error.getField(), error.getDefaultMessage())
);
return ResponseEntity.badRequest().body(errors);
}
}
```

Benefits of Filtering Validators

1. Data Integrity: Ensures valid inputs, reducing errors in business logic.
2. Simplified Error Handling: Automatically provides error messages for invalid inputs.
3. Reusability: Custom validators may be reused by several different controllers or services.
4. Better Security: Filters bad or malicious data, minimizing risks.

## 10.7 Spring paging validators

Pagination Validators: Pagination validators have been used to verify the validity of the incoming pagination parameters (page and size) prior to query execution or data retrieval in Spring applications. This validation allows errors such as invalid page numbers or sizes, negative numbers, or sizes that are too large and thus that would affect the performance.

Validation Approaches

1. Controller-Level Validation

   ```
   @GetMapping("/items")
   ```

```
public ResponseEntity<List<Item>>getPagedItems(
@RequestParam(defaultValue = "0") @Min(0) int page,
@RequestParam(defaultValue = "10") @Min(1) @Max(100) int size
) {
Pageable pageable = PageRequest.of(page, size);
Page<Item>itemsPage = itemService.getPagedItems(pageable);
return ResponseEntity.ok(itemsPage.getContent());
}
```

2. Custom Annotation for Paging Validation

```
@Target(ElementType.TYPE)
@Retention(RetentionPolicy.RUNTIME)
@Constraint(validatedBy = PagingValidator.class)
public @interface ValidPaging {
String message() default "Invalid paging parameters";
Class<?>[] groups() default {};
Class<? extends Payload>[] payload() default {};
}
```

3. Custom Validator Implementation

```
public class PagingValidator implements ConstraintValidator<ValidPaging,
PagingRequest> {
@Override
public booleanisValid(PagingRequest request, ConstraintValidatorContext context) {
if (request.getPage() < 0) {
context.buildConstraintViolationWithTemplate("Page index must be 0 or greater")
.addPropertyNode("page").addConstraintViolation();
return false;
}
if (request.getSize() < 1 || request.getSize() > 100) {
context.buildConstraintViolationWithTemplate("Page size must be between 1 and 100")
.addPropertyNode("size").addConstraintViolation();
return false;
}
return true;
}
}
```

4. Paging Request Object

```
@ValidPaging
public class PagingRequest {
private int page;
private int size;
```

```
// Getters and Setters
}
```

5. Service-Level Validation

```
@Service
public class ItemService {
public Page<Item>getPagedItems(Pageable pageable) {
if (pageable.getPageNumber() < 0 || pageable.getPageSize() < 1 || pageable.getPageSize() >
100) {
throw new IllegalArgumentException("Invalid paging parameters");
}
return itemRepository.findAll(pageable);
}
}
```

6. Global Exception Handling

```
@RestControllerAdvice
public class PagingValidationExceptionHandler {
@ExceptionHandler(MethodArgumentNotValidException.class)
public ResponseEntity<Map<String, String>>handleValidationExceptions(Method
ArgumentNotValidException ex) {
Map<String, String> errors = new HashMap<>();
ex.getBindingResult().getFieldErrors().forEach(error ->
errors.put(error.getField(), error.getDefaultMessage())
);
return ResponseEntity.badRequest().body(errors);
}
@ExceptionHandler(IllegalArgumentException.class)
public ResponseEntity<String>handleIllegalArgumentException(IllegalArgument
Exception ex) {
return ResponseEntity.badRequest().body(ex.getMessage());
}
}
```

## 10.8 Spring sorting validators

1. Controller-Level Validation

```
@GetMapping("/items")
public ResponseEntity<List<Item>>getSortedItems(
@RequestParam(defaultValue = "id") String sortBy,
@RequestParam(defaultValue = "ASC") @Pattern(regexp = "ASC|DESC", message = "Sort
direction must be ASC or DESC") String direction
```

```
) {
Sort sort = direction.equalsIgnoreCase("ASC") ? Sort.by(sortBy).ascending() : Sort.by
(sortBy).descending();
List<Item> items = itemService.getSortedItems(sort);
return ResponseEntity.ok(items);
}
```

2. Custom Annotation

```
@Target(ElementType.TYPE)
@Retention(RetentionPolicy.RUNTIME)
@Constraint(validatedBy = SortingValidator.class)
public @interface ValidSorting {
String message() default "Invalid sorting parameters";
Class<?>[] groups() default {};
Class<? extends Payload>[] payload() default {};
}
```

3. Custom Validator Implementation

```
public class SortingValidator implements ConstraintValidator<ValidSorting,
SortingRequest> {
private static final List<String> ALLOWED_FIELDS = Arrays.asList("id", "name", "price");
@Override
public booleanisValid(SortingRequest request, ConstraintValidatorContext context) {
if (!ALLOWED_FIELDS.contains(request.getSortBy())) {
context.buildConstraintViolationWithTemplate("Invalid sortBy field")
.addPropertyNode("sortBy").addConstraintViolation();
return false;
}
if (!request.getDirection().equalsIgnoreCase("ASC") &&
!request.getDirection().equalsIgnoreCase("DESC")) {
context.buildConstraintViolationWithTemplate("Invalid sort direction")
.addPropertyNode("direction").addConstraintViolation();
return false;
}
return true;
}
}
```

4. Sorting Request Object

```
@ValidSorting
public class SortingRequest {
private String sortBy;
private String direction;
```

```
// Getters and Setters
}
```

5. Service-Level Validation

```
@Service
public class ItemService {
private static final List<String> ALLOWED_FIELDS = Arrays.asList("id", "name", "price");
public List<Item>getSortedItems(Sort sort) {
String sortBy = sort.toString().split(":")[0].trim();
if (!ALLOWED_FIELDS.contains(sortBy)) {
throw new IllegalArgumentException("Invalid sortBy field: " + sortBy);
}
return itemRepository.findAll(sort);
}
}
```

6. Global Exception Handling

```
@RestControllerAdvice
public class ValidationExceptionHandler {
@ExceptionHandler(MethodArgumentNotValidException.class)
public ResponseEntity<Map<String, String>>handleValidationExceptions(Method
ArgumentNotValidException ex) {
Map<String, String> errors = new HashMap<>();
ex.getBindingResult().getFieldErrors().forEach(error ->
errors.put(error.getField(), error.getDefaultMessage())
);
return ResponseEntity.badRequest().body(errors);
}
@ExceptionHandler(IllegalArgumentException.class)
public ResponseEntity<String>handleIllegalArgumentException(IllegalArgument
Exception ex) {
return ResponseEntity.badRequest().body(ex.getMessage());
}
}
```

## 10.9 Filtering types

In Spring, filtering allows developers to narrow down the data returned from a query based on specific conditions. Here are the common types of filtering in Spring applications:

1. Request Parameter Filtering
   - Filters data based on query parameters provided in the request.

- Typically used in REST APIs to provide dynamic filtering options.

  Example Syntax:
  ```
  @GetMapping("/items")
  public List<Item>filterItems(@RequestParam(required = false) String name,
  @RequestParam(required = false) String category) {
  return itemService.filterItems(name, category);
  }
  ```

2. Path Variable Filtering
   - Filters data based on values in the URL path.

     Example Syntax:
     ```
     @GetMapping("/items/{category}")
     public List<Item>getItemsByCategory(@PathVariable String category) {
     return itemService.getItemsByCategory(category);
     }
     ```

3. Dynamic Filtering with Spring Data Specifications
   - Uses the JPA Criteria API for dynamic and advanced filtering.

     Example Syntax:
     ```
     public class ItemSpecification implements Specification<Item> {
     private SearchCriteriacriteria;
     @Override
     public Predicate toPredicate(Root<Item> root, CriteriaQuery<?> query, CriteriaBuilder
     builder) {
     if (criteria.getOperation().equalsIgnoreCase("=")) {
     return builder.equal(root.get(criteria.getKey()), criteria.getValue());
     }
     return null;
     }
     }
     ```

4. Filter Chains (Servlet Filters)
   - Used to process requests and responses, typically at a low level for tasks like authentication, authorization, or request preprocessing.

     Example Syntax:
     ```
     @Component
     public class CustomFilter implements Filter {
     @Override
     public void doFilter(ServletRequest request, ServletResponse response, FilterChain
     chain)
     throws IOException, ServletException {
     HttpServletRequest req = (HttpServletRequest) request;
     ```

```
System.out.println("Request URI: " + req.getRequestURI());
chain.doFilter(request, response);
}
}
```

5. DTO-Based Filtering
   - Filters data by transferring only the relevant fields to the client.

   Example Syntax:
   ```
   public class ItemDTO {
   private String name;
   private String category;
   // getters and setters
   }
   ```

6. Filtering with Spring Data Query Methods
   - Filters data directly in the repository layer with method naming conventions.

   Example Syntax:
   ```
   @Repository
   public interface ItemRepository extends JpaRepository<Item, Long> {
   List<Item>findByCategory(String category);
   List<Item>findByNameContaining(String name);
   }
   ```

7. Global Exception Handling for Filters
   - Ensures proper handling of filter-specific errors.

Example Syntax:
```
@RestControllerAdvice
public class GlobalExceptionHandler {
@ExceptionHandler(IllegalArgumentException.class)
public ResponseEntity<String>handleInvalidFilters(IllegalArgumentException ex) {
return ResponseEntity.badRequest().body("Invalid filter parameter: " + ex.getMessage());
}
}
```

These types of filtering mechanisms can be combined to create flexible and powerful data retrieval systems in Spring applications.

## 10.10 Sorting types

In Spring, sorting refers to arranging data in a specific order (ascending or descending) based on one or more fields. Here are the common types of sorting mechanisms in Spring applications:

1. Sorting with Spring Data Query Methods
   - Sorting is done by specifying fields and sort directions in method names.

     Example Syntax:
     ```
     @Repository
     public interface ItemRepository extends JpaRepository<Item, Long> {
     List<Item>findByCategoryOrderByNameAsc(String category);
     List<Item>findByCategoryOrderByPriceDesc(String category);
     }
     ```
2. Sorting with Sort Object
   - The Sort object provided by Spring Data allows dynamic sorting.

     Example Syntax:
     ```
     @GetMapping("/items")
     public List<Item>getItems(@RequestParam String sortBy) {
     return itemRepository.findAll(Sort.by(Sort.Direction.ASC, sortBy));
     }
     ```
3. Sorting with Pageable
   - Combines pagination and sorting using the Pageable interface.

     Example Syntax:
     ```
     @GetMapping("/items")
     public Page<Item>getItems(Pageable pageable) {
     return itemRepository.findAll(pageable);
     }
     // Example Pageable usage
     Pageable pageable = PageRequest.of(0, 10, Sort.by("price").descending());
     ```
4. Sorting with Native Queries
   - Sorting is directly embedded in native SQL or JPQL queries.

     Example Syntax:
     ```
     @Query("SELECT i FROM Item i WHERE i.category = :category ORDER BY i.name
     ASC")
     List<Item>findItemsByCategory(@Param("category") String category);
     ```
5. Sorting in Controller Using Query Parameters
   - Dynamic sorting based on query parameters passed in HTTP requests.

     Example Syntax:
     ```
     @GetMapping("/items")
     public List<Item>getSortedItems(@RequestParam String sortBy, @RequestParam
     String direction) {
     Sort sort = direction.equalsIgnoreCase("asc") ? Sort.by(sortBy).ascending() : Sort.by
     (sortBy).descending();
     return itemRepository.findAll(sort);
     ```

```
}
```

6. Sorting with Multiple Fields
   - Sorting by more than one field (multi-level sorting).

     Example Syntax:
     ```
     Sort sort = Sort.by(Sort.Order.asc("price"), Sort.Order.desc("name"));
     List<Item> items = itemRepository.findAll(sort);
     ```
7. Sorting in UI with Thymeleaf

- Sorting links can be dynamically generated in the UI.

  Example Syntax (Thymeleaf):
  ```
  <a href="/items?sortBy=price&direction=asc">Sort by Price (Ascending)</a>
  <a href="/items?sortBy=price&direction=desc">Sort by Price (Descending)</a>
  ```

8. Global Sorting Defaults
   - Use default sorting in the application configuration for specific repositories or services.

   Example Syntax:
   ```
   @Configuration
   public class RepositoryConfig {
   @Bean
   public Sort defaultSort() {
   return Sort.by("name").ascending();
   }
   }
   ```

These sorting types can be mixed and matched to implement flexible sorting logic for Spring applications, allowing both static and dynamic sorting based on the application's requirements.

## 10.11 Pagination types

In Spring, pagination refers to breaking large datasets into smaller chunks (pages) for efficient processing and display. Different types of pagination can be implemented depending on the use case and dataset characteristics. Here are the common types of pagination in Spring:

1. Offset-Based Pagination
   - This is the most common type of pagination. It uses a starting point (page) and the number of records per page (size) to fetch the data.
   - Suitable for smaller datasets or when the dataset doesn't change frequently.

     Syntax:
     ```
     Pageable pageable = PageRequest.of(page, size);
     Page<Item> items = itemRepository.findAll(pageable);
     ```

2. Cursor-Based Pagination
    - It is commonly applied in real-time applications in which changes in the data occur too often.
    - Ideal large real-time datasets where consistent results may be undermined by offset-based pagination.

    Syntax:
    ```
    @Query("SELECT i FROM Item i WHERE i.id > :cursor ORDER BY i.id ASC")
    List<Item>getItemsByCursor(@Param("cursor") Long cursor, Pageable pageable);
    ```
3. Keyset Pagination
    - Fetches data using a unique key, which is a primary key rather than an offset. It is more effective with big datasets as large dataset rows not in the result are not scanned.
    - Applicable in large scale applications that need high performance.

    Syntax:
    ```
    @Query("SELECT i FROM Item i WHERE i.createdAt> :lastSeen ORDER BY i.createdAt
    ASC")
    List<Item>getItemsAfterTimestamp(@Param("lastSeen") Timestamp lastSeen,
    Pageable pageable);
    ```
4. Infinite Scroll Pagination
    - Variation that fetches small bits of information as the user scrolls the application (lazy loading).
    - Usually deployed in the web and mobile applications to load data in a friendly and seamless way.

    Syntax:
    ```
    @GetMapping("/items")
    public List<Item>getItemsForScroll(@RequestParam int size, @RequestParam(required
    = false) Long lastItemId) {
    if (lastItemId == null) {
    return itemRepository.findTopN(size);
    } else {
    return itemRepository.findNextItems(lastItemId, size);
    }
    }
    ```
5. Hybrid Pagination
    - Brings together offset-based and cursor-based methods to simplify and speed efficiency.
    - Useful in complicated systems where diverse components of the application demand varied pagination techniques.

    Syntax:
    ```
    Pageable pageable = PageRequest.of(page, size, Sort.by("createdAt").descending());
    Page<Item> items = itemRepository.findAll(pageable);
    ```

6. Client-Side Pagination
   - The complete data is not accessed again, and pagination is done on the client (browsers or front-end applications).
   - Suitable for small datasets.

   Syntax (Controller):
   ```
   @GetMapping("/items")
   public List<Item>getAllItems() {
   return itemRepository.findAll();
   }
   ```
7. Server-Side Pagination
   - Only the necessary page data is transferred between the server and the client.
   - Favored when working with large datasets in order to reduce memory needs and network bandwidth.

   Syntax (Controller):
   ```
   @GetMapping("/items")
   public Page<Item>getPaginatedItems(Pageable pageable) {
   return itemRepository.findAll(pageable);
   }
   ```
8. Sorting with Pagination
   - Integrates pagination and sorting, giving the user the ability to retrieve sorted data in batches.
   - Paged and useful in sorting big datasets.

   Syntax:
   ```
   Pageable pageable = PageRequest.of(page, size, Sort.by("price").ascending());
   Page<Item> items = itemRepository.findAll(pageable);
   ```

These forms of pagination enable Spring applications to easily process datasets of different sizes and natures and enhance user experience and system overall performance.

# Bibliography

IBM (2024). Data Filtering. https://www.ibm.com/docs.

Oracle (2024). Sorting Algorithms. https://docs.oracle.com.

Spring (2024). Pageable Interface. https://docs.spring.io.

Spring Data (2024). Pagination Docs. https://docs.spring.io.

# 11

# Integrating microservices with Spring Boot and Spring Cloud

## 11.1 Microservices

Microservices is an architectural style in which an application is designed as a collection of small, independent, and loosely coupled services. Each service focuses on a specific business capability, is self-contained, and communicates with other services via lightweight protocols (e.g., REST APIs, messaging).

How Spring Helps Build Microservices

1. Spring Boot:
   - Simplifies microservice development with features like embedded servers (Tomcat/Jetty), auto-configuration, and minimal boilerplate code.
2. Spring Cloud:
   - Provides tools for distributed systems, including
   - Service Discovery: Eureka, Consul.
   - Load Balancing: Ribbon, Spring Cloud Gateway.
   - Configuration Management: Spring Cloud Config.
   - Resilience: Circuit breakers (Hystrix, Resilience4j).
   - Distributed Tracing: Sleuth, Zipkin.
3. Spring Security:
   - Offers robust authentication and authorization mechanisms for securing microservices.
4. Spring Data:
   - Simplifies database interactions in each microservice.
5. Spring Messaging:
   - Enables asynchronous communication between microservices using Kafka, RabbitMQ, or other message brokers.

## 11.2 Microservices with Spring Boot implementation

To run a Spring Boot application with a microservices architecture step by step, follow this procedure with relevant syntax:

**Step 1:** Set Up a Spring Boot Project

You need to create a Spring Boot project with dependencies for Spring Web, Spring Data JPA, Spring Cloud, Eureka Server (for service discovery), and other required dependencies. You can use Spring Initializr to generate a base project.

**Mastering Java Full Stack Development. DOI: https://doi.org/10.1016/B978-0-443-51683-2.00014-X**

Example: Maven pom.xml

```
<dependencies>
<dependency>
<groupId>org.springframework.boot</groupId>
<artifactId>spring-boot-starter-web</artifactId>
</dependency>
<dependency>
<groupId>org.springframework.cloud</groupId>
<artifactId>spring-cloud-starter-netflix-eureka-server</artifactId>
</dependency>
<dependency>
<groupId>org.springframework.cloud</groupId>
<artifactId>spring-cloud-starter-netflix-eureka-client</artifactId>
</dependency>
<dependency>
<groupId>org.springframework.boot</groupId>
<artifactId>spring-boot-starter-data-jpa</artifactId>
</dependency>
<dependency>
<groupId>org.springframework.boot</groupId>
<artifactId>spring-boot-starter-thymeleaf</artifactId>
</dependency>
</dependencies>
```

**Step 2:** Set Up Eureka Server (Service Registry)

The Eureka Server acts as a service registry where all microservices register themselves, allowing for easy discovery.

Application Class (EurekaServerApplication.java):

```
@SpringBootApplication
@EnableEurekaServer
public class EurekaServerApplication {
public static void main(String[] args) {
SpringApplication.run(EurekaServerApplication.class, args);
}
}
```

application.properties for Eureka Server:

```
server.port=8761
spring.application.name=eureka-server
eureka.client.register-with-eureka=false
eureka.client.fetch-registry=false
```

**Step 3:** Create a Microservice (Product Service)

The product service will be a simple REST API that returns product information.

Application Class (ProductServiceApplication.java):

```
@SpringBootApplication
@EnableEurekaClient
@RestController
public class ProductServiceApplication {
public static void main(String[] args) {
SpringApplication.run(ProductServiceApplication.class, args);
}
@RequestMapping("/products")
public List<Product> getAllProducts() {
return Arrays.asList(new Product(1, "Product A"), new Product(2, "Product B"));
}
}
```

Product Entity (Product.java):

```
public class Product {
private int id;
private String name;
public Product(int id, String name) {
this.id = id;
this.name = name;
}
// Getters and setters
}
```

application.properties for Product Service:

```
spring.application.name=product-service
server.port=8081
eureka.client.serviceUrl.defaultZone=http://localhost:8761/eureka/
```

**Step 4:** Set Up Another Microservice (Order Service)

The Order Service will use the product service and return an order with product details.

Application Class (OrderServiceApplication.java):

```
@SpringBootApplication
@EnableEurekaClient
@RestController
public class OrderServiceApplication {
public static void main(String[] args) {
SpringApplication.run(OrderServiceApplication.class, args);
}
```

```
@Autowired
private RestTemplate restTemplate;
@RequestMapping("/orders")
public Order getOrderDetails() {
Product product = restTemplate.getForObject("http://product-service/products",
Product.class);
return new Order(1, product);
}
}
```

Order Entity (Order.java):

```
public class Order {
private int id;
private Product product;
public Order(int id, Product product) {
this.id = id;
this.product = product;
}
// Getters and setters
}
```

application.properties for Order Service:

```
spring.application.name=order-service
server.port=8082
eureka.client.serviceUrl.defaultZone=http://localhost:8761/eureka/
```

**Step 5:** Enable Service Discovery with @EnableEurekaClient

For each microservice (such as ProductServiceApplication and OrderService Application), add

@EnableEurekaClient to enable the services to register themselves with the Eureka server.

```
@EnableEurekaClient
```

**Step 6:** Set Up RestTemplate for Communication between Microservices

In the OrderServiceApplication, use RestTemplate to communicate with the ProductService.

Define RestTemplate Bean in a Configuration Class (Config.java):

```
@Configuration
public class Config {
@Bean
public RestTemplate restTemplate() {
return new RestTemplate();
}
}
```

**Step 7:** Run Eureka Server
Run the Eureka Server first by executing the following:

```
mvn spring-boot:run
```

Once the server is up, it will be available at http://localhost:8761.
**Step 8:** Run Product Service
Now, run the Product Service:

```
mvn spring-boot:run
```

It will be available at http://localhost:8081.
**Step 9:** Run Order Service
Finally, run the Order Service:

```
mvn spring-boot:run
```

It will be available at http://localhost:8082.
**Step 10:** Testing the Microservices

- Product Service: Access the list of products at http://localhost:8081/products.
- Order Service: Access the order details at http://localhost:8082/orders. It will fetch the product information from the Product Service.

**Step 11:** Verify Service Registration
After running the microservices, you can verify that both services are registered with Eureka by visiting the Eureka dashboard at http://localhost:8761. Both the Product Service and Order Service should appear in the list of registered services.
**Step 12:** Handle Circuit Breaker (Optional)
You can add a circuit breaker (e.g., using Hystrix or Resilience4j) to gracefully handle failures when one service is down or unresponsive.
**Step 13:** Conclusion
You have now created and run a basic Spring Boot application with microservices. The Product Service and Order Service are registered with Eureka and can communicate with each other.

By following these steps, you can create more microservices, extend the communication with message brokers, handle interservice security, and scale your application.

## 11.3 Microservices with Spring Cloud: working procedure and architecture

Spring Cloud is the simplest in development of microservices as it offers the necessary tools to deal with the service discovery, client-side load balancing, configuration management, fault tolerance, and others. With several ingredients such as Eureka, Ribbon, Hystrix, and Spring Cloud Config, it is possible to build a strong and scalable microservices system.

Architecture of Microservices with Spring Cloud

1. API Gateway:
   - Handles incoming requests from the client.
   - Routes requests to appropriate microservices.
   - Provides additional functionality like load balancing, security, and logging.
   - Examples: Zuul, Spring Cloud Gateway
2. Service Registry (Eureka Server):
   - A central server where all microservices register themselves.
   - Services can discover other services by querying the registry.
   - Provides dynamic service discovery, eliminating the need for hard-coded service URLs.
3. Microservices:
   - Individual services that perform a specific business function.
   - Each microservice has its own database, data model, and logic.
   - Services can communicate with each other via HTTP (REST), gRPC, or messaging systems.
4. Service-to-Service Communication:
   - Services communicate using REST APIs, Feign Client, or Message Queues (e.g., Kafka or RabbitMQ).
   - Communication is often made resilient using Hystrix (circuit breaker) and Ribbon (client-side load balancing).
5. Configuration Server:
   - Centralized configuration management using Spring Cloud Config.
   - All microservices can pull configuration from the configuration server, which stores application properties in a Git repository or filesystem.
6. Service Discovery:
   - Services can automatically discover and communicate with each other using Eureka or Consul.
   - Provides load balancing by routing requests to different service instances.
7. Circuit Breaker and Fault Tolerance:
   - Hystrix or Resilience4J protects services from failure by implementing a circuit breaker pattern.
   - Ensures that requests to a failing service do not affect the overall system.
8. Distributed Tracing and Logging:
   - Spring Cloud Sleuth and Zipkin provide distributed tracing across microservices.
   - Logs from different services can be correlated, making it easier to trace the flow of requests through the system.
9. Monitoring and Metrics:
   - Spring Cloud is also compatible with such tools as Prometheus, Grafana, and Micrometer to reveal metrics that monitor the health and performance of microservices.

**10.** Database:
- Each microservice can be associated with its database, according to the Database per Service pattern, which will guarantee a loose service-service relationship.
- This may be a classic relational database (e.g., MySQL) or a NoSQL database (e.g., MongoDB) or a mix of the two based on the requirements of a service.

**Spring Cloud layer Representation of Microservices architecture**
(Fig. 11–1)

**1.** The Client Layer (Presentation Layer):
- The duty of this layer is to accept requests on behalf of end users or clients (mobile apps, web apps, external systems). It interacts with the routing API gateway.
- Components:
  - Web Clients (Browsers, Mobile Devices, etc.)
  - API Gateway (Spring Cloud Gateway, Zuul)
  - Load Balancer (Client-Side Load Balancing with Ribbon)
- Technologies:
  - HTTP/REST
  - WebSockets
  - GraphQL (optional)

**2.** API Gateway Layer:
- This layer also performs routing of the incoming requests to the corresponding microservice. It uses an abstraction of internal microservices and presents a single API.
- Components:
  - Zuul or Spring Cloud Gateway: Responsible for routing, authentication, authorization, and load balancing
- Technologies:
  - Spring Cloud Gateway
  - Zuul
  - Spring Security (for API security)

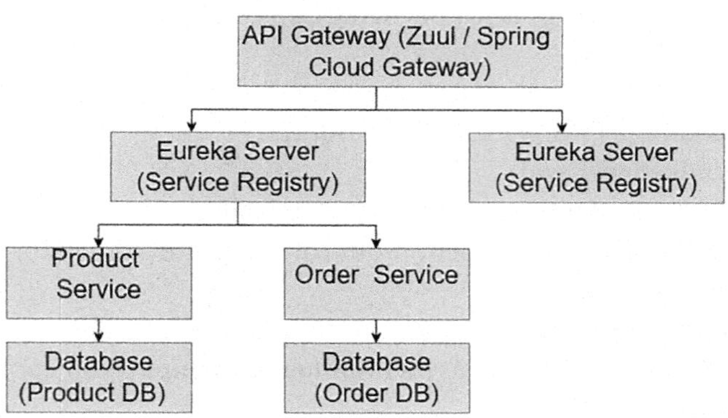


**FIGURE 11–1** Spring cloud layers.

3. Service Discovery Layer:
   - The dynamically registered and discovered microservices are done in this layer. Each of the services registers itself in a Service Registry such as Eureka that enables them to locate and communicate with other services.
   - Components:
     - Eureka Server: A central registry for services
     - Eureka Clients: Microservices that register themselves with Eureka
   - Technologies:
     - Spring Cloud Netflix Eureka
     - Consul (optional for service discovery)
4. Microservices Layer:
   - This is the innermost layer, and each microservice is independent and manages given business logic. It interacts with other services via REST APIs or queuing systems.
   - Components:
     - Product Service: Deals with all business logic pertaining to product
     - Order Service: Deals with processing orders
     - Payment Service: Provides payment solutions
   - Technologies:
     - Spring Boot (microservices implementation)
     - Spring Web (for REST APIs)
     - Spring Data JPA (to connect with database)
     - Spring Cloud Feign (inter-service communication)
5. Database Layer:
   - To achieve loose coupling, the Database per Service pattern is used, whereby each microservice operates its database. This makes individual services free to determine their data model and schema.
   - Components:
     - Product Database: Contains product-related information (e.g., MySQL, PostgreSQL, MongoDB)
     - Order Database: Holds order-related information
     - Payment Database: Archives payment transactions.
   - Technologies:
     - Relational databases (MySQL, PostgreSQL)
     - NoSQL databases (MongoDB, Cassandra)
6. Service Communication Layer:
   The layer takes care of microservice communication with one another. It might be synchronous (REST/HTTP) or asynchronous (message queues, such as Kafka, RabbitMQ).
   - Components:
     - REST APIs: Microservice communication direct by HTTP
     - Message Brokers: Used in asynchronous communication (Spring Cloud Stream, Kafka, RabbitMQ)

- Technologies:
  - Spring Cloud Feign (declarative HTTP communication)
  - Spring Cloud Stream (messaging and event-driven architecture)
  - Kafka/RabbitMQ (Asynchronous Communication): Message queues

7. Fault Tolerance/Resilience Layer:
   - This layer also provides the consideration that the failure of one service will not affect the whole system. It offers circuit breakers, retries, and fallback.
   - Components:
     - Hystrix (or Resilience4J): Circuit breaker to deal with service failures
     - Ribbon: Distributed service client-side load balancing
   - Technologies:
     - Spring Cloud Hystrix (circuit breaker)
     - Spring Cloud Resilience4J (more complex fault tolerance)
     - Ribbon (client-side load balancing)
8. Configuration Layer: Distributed:
   - This layer offers a centralized configuration control of microservices, enabling all the services to access and update their configurations through a central source.
   - Components:
     - Spring Cloud Config Server: A centralized configuration server in which all the service configurations are stored.
     - Config Clients: Those microservices that read configuration out of the config server.
   - Technologies:
     - Spring Cloud Config Server
     - Git (as a place of configuration)
9. Monitoring and Logging Layer:
   - This layer controls the health, performance, and status of microservices. It is also used to record details of troubleshooting and tracing of requests between services.
   - Components:
     - Spring Cloud Sleuth: Puts trace IDs and span IDs on logs to trace requests.
     - Zipkin: A distributed tracing system to draw service interactions.
     - Prometheus/Grafana: To monitor and see.
   - Technologies:
     - Spring Cloud Sleuth (trace).
     - Tracing (dist. tracing): Zipkin.
     - Prometheus (metrics and monitoring).
     - Grafana (for visualization).
10. Security Layer:
    - This layer makes certain that the microservices are secured by using authentication and authorization.
    - Components:
      - OAuth2/JWT: To provide safe authentication.
      - Spring security: To secure API endpoints and role management.

**FIGURE 11–2** Layered architecture diagram.

- Technologies:
  - Spring Security.
  - OAuth2 / JWT (to authenticate using tokens).

This layered architecture will guarantee that microservices are loosely coupled and independent of each other, and can be scaled. Spring Cloud eases the binding and maintenance of such architecture by offering service discovery, management, security, and fault tolerance tools. Through this structure, organizations are able to create strong, scalable, and resilient microservice-based applications (Fig. 11–2).

## 11.4 Microservices with Spring Cloud

In order to deploy microservices using Spring Cloud, do the following:

Step 1: Spring Boot Project Set Up

You should develop several Spring Boot applications, one of them being the Eureka Server (Service Registry) and the other ones being the microservices.

1. Create projects with Spring Initializr:
   - Use Spring Initializr to develop the base projects of Eureka Server, Product Service, and Order Service.
   - Select dependencies: Spring Web, Spring Cloud Eureka Server, Spring Cloud Eureka Client, Spring Boot DevTools, Spring Data JPA, and so on.

   Step 2: Installing Eureka Server (Service Registry)
   The Eureka Server does the registration and discovery of microservices.

**2.1** Develop Eureka Server Application
Start a Spring Boot Eureka Server:
EurekaServerApplication.java:

```
@SpringBootApplication
@EnableEurekaServer
class EurekaServerApplication is public.
static void main(String[])
SpringApplication.run(EurekaServerApplication.class, args);
}
}
```

**2.2** Configure Eureka Server (application.properties):

```
server.port=8761
spring.application.name=eureka-server
eureka.client.register-with-eureka=false
eureka.client.fetch-registry=false
```

Step 3: Set Up Product Service (Microservice 1)
This will be a simple REST API microservice that returns a list of products.

**3.1** Create Product Service Application
ProductServiceApplication.java:

```
@SpringBootApplication
@EnableEurekaClient
@RestController
public class ProductServiceApplication {
public static void main(String[] args) {
SpringApplication.run(ProductServiceApplication.class, args);
}
@RequestMapping("/products")
public List<Product> getProducts() {
return Arrays.asList(new Product(1, "Product A"), new Product(2, "Product B"));
}
}
```

**3.2** Create Product Entity
Product.java:

```
public class Product {
private int id;
private String name;
// Constructor, getters, setters
}
```

**3.3** Configure Product Service (application.properties)

```
spring.application.name=product-service
server.port=8081
eureka.client.serviceUrl.defaultZone=http://localhost:8761/eureka/
```

**Step 4:** Set up Order Service (Microservice 2)
This will consume the Product Service via REST and return an order with product details.

**4.1** Create Order Service Application
OrderServiceApplication.java:

```
@SpringBootApplication
@EnableEurekaClient
@RestController
public class OrderServiceApplication {
public static void main(String[] args) {
SpringApplication.run(OrderServiceApplication.class, args);
}
@Autowired
private RestTemplate restTemplate;
@RequestMapping("/orders")
public Order getOrderDetails() {
Product product = restTemplate.getForObject("http://product-service/products", Product.
class);
return new Order(1, product);
}
}
```

**4.2** Create Order Entity
Order.java:

```
public class Order {
private int id;
private Product product;
// Constructor, getters, setters
}
```

**4.3** Define RestTemplate Bean (Config.java)

```
@Configuration
public class Config {
@Bean
public RestTemplate restTemplate() {
return new RestTemplate();
}
}
```

**4.4** Configure Order Service (application.properties)

```
spring.application.name=order-service
server.port=8082
eureka.client.serviceUrl.defaultZone=http://localhost:8761/eureka/
```

**Step 5:** Enable Service Discovery with @EnableEurekaClient

In both ProductServiceApplication and OrderServiceApplication, annotate the classes with @EnableEurekaClient to enable service registration.

```
@EnableEurekaClient
```

**Step 6**: Run Eureka Server

- Run the Eureka Server by executing the following Maven command:
  mvn spring-boot:run.
- Verify the Eureka Server is running by visiting http://localhost:8761. It will show a dashboard of registered services.

**Step 7:** Run Product Service

- Run the Product Service by executing the following Maven command:
  mvn spring-boot:run.
- The Product Service should be available at http://localhost:8081.

**Step 8:** Run Order Service

- Run the Order Service by executing the following Maven command:
  mvn spring-boot:run.
- The Order Service should be available at http://localhost:8082.

**Step 9:** Access the Microservices

1. Product Service: You can access the products by going to http://localhost:8081/products.
2. Order Service: You can access the order details by going to http://localhost:8082/orders. This will fetch product details from Product Service using RestTemplate.

**Step 10:** Verify Service Registration

- After starting both the Product Service and Order Service, you can go to the Eureka dashboard at http://localhost:8761.
- The Product Service and Order Service should appear in the list of registered services.

**Step 11:** Handle Circuit Breaker (Optional)

You can add a circuit breaker using Resilience4j or Hystrix to handle failures in communication between services gracefully.

Add Resilience4j Dependency (pom.xml):

```
<dependency>
<groupId>io.github.resilience4j</groupId>
<artifactId>resilience4j-spring-boot2</artifactId>
<version>1.7.0</version>
</dependency>
```

Configure Circuit Breaker (@CircuitBreaker):

```
@CircuitBreaker(name = "productService", fallbackMethod = "fallback")
public Product getProduct() {
return restTemplate.getForObject("http://product-service/products", Product.class);
}
public Product fallback(Exception ex) {
return new Product(0, "Fallback Product");
}
```

**Step 12:** Conclusion

- You've set up and run a basic microservices architecture using Spring Cloud with Eureka as a service registry.
- Product Service registers with Eureka and can be discovered by other services like Order Service.
- The Order Service fetches product information from the Product Service using RestTemplate.

# Bibliography

AWS. (2024). Microservices on AWS, https://aws.amazon.com.

IBM. (2024). Microservices, https://www.ibm.com/topics/microservices.

Microsoft. (2024). Microservices Architecture, https://learn.microsoft.com.

Newman, S. (2021). *Building microservices: designing fine-grained systems.* O'Reilly Media, Inc.

Red Hat. (2024). Microservices Guide, https://www.redhat.com.

Spring. (2024). Spring Boot Docs, https://docs.spring.io/spring-boot.

Spring. (2024). Spring Cloud Docs, https://docs.spring.io/spring-cloud.

# 12 Handling communication between microservices

## 12.1 Communication in microservices

Microservice communication is a set of techniques and protocols that microservices are registered with to communicate with one another in a microservices-based architecture. Microservices are usually distributed systems, which do not work together but require collaboration with each other; hence communication is necessary to share data, invoke operations, and offer services. The communication of microservices can either be asynchronous or synchronous depending on the application.

Microservices communication is a very important feature of distributed systems, and it is necessary to select the appropriate methodology depending on your application. Quick communications that require fast and immediate responses can use synchronous communication techniques (e.g., HTTP/representational state transfer [REST] and Google Remote Procedure Call [gRPC]), whereas asynchronous communication techniques (e.g., message brokers and event-driven architecture) are appropriate in decoupled and scalable systems where the sequence and timeliness of responses are less significant. Each of these has its own pros and cons, and most of the time, a mixture of the two methods is employed in a microservices architecture in the real world.

Types of Microservice Communication

1. Synchronous Communication
2. Asynchronous Communication
   - Synchronous Communication
     In synchronous communication, one microservice sends a request to another microservice and waits for a response before continuing its execution. This type of communication is blocking, meaning the client service has to wait for the response before proceeding further. Common examples of synchronous communication protocols include HTTP (RESTful APIs) and gRPC.
     a. HTTP/RESTful APIs (Representational State Transfer)
        HTTP/REST is one of the most commonly used synchronous communication methods in microservices. In this approach, microservices expose endpoints (URLs) to provide specific functionalities. Other microservices can make HTTP requests to these endpoints to retrieve or manipulate data.

Mastering Java Full Stack Development. DOI: https://doi.org/10.1016/B978-0-443-51683-2.00002-3

Example in Spring Boot (REST API):

Controller Layer (Providing REST endpoint):

```
@RestController
@RequestMapping("/api/items")
public class ItemController {
@Autowired
private ItemService itemService;
@GetMapping("/{id}")
public ResponseEntity<Item> getItem(@PathVariable("id") Long id) {
Item item = itemService.getItemById(id);
return ResponseEntity.ok(item);
}
}
```

Service Layer (Business Logic):

```
@Service
public class ItemService {
@Autowired
private ItemRepository itemRepository;
public Item getItemById(Long id) {
return itemRepository.findById(id).orElse(null);
}
}
```

Repository Layer (Data Access):

```
@Repository
public interface ItemRepository extends JpaRepository<Item, Long> {
}
```

In this example, the ItemController exposes an HTTP endpoint for retrieving item information. Another microservice can send an HTTP request to the endpoint to get the data.

Advantages:

- Simple to implement.
- Easy to scale with load balancers and service discovery.

Disadvantages:

- It can lead to tight coupling between microservices.
- If one service is down or slow, it can affect others, leading to latency or failures.

**b.** Google Remote Procedure Call (gRPC)

gRPC is a high-performance, open-source RPC framework that uses HTTP/2 and Protocol Buffers (Protobuf) to communicate between microservices. It's faster and more efficient than traditional HTTP/REST for many use cases and supports bidirectional streaming.

gRPC Example:

Define Service in Protobuf:

```
syntax = "proto3";
service ItemService {
rpc GetItem (ItemRequest) returns (ItemResponse);
}
message ItemRequest {
int32 id = 1;
}
message ItemResponse {
string name = 1;
}
```

1. Spring Boot gRPC Server:

Use grpc-spring-boot-starter to integrate gRPC with Spring Boot.

Service Implementation:

```
@GrpcService
public class ItemServiceImpl extends ItemServiceGrpc.ItemServiceImplBase {
@Override
public void getItem(ItemRequest request, StreamObserver<ItemResponse>
responseObserver) {
// Business logic to fetch item by ID
ItemResponse response = ItemResponse.newBuilder().setName("Item Name").build();
responseObserver.onNext(response);
responseObserver.onCompleted();
}
}
```

gRPC Client:

Calling gRPC service:

```
ManagedChannel channel = ManagedChannelBuilder.forAddress("localhost",
50051).usePlaintext().build();

ItemServiceGrpc.ItemServiceBlockingStub stub = ItemServiceGrpc.newBlockingStub
(channel);

ItemRequest request = ItemRequest.newBuilder().setId(1).build();

ItemResponse response = stub.getItem(request);
```

Advantages:

- Faster and more efficient than REST, especially for large payloads.
- Supports bidirectional streaming and multiplexing.

Disadvantages:

- Requires a bit more setup compared to RESTful services.
- More difficult to implement across different technology stacks.

2. Asynchronous Communication

   In asynchronous communication, one microservice sends a request to another microservice and does not wait for a response. Instead, it continues executing while the receiving microservice processes the request in the background. The requester may receive a callback or listen for an event once the processing is complete.

   a. Message Brokers (e.g., RabbitMQ, Kafka)

Message brokers facilitate asynchronous communication by allowing microservices to send messages that other microservices can consume at a later time. These messages are placed in a queue, and consumers process them independently.

Example using RabbitMQ with Spring Boot:

Producer (Sender) Service:

Define a service that sends messages to RabbitMQ:

@Service

public class MessageProducer {

3. @Autowired

private RabbitTemplate rabbitTemplate;

public void sendMessage(String message) {

rabbitTemplate.convertAndSend("queueName", message);

}

}

Consumer (Receiver) Service:

Define a service that consumes messages from RabbitMQ:

@Service

public class MessageListener {

@RabbitListener(queues = "queueName")

```
public void receiveMessage(String message) {
System.out.println("Received message: " + message);
}
}
```

Advantages:

- Decouples microservices, allowing them to function independently.
- Suitable for high-volume data streams and event-driven architectures.

Disadvantages:

- Requires additional infrastructure (e.g., RabbitMQ, Kafka).
- May require complex error handling and retries.

**b.** Event-Driven Communication (Event Sourcing, CQRS)

In event-driven communication, microservices emit events when certain actions occur (e.g., an item is created, updated, or deleted). Other microservices can listen for these events and take appropriate actions.

Example using Spring Cloud Stream:

Producer (Emitting an Event):

```
@EnableBinding(Sink.class)
public class ItemEventPublisher {
@Autowired
private MessageChannel output;
public void publishEvent(ItemEvent itemEvent) {
output.send(MessageBuilder.withPayload(itemEvent).build());
}
}
```

Consumer (Listening for Events):

```
@EnableBinding(Source.class)
public class ItemEventListener {
@StreamListener(Sink.INPUT)
public void handleEvent(ItemEvent itemEvent) {
// Business logic to process the event
}
}
```

Advantages:

- Highly scalable and decoupled.
- Supports complex workflows and domain-driven design.

Disadvantages:

- Event consistency and message duplication can be issues.
- Eventual consistency may lead to complexity in certain scenarios.

## 12.2 Synchronous communication

In a microservices architecture, synchronous communication refers to a communication method where one microservice sends a request to another microservice and waits for a response before continuing its execution. The client service (requester) sends a request to the server service (provider) and is blocked until the server responds with the necessary information.

A simple and frequent method in microservices is synchronous communication, in which the client anticipates a prompt answer in the server. Although it is simple to apply and comprehend, it has drawbacks in scalability and strength against asynchronous communication. Error control and time management are critical for ensuring the reliability of synchronous communication in a production environment.

This is typically used when real-time, immediate responses are necessary. The communication is usually done using HTTP (REST APIs), gRPC, or similar protocols. The client and server interact in a tightly coupled way in synchronous communication, meaning if the server service is slow or unavailable, the client will be affected (i.e., it can result in timeouts or errors).

Procedure of Synchronous Communication:

1. Client Request:
   - The client (requester) initiates the communication by sending an HTTP request (or another protocol like gRPC) to the server.
   - The request contains the necessary parameters (e.g., item ID, query data) that the server needs to process the request.
2. Server Response:
   - The server receives the request and processes it. This might involve querying a database, interacting with other services, or performing business logic.
   - Once the server has the necessary data, it responds to the client with the result in the expected format (e.g., JSON, XML, etc.).
3. Client Waits:
   - The client waits for the server's response. During this time, the client is blocked, meaning it cannot perform other tasks until it receives the response.
   - If the server takes too long to respond or fails to respond, the client may encounter timeouts or errors.

4. Handling Errors:
   - In case of errors or timeouts, the client needs to handle these exceptions by retrying the request, returning an error message to the user, or implementing a fallback strategy.
   - This can be done through proper exception handling mechanisms, such as HTTP status codes (404, 500) or custom error responses.
5. Processing Response:
   - Once the client receives the response from the server, it processes the response data (e.g., displays it to the user, updates the UI, or performs further operations).

Architecture of Synchronous Communication:

The architecture of synchronous communication generally follows a request–response pattern, where the requester waits for the response from the provider before continuing. Here's an overview of the architecture:

Components in Synchronous Communication:

1. Client (Requester):
   - The client initiates the communication by sending a request to a server.
   - It waits for a response and processes the result.
   - Typically a web browser, mobile app, or another service that needs to consume data.
2. API Gateway (Optional):
   - An API gateway can serve as a single entry point to various microservices.
   - It routes requests to the appropriate microservice based on the request type (e.g., GET, POST).
   - It can also handle authentication, rate limiting, load balancing, and request aggregation.
3. Server (Provider):
   - The server (or microservice) processes the incoming request and sends back a response.
   - It may interact with databases, other microservices, or perform complex calculations to fulfill the request.
4. Database (Optional):
   - The server might interact with a database to retrieve or store data in response to the request.
   - This could be a relational database (e.g., MySQL, PostgreSQL) or a NoSQL database (e.g., MongoDB).
5. Load Balancer (Optional):
   - In high-traffic environments, a load balancer distributes incoming requests across multiple instances of the server (microservice) to improve scalability and availability.
   - It ensures that requests are routed efficiently to available instances.

Synchronous Communication Architecture Flow:

1. Request Initiation:
   - The client sends an HTTP request (e.g., GET/POST) to the server, requesting data or triggering an operation.
2. Routing Request (API Gateway/Load Balancer):
   - If there's an API Gateway, it routes the request to the appropriate microservice.
   - If there's a Load Balancer, it ensures the request is sent to one of the healthy instances of the service.
3. Service Logic:
   - The server microservice receives the request and processes it. It may query a database or interact with other microservices (synchronously or asynchronously) to gather the required data.
4. Database Interaction (Optional):
   - The server may interact with a database to retrieve or store information based on the request.
5. Response Generation:
   - Once the server has gathered the necessary data, it generates a response (e.g., JSON or XML) and sends it back to the client.
6. Client Receives Response:
   - The client receives the response and processes it (e.g., displays data on the user interface, updates internal state, etc.).
   - If the response is an error or a timeout occurs, the client handles it gracefully by retrying the request or showing an error message.

A basic example of synchronous communication using Spring Boot with REST APIs:

Controller Layer (Client Request):

```
@RestController
@RequestMapping("/api/items")
public class ItemController {
@Autowired
private ItemService itemService;
@GetMapping("/{id}")
public ResponseEntity<Item> getItem(@PathVariable("id") Long id) {
Item item = itemService.getItemById(id);
return ResponseEntity.ok(item);
}
}
```

Service Layer (Processing Request):

```
@Service
public class ItemService {
```

```
@Autowired
private ItemRepository itemRepository;
public Item getItemById(Long id) {
return itemRepository.findById(id).orElseThrow(() -> new ItemNotFoundException("Item
not found"));
}
}
```

Repository Layer (Database Interaction):

```
@Repository
public interface ItemRepository extends JpaRepository<Item, Long> {
}
Client-side HTTP Request (Using RestTemplate):
@Service
public class ClientService {
@Autowired
private RestTemplate restTemplate;
public Item getItem(Long id) {
String url = "http://localhost:8080/api/items/" + id;
return restTemplate.getForObject(url, Item.class);
}
}
```

Advantages:

- Simple to implement and understand.
- Immediate and predictable response time for the client.
- Easy to monitor, as the request-response pattern is easy to track.
  Disadvantages:
- The client is blocked until the response is received, which can cause delays if the server is slow.
- Tight coupling between services: The client relies on the availability and speed of the server.
- If the server service is down or facing performance issues, it can directly impact the client's functionality.

The steps involved in synchronous communication within a Spring Boot microservice:
Components of the Architecture

1. Client (UI): The user interacts with the UI and initiates a request for an item by ID.
2. API Gateway (optional): API Gateway directs the request to the appropriate service in the case it is used.
3. ItemController (REST): Controller layer in the service receives the request, processes the request, and sends it to the service layer.
4. ItemService: Service layer: Business logic and requests, which also interacts with the database where the interaction is required.

5. ItemRepository (DB): This layer interacts with the database (fetched item details in this case).
6. Response Sent to Client: After the data has been read, it is returned to the client by a response (typically in the form of JSON).
7. Client (UI): The data is sent to the client who then presents it to the user.

In synchronous communication, the client pauses until the server responds to it. All the layers play a particular role to make sure that the request is handled in the most efficient manner and the correct information is sent back to the client.

## 12.3 Synchronous communication implementation

Synchronous communication between microservices involves sending requests to a service and waiting for a response before proceeding. Below is a step-by-step guide to set up and run synchronous communication with Spring Boot, including the necessary code syntax.

1. Create a Spring Boot Application
   Start by creating a Spring Boot application using either Spring Initializr (<underline>https://start.spring.io/</underline>) or manually setting up the dependencies.
   - Dependencies to include:
   - Spring Web
   - Spring Boot DevTools (optional for easier development)
   - Spring Data JPA (if you want database interaction)
   - H2 Database (or any other database for persistence)
2. Set Up the Model (Entity Class)
   In synchronous communication, we typically send requests to a service that processes data, such as retrieving information from a database. Below is an example of an Item entity class.

```
import javax.persistence.Entity;
import javax.persistence.Id;
@Entity
public class Item {
@Id
private Long id;
private String name;
// Constructors, Getters, and Setters
public Item(Long id, String name) {
this.id = id;
this.name = name;
}
public Long getId() {
```

```
return id;
}
public void setId(Long id) {
this.id = id;
}
public String getName() {
return name;
}
public void setName(String name) {this.name = name;
}
}
```

3. Set Up the Repository Layer
   The repository layer interacts with the database to perform CRUD operations. This example uses Spring Data JPA's JpaRepository interface for easy database interaction.

```
import org.springframework.data.jpa.repository.JpaRepository;
import org.springframework.stereotype.Repository;
@Repository
public interface ItemRepository extends JpaRepository<Item, Long> {
}
```

4. Create the Service Layer
   The service layer contains business logic. Here, the ItemService class will interact with the repository to fetch the data.

```
import org.springframework.beans.factory.annotation.Autowired;
import org.springframework.stereotype.Service;
@Service
public class ItemService {
@Autowired
private ItemRepository itemRepository;
public Item getItemById(Long id) {
return itemRepository.findById(id).orElseThrow(() -> new ItemNotFoundException("Item
not found"));
}
}
```

5. Controller Layer (Synchronous Communication Endpoint)
   The controller layer handles HTTP requests and forwards them to the service layer. It returns a response after receiving the data from the service.

```
import org.springframework.beans.factory.annotation.Autowired;
import org.springframework.http.ResponseEntity;
import org.springframework.web.bind.annotation.*;
```

```
@RestController
@RequestMapping("/api/items")
public class ItemController {
@Autowired
private ItemService itemService;
// Synchronous communication: Get Item by ID
@GetMapping("/{id}")
public ResponseEntity<Item> getItem(@PathVariable("id") Long id) {
Item item = itemService.getItemById(id);
return ResponseEntity.ok(item); // Response sent back after synchronous communication
}
}
```

6. Run the Application
   You can now run the Spring Boot application using the following command (in your project directory):
   - For Maven:
     mvn spring-boot:run
   - For Gradle:
     gradle bootRun
     This will start the application, and it will listen on the default port 8080.
7. Testing the Synchronous Communication
   Once the application is running, you can test the synchronous communication by making a GET request to the /api/items/{id} endpoint. This can be done via:
   - Web Browser: Open http://localhost:8080/api/items/1 (replace 1 with the actual item ID).
   - Postman: Send a GET request to http://localhost:8080/api/items/1.

The service will process the request and return a JSON response like:

```
{
"id": 1,
"name": "Item Name"
}
```

8. Handling Errors
   If the item with the given ID does n't exist, the service will throw a custom exception. Below is the custom exception handler for ItemNotFoundException.

```
import org.springframework.http.HttpStatus;
import org.springframework.web.bind.annotation.ExceptionHandler;
import org.springframework.web.bind.annotation.ResponseStatus;
import org.springframework.web.bind.annotation.RestControllerAdvice;
@RestControllerAdvice
```

```
public class GlobalExceptionHandler {
@ExceptionHandler(ItemNotFoundException.class)
@ResponseStatus(HttpStatus.NOT_FOUND)
public String handleItemNotFoundException(ItemNotFoundException ex) {
return ex.getMessage(); // Return error message to the client
}
}
```

**9.** Client-Side Request (Simulating the Client)

To simulate the client-side request (making a synchronous request to another service), you can use RestTemplate in Spring.

**1.** ClientService Class (Request to Another Service):

```
import org.springframework.beans.factory.annotation.Autowired;
import org.springframework.stereotype.Service;
import org.springframework.web.client.RestTemplate;
@Service
public class ClientService {
@Autowired
private RestTemplate restTemplate;
public Item getItem(Long id) {
String url = "http://localhost:8080/api/items/" + id; // URL to the ItemService
return restTemplate.getForObject(url, Item.class); // Blocking call, waits for response
}
}
```

**2.** Configuration for RestTemplate (Add to Main Configuration):

```
import org.springframework.context.annotation.Bean;
import org.springframework.context.annotation.Configuration;
import org.springframework.web.client.RestTemplate;
@Configuration
public class AppConfig {
@Bean
public RestTemplate restTemplate() {
return new RestTemplate();
}
}
```

**3.** Test Synchronous Client Request:

Call the getItem method in your client service to make a synchronous request to your /api/items/{id} endpoint.

## 12.4 Asynchronous communication procedure

In synchronous communication, the client sends a request to the server, and the server processes the request and returns a response immediately. The client is blocked during this entire process, meaning the client has to wait for the server to finish its task before it can continue with further operations. This type of communication follows a request–response model.

The architecture of an asynchronous communication system with Spring Boot tends to have a number of layers that deal with various tasks.

1. Client Layer: The client is the one who pours a request to the Spring Boot application, which normally is through HTTP. This may be a browser, a mobile application, or any other client that accesses the service by a REST API.
2. Controller Layer: The controller layer gets the request, and it handles the flow of application. It also assigns the time-consuming activities to the service layer as is the case of asynchronous communication, and the response can be immediate even before the activity is done.

   Key Component: @RestController or @Controller.

3. Service Layer: Service layer entails the application business logic. It processes the asynchronous tasks. Methods within this layer have annotations of the form, which allows them to reside in a different thread. Such techniques transform Future, CompletableFuture, or ListenableFuture to reflect the outcome of the work.

   Critical Element: @Service, @Async.

4. Async Executor (Thread Pool): The Spring Boot annotation of asynchronous execution is called @EnableAsync. You are free to set an Executor bean to get control over the threads used to perform the asynchronous methods. This might be a custom thread pool that has been customized to support several tasks at once, thereby making sure that resources are well managed and there is no blocking operation.

   Implant: AsyncConfigurer, Executor.

5. Response Layer: The controller layer is in a position to send a response to the client instantly as the asynchronous task is being run in the background. The client can be notified that the task has been started or given some other form of reply, which tells him that the task is being executed in the background.
6. Background Processing: The process is one that executes concurrently and does not block the main process. This might include activities such as emailing, handling data volumes, or calling other external services which depend on the logic of the business.
7. Logging/Monitoring (Optional): The monitoring and logging of the progress and completion of the asynchronous tasks is necessary, particularly when they are long-running or resource-intensive operations. Spring supports logging and monitoring of asynchronous processes with support tools, such as Spring AOP or custom interceptors.

## 12.5 Asynchronous communication implementation

To support asynchronous communication in a Spring Boot application, you normally rely on features such as Spring annotation, the Spring annotation of Async, message queues, or event driving such as Spring Integration or Spring Cloud Stream. A stepwise process involved the use of the Spring annotation of asynchronous (Springs, 2018) by annotation in running tasks asynchronously in a Spring application (Figs. 12.1 and 12.2).

1. Install Spring Boot Application:
   - Not only do you have to create a Spring Boot application in Spring Initializr or the IDE of your choice with the required dependencies, but you also have to start with a blank project.
   - You should not forget to add the following dependencies:
     - spring-boot-starter-web
     - spring-boot-starter-async
2. Asynchronous Execution:
   - Add the annotation @EnableAsync to the main application class to start the execution of the asynchronous methods of Spring.

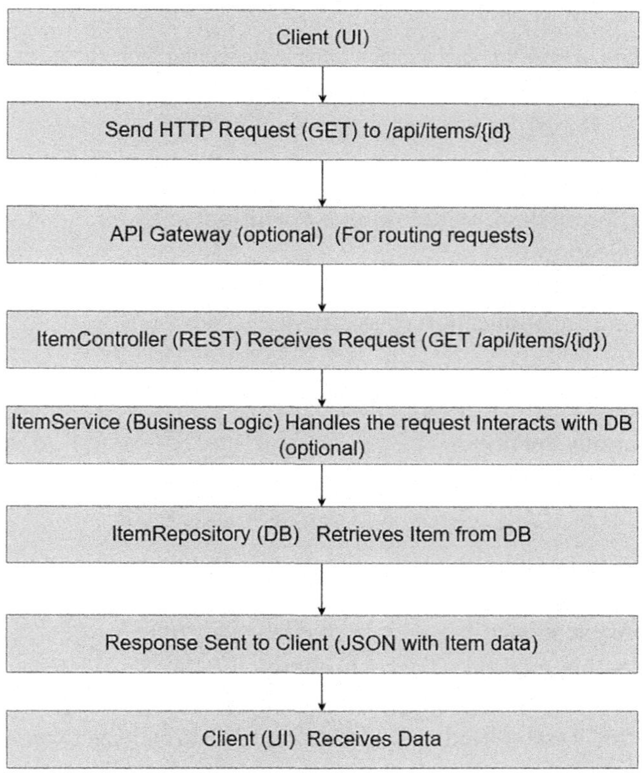


**FIGURE 12–1** Architecture of synchronous communication.

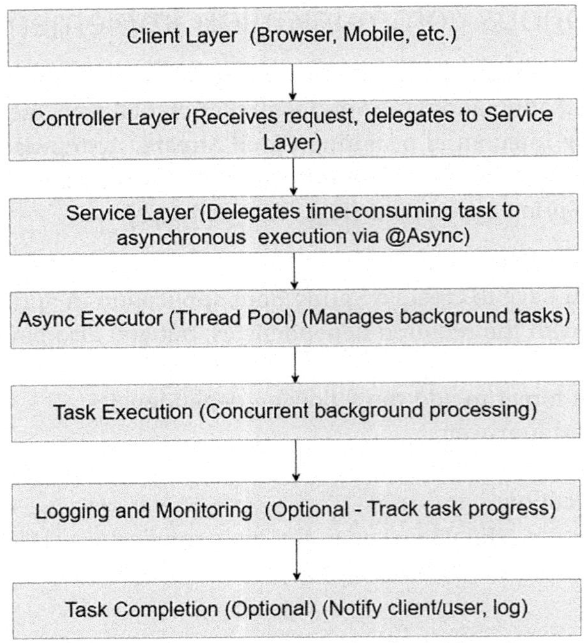


**FIGURE 12–2** Architecture of asynchronous communication system using spring boot.

Example:

```
@SpringBootApplication
EnableAsync // Spring boot asynchronous execution.
public class Application {
static void main (String[] args)
SpringApplication.run(Application.class, args);
}
}
```

**3.** Create Asynchronous Service:
- In the service layer, create a method annotated with @Async to execute it asynchronously.
- Example:

```
@Service
public class MyAsyncService {
@Async // Marks this method as asynchronous
public CompletableFuture<String> processTask() throws InterruptedException {
System.out.println("Task started: " + Thread.currentThread().getName());
```

```
Thread.sleep(5000); // Simulate a time-consuming task
return CompletableFuture.completedFuture("Task Completed");
}
}
```

4. Call the Asynchronous Method in Controller:
   - You can call the asynchronous method from a controller and return a response. The controller won't wait for the asynchronous method to finish; it will return immediately.
   - Example:

```
@RestController
@RequestMapping("/async")
public class MyController {
@Autowired
private MyAsyncService myAsyncService;
@GetMapping("/execute")
public String startAsyncTask() throws InterruptedException {
myAsyncService.processTask(); // Initiates the async task
return "Task Started"; // Immediate response to the client
}
}
```

5. Create a ThreadPool for Asynchronous Execution (Optional):
   - You can configure a custom Executor for handling asynchronous tasks in a separate thread pool.
   - Example:

```
@Configuration
public class AsyncConfig implements AsyncConfigurer {
@Override
public Executor getAsyncExecutor() {
return new SimpleAsyncTaskExecutor(); // Custom Executor for async tasks
}
}
```

6. Run the Application:
   - Build the project and run it using Maven or Gradle:
   - For Maven:

     ```
     mvn spring-boot:run
     ```
   - For Gradle:

```
gradle bootRun
```

7. Test the Application:
   - Open a browser or use Postman to test the asynchronous endpoint.
   - Example:
   - http://localhost:8080/async/execute
   - The response will be immediate with "Task Started," and the actual processing of the task will happen in the background.

Final Project Structure:

```
Main Class (Application.java):
@SpringBootApplication
@EnableAsync
public class Application {
public static void main(String[] args) {
SpringApplication.run(Application.class, args);
}
}
```

Service Class (MyAsyncService.java):

```
@Service
public class MyAsyncService {
@Async
public CompletableFuture<String> processTask() throws InterruptedException {
System.out.println("Task started: " + Thread.currentThread().getName());
Thread.sleep(5000); // Simulate a time-consuming task
return CompletableFuture.completedFuture("Task Completed");
}
}
```

Controller Class (MyController.java):

```
@RestController
@RequestMapping("/async")
public class MyController {
@Autowired
private MyAsyncService myAsyncService;
@GetMapping("/execute")
public String startAsyncTask() throws InterruptedException {
myAsyncService.processTask(); // Initiates the async task
return "Task Started"; // Immediate response to the client
}
}
```

# Bibliography

AWS. (2024). Messaging Services. https://aws.amazon.com.

IBM. (2024). Microservices Communication. https://www.ibm.com/docs.

Kafka. (2024). Apache Kafka Docs. https://kafka.apache.org.

Microsoft. (2024). Sync vs Async. https://learn.microsoft.com.

Red Hat. (2024). Messaging Architecture. https://www.redhat.com.

Spring. (2024). Messaging Docs. https://docs.spring.io.

# 13

# Testing and deploying Spring Boot applications

## 13.1 Testing Spring Boot

Testing Spring Boot applications involves ensuring that the components of your application (controllers, services, repositories, etc.) work as expected. You can achieve this using various testing methods like unit testing, integration testing, and end-to-end testing. Below is the step-by-step procedure with syntax for testing a Spring Boot application.

1. Set Up Testing Dependencies
   First, include the required dependencies for testing in your pom.xml (Maven) or build.gradle (Gradle) file.
   Maven Dependencies:

```
<dependency>
<groupId>org.springframework.boot</groupId>
<artifactId>spring-boot-starter-test</artifactId>
<scope>test</scope>
</dependency>
```

   Gradle Dependencies:

```
testImplementation 'org.springframework.boot:spring-boot-starter-test'
```

   This dependency includes the necessary libraries for unit testing, integration testing, and mocking.

2. Writing Unit Tests
   Unit tests are typically written using JUnit and Mockito. They allow testing individual components like services, controllers, or repositories.
   Service Layer Test:

```
@ExtendWith(SpringExtension.class)
@SpringBootTest
class ItemServiceTest {
@MockBean
private ItemRepository itemRepository;
@Autowired
private ItemService itemService;
@Test
void testGetItemById() {
```

Mastering Java Full Stack Development. DOI: https://doi.org/10.1016/B978-0-443-51683-2.00008-4

```
Item mockItem = new Item(1L, "Item 1", "Description");
Mockito.when(itemRepository.findById(1L)).thenReturn(Optional.of(mockItem));
Item item = itemService.getItemById(1L);
assertEquals("Item 1", item.getName());
}
}
```

**3.** Controller Testing
Controller tests involve sending HTTP requests to the controller and verifying the response.
MockMvc Test:

```
@WebMvcTest(ItemController.class)
class ItemControllerTest {
@Autowired
private MockMvc mockMvc;
@MockBean
private ItemService itemService;
@Test
void testGetItemById() throws Exception {
Item mockItem = new Item(1L, "Item 1", "Description");
Mockito.when(itemService.getItemById(1L)).thenReturn(mockItem);
mockMvc.perform(get("/items/1"))
.andExpect(status().isOk())
.andExpect(jsonPath("$.name").value("Item 1"));
}
}
```

**4.** Integration Testing
Integration tests involve testing the components together, such as the controller, service, and repository layers interacting with a real or in-memory database.
This integration test uses @SpringBootTest as a component.<|human|>Notes: This is an integration test that will use the component, @SpringBootTest.

```
@SpringBootTest
@Transactional
class ItemIntegrationTest {
@Autowired
private ItemRepository itemRepository;
@Test
void testSaveItem() {
Item item = new Item("Item 1", "Description");
itemRepository.save(item);
Item fetchedItem = itemRepository.findById(item.getId()).get();
assertEquals("Item 1", fetchedItem.getName());
```

```
}
}
```

5. Mocking External Services
   For external services (e.g., APIs or other microservices), you can use @MockBean to mock service calls.
   Mocking External Service in Integration Test:

```
@SpringBootTest
class ExternalServiceTest {
@MockBean
private ExternalService externalService;
@Autowired
private MyService myService;
@Test
void testCallExternalService() {
Mockito.when(externalService.call()).thenReturn("Response from external service");
String result = myService.callExternalService();
assertEquals("Response from external service", result);
}
}
```

6. Running Tests
   Once your tests are written, you can run them using Maven or Gradle.
   For Maven:
   mvn test
   For Gradle:
   gradle test
   These commands will run all the tests in your project, and the test results will be shown in the terminal.
7. Test Report
   After running the tests, Maven and Gradle generate test reports. For Maven, the reports are stored in the target/test-classes folder, and for Gradle, they are in the build/reports/tests/test folder.

## 13.2 Deploying

Deploying a Spring Boot application into various platforms can be done using several methods, such as deploying on a local server, cloud platforms, or containerized environments.

1. Local Deployment (Running on Your Local Machine)

To deploy a Spring Boot application locally, you simply need to run the application on your local machine.

1. Build the Project:
   - For Maven:
     mvn clean install
   - For Gradle:

   gradle build

2. Run the Application: After building the project, run the Spring Boot application.
   - For Maven:
     mvn spring-boot:run
   - For Gradle:

   gradle bootRun

3. Access the Application: The application will typically run on port 8080 by default. You can access it via the browser by navigating to:

http://localhost:8080

2. Deploying Spring Boot Application on Heroku:
   Heroku is a popular cloud platform to deploy Java applications.
   Create a Procfile: This file tells Heroku how to run your application. Create a file named Procfile in the root directory of your project with the following content:
   web: java -Dserver.port=$PORT -jar target/your-app.jar
   Install Heroku CLI: Download and install the Heroku CLI from Heroku CLI.
   Log In to Heroku: Run the following command to log in to Heroku from the command line:
   heroku login
   Initialize a Git Repository: If you haven't already initialized your project as a git repository, run the following:
   git init
   Add and Commit Changes: Add all files to git and commit:
   git add.
   git commit -m "First commit"
   Create a Heroku Application: Create a new Heroku application:
   heroku create your-app-name
   Deploy the Application: Push the application to Heroku:
   git push heroku master
   Open the Application: After deployment is complete, you can open your application in the browser:
   heroku open
3. Deploying Spring Boot on Amazon Web Services Elastic Beanstalk
   Elastic Beanstalk is a Platform as a Service by Amazon Web Services (AWS) that makes it easy to deploy and manage applications.
   Package Your Application: Build the project into a .jar file.

For Maven:

mvn clean install
For Gradle:
gradle build
Install AWS CLI: Install the AWS CLI from AWS CLI.
Configure AWS CLI: Configure AWS CLI with your credentials:
aws configure
Create an Elastic Beanstalk Application: Use the AWS Elastic Beanstalk CLI to create an application:
eb init -p java -r us-east-1 your-app-name
Create Environment and Deploy: Create an environment and deploy the application:
eb create your-app-environment
eb deploy
Access the Application: After the deployment, you can open the application:
eb open

**4** Deploying Spring Boot on Docker
Docker is a platform for developing, shipping, and running applications in containers.
Create a Dockerfile: Create a Dockerfile in the root directory of your Spring Boot application:

FROM openjdk:11-jre-slim
COPY target/your-app.jar /app.jar
ENTRYPOINT ["java", "-jar", "/app.jar"]
Build Docker Image: Use the following command to build the Docker image:
docker build -t your-app-name.
Run the Docker Container: After building the Docker image, run the container:
docker run -p 8080:8080 your-app-name
Access the Application: Open your browser and navigate to:
http://localhost:8080

**5** Deploying Spring Boot on Kubernetes

**Kubernetes is an open-source system for automating deployment, scaling, and management of containerized applications.**
Create a Dockerfile (same as above in Docker section).
Build Docker Image:
docker build -t your-app-name.
Push Image to Docker Hub: First, log in to Docker Hub, then push the image:
docker login
docker push your-dockerhub-username/your-app-name
Create Kubernetes Deployment YAML: Create a deployment.yaml file for Kubernetes:
apiVersion: apps/v1

```
kind: Deployment
metadata:
name: your-app-deployment
spec:
replicas: 1
selector:
matchLabels:
app: your-app
template:
metadata:
labels:
app: your-app
spec:
containers:
name: your-app
image: your-dockerhub-username/your-app-name:latest
ports:
containerPort: 8080
```

Create Kubernetes Service YAML: Create a service.yaml file for exposing the deployment as a service:

```
apiVersion: v1
kind: Service
metadata:
name: your-app-service
spec:
selector:
app: your-app
ports:
protocol: TCP
port: 80
targetPort: 8080
type: LoadBalancer
```

Apply Deployment and Service to Kubernetes: Apply the deployment and service to your Kubernetes cluster:

```
kubectl apply -f deployment.yaml
kubectl apply -f service.yaml
```

Access the Application: If you're using a cloud provider, Kubernetes will assign an external IP to access your application:

```
kubectl get services
```

Each platform requires different configurations, but the core principle is the same: package the application into a deployable unit and push it to the respective platform for running in a production environment.

## 13.3 Deployment on GitHub

Deploying a Spring Boot application on GitHub typically refers to pushing your code to GitHub for version control, and then using GitHub Actions to automate deployment to a platform like AWS, Heroku, Docker, etc. GitHub itself is not a hosting platform for running Spring Boot applications directly, but it can serve as the source repository where your code is stored, and you can automate the build and deployment process using GitHub Actions.

1. Prepare Your Spring Boot Application
   Before deploying, make sure your Spring Boot application is built and ready for deployment.
   1. Build the application using Maven or Gradle:
      - For Maven:
        mvn clean install
      - For Gradle:
        gradle build
   1. Create a .gitignore file: Ensure that files you don't want to push to GitHub (like target/ or build/) are ignored by adding them to .gitignore.
   2. Initialize Git and push to GitHub: Initialize a git repository, commit your code, and push it to GitHub.
      git init
      git add.
      git commit -m "Initial commit"
      git remote add origin https://github.com/your-username/your-repo-name.git
      git push -u origin master
2. Setting Up GitHub Actions for Continuous Integration (CI)/Deployment (CD)
   GitHub Actions allows you to automate the process of building, testing, and deploying your application.
   1. Create a .github/workflows directory in your project root:
      - Inside the .github/workflows/ directory, create a YAML file, for example, deploy.yml.
   2. Define your workflow for continuous integration (CI) and deployment (CD):
      name: Spring Boot CI/CD Pipeline
      on:
      push:
      branches:
      master
      pull_request:
      branches:
      master
      jobs:
      build:
      runs-on: ubuntu-latest
      steps:
      # Checkout the code

```
name: Checkout code
uses: actions/checkout@v2
# Set up JDK (Java)
name: Set up JDK 11
uses: actions/setup-java@v2
with:
java-version: '11'
# Build with Maven
name: Build with Maven
run: mvn clean install
# Deploy to Heroku
name: Deploy to Heroku
env:
HEROKU_API_KEY: ${{ secrets.HEROKU_API_KEY }}
run: |
heroku -version
heroku login -i
git remote add heroku https://git.heroku.com/your-heroku-app.git
git push heroku master
```

1. Set up secrets in GitHub:
   - In your GitHub repository, go to Settings → Secrets.
   - Add your Heroku API key as a secret with the name HEROKU_API_KEY.

     To get the Heroku API key:
   - Log in to your Heroku account.
   - Go to Account Settings → API Key → Reveal.

1 Commit and push the changes: After configuring the GitHub Actions workflow, commit and push the changes to GitHub.
2 git add .github/workflows/deploy.yml
3 git commit -m "Add CI/CD pipeline for deployment"
4 git push origin master

3. GitHub Actions Workflow Execution

   Once the code is pushed to GitHub, the GitHub Actions workflow will automatically trigger and run the CI/CD pipeline.
   1. Check out the code: The workflow checks out your Spring Boot project code.
   2. Set up JDK 11: The appropriate JDK version is set up for building the project.
   3. Build the project with Maven: It runs mvn clean install to build the Spring Boot application.
   4. Deploy to Heroku: The application is deployed to Heroku using the Heroku CLI. It pushes the built project to the Heroku app's remote repository.
4. Access the Application

   After the deployment completes successfully, the Spring Boot application will be hosted on Heroku (or any other platform you use in your workflow). You can access it via the URL

provided by Heroku, for example:
https://your-heroku-app.herokuapp.com

5. Optional: Deploy to Other Platforms (AWS, Docker, etc.)
   You can modify the GitHub Actions pipeline to deploy to other platforms such as AWS Elastic Beanstalk, Docker, Kubernetes, or Google Cloud. You would need to:
   - Change the deployment part of the deploy.yml file to use the respective platform's deployment CLI or API.
   - Set appropriate secrets (like AWS credentials, DockerHub credentials) in GitHub.
     For instance, to deploy to AWS Elastic Beanstalk, you would use AWS CLI commands in the deploy.yml file to interact with AWS services.
6. Monitoring the Deployment

Each step has its logs in GitHub Actions. Once the workflow is complete, it is possible to visit the Actions tab of your GitHub repository and observe the output of your deployment, including the errors or warnings that may have been encountered in the process.

## 13.4 Testing Spring Boot applications

A very important process in creating strong and trusted Spring Boot applications is testing. Spring Boot offers numerous methods of testing different components, including controllers, services, and repositories, among others. The testing can be divided into unit testing, integration testing, and end-to-end testing.

The testing of Spring Boot application entails the various layers, such as unit, integration, and end-to-end testing. Spring Boot supports several annotations and testing tools like:

|human|>Spring boot supports testing including: @WebMvcTest in testing controllers, @ SpringBootTest in testing full integration and finally, @DataJpaTest testing repository. It is easy to run with Maven or Gradle commands, and the tests can be useful in ensuring the reliability and correctness of your application prior to deployment.

*Testing in the Spring Boot*

1 Unit Testing: Unit testing aims at testing the parts (methods or classes) of a system separately. The important aspect in unit testing is mocking dependencies and testing in isolation the code logic.
2 Integration Testing: Integration tests confirm the integration of various components of one application (e.g., databases, APIs, services). These tests tend to be more complicated than unit tests and entail the execution of components of the Spring context, for example, repositories or services.
3 End-to-End (E2E) Testing: End-to-end tests simulate real-world user scenarios by testing the application as a whole. This includes testing controllers, services, and repositories together, often with external dependencies like databases.
   Procedure for Testing Spring Boot Applications

1 Set Up Dependencies in pom.xml (For Maven) or build.gradle (For Gradle)
Make sure to include the necessary testing dependencies. For Maven, add the following dependencies:

```
<dependencies>
<!– Spring Boot Starter Test for unit/integration tests –>
<dependency>
<groupId>org.springframework.boot</groupId>
<artifactId>spring-boot-starter-test</artifactId>
<scope>test</scope>
</dependency>
<!– Mockito for mocking dependencies in tests –>
<dependency>
<groupId>org.mockito</groupId>
<artifactId>mockito-core</artifactId>
<version>4.0.0</version>
<scope>test</scope>
</dependency>
</dependencies>
```

For Gradle:

```
dependencies {
testImplementation 'org.springframework.boot:spring-boot-starter-test'
testImplementation 'org.mockito:mockito-core:4.0.0'
}
```

2 Write Unit Test for Controller (Using @WebMvcTest)
@WebMvcTest is used to test the Spring MVC components, primarily controllers, by mocking the service layer.

Example:

```
@RunWith(SpringRunner.class)
@WebMvcTest(ItemController.class)
public class ItemControllerTest {
@Autowired
private MockMvc mockMvc;
@MockBean
private ItemService itemService;
@Test
public void testGetItems() throws Exception {
// Mock the service layer
when(itemService.getAllItems()).thenReturn(List.of(new Item(1L, "Item 1")));
// Test the GET request to the controller endpoint
mockMvc.perform(get("/items"))
```

```
.andExpect(status().isOk())
.andExpect(jsonPath("$[0].name", is("Item 1")));
}
}
```

The test mocks the ItemService and uses MockMvc to simulate an HTTP request to the /items endpoint. The @WebMvcTest annotation focuses only on Spring MVC components like controllers.

**3** Write Service Layer Test (Using @MockBean **and** @SpringBootTest**)**
@SpringBootTest is used for integration tests and starts the full Spring context, including the service layer, repository, and configuration.

Example:

```
@RunWith(SpringRunner.class)
@SpringBootTest
public class ItemServiceTest {
@Autowired
private ItemService itemService;
@MockBean
private ItemRepository itemRepository;
@Test
public void testGetItemById() {
// Mock repository behavior
Item mockItem = new Item(1L, "Mock Item");
when(itemRepository.findById(1L)).thenReturn(Optional.of(mockItem));
// Call the service method
Item item = itemService.getItemById(1L);
// Assert the result
assertEquals("Mock Item", item.getName());
}
}
```

@SpringBootTest annotation starts the full application context, making it useful for integration tests. @MockBean is used to mock the repository layer, allowing you to test the service in isolation.

**4** Repository Layer Testing (Using @DataJpaTest**)**
@DataJpaTest is used for testing repository layers, which focus on testing the interaction with the database.

Example:

```
@RunWith(SpringRunner.class)
@DataJpaTest
public class ItemRepositoryTest {
@Autowired
```

```
private TestEntityManager entityManager;
@Autowired
private ItemRepository itemRepository;
@Test
public void testFindById() {
// Given
Item savedItem = entityManager.persistFlushFind(new Item(1L, "Test Item"));
// When
Optional<Item> foundItem = itemRepository.findById(savedItem.getId());
// Then
assertTrue(foundItem.isPresent());
assertEquals("Test Item", foundItem.get().getName());
}
}
```

@DataJpaTest is used to test JPA repositories, ensuring that the database interaction works as expected. It initializes an in-memory database by default and performs tests.

5 Running Tests

To run the tests, use the following commands:

- For Maven:

```
mvn test
```

- For Gradle:

```
gradle test
```

## 13.5 Autoconfigured tests

Here is the syntax for autoconfigured tests in Spring Boot:

1 Unit Testing with @SpringBootTest:

```
@SpringBootTest
public class YourServiceTest {
@Autowired
private YourService yourService;
@Test
public void testServiceMethod() {
// Test logic
}
}
```

2 Mocking Beans with @MockBean:

```
@RunWith(SpringRunner.class)
@SpringBootTest
```

```
public class YourServiceTest {
@MockBean
private YourRepository yourRepository;
@Autowired
private YourService yourService;
@Test
public void testServiceMethod() {
// Mock repository method
when(yourRepository.someMethod()).thenReturn(someValue);
// Test your service method
}
}
```

3 Web Layer Testing with @WebMvcTest:

```
@RunWith(SpringRunner.class)
@WebMvcTest(YourController.class)
public class YourControllerTest {
@Autowired
private MockMvc mockMvc;
@MockBean
private YourService yourService;
@Test
public void testGetEndpoint() throws Exception {
// Mock service method
when(yourService.someMethod()).thenReturn(someValue);
// Perform GET request
mockMvc.perform(get("/your-endpoint"))
.andExpect(status().isOk())
.andExpect(jsonPath("$.someField", is(someValue)));
}
}
```

4 Data Layer Testing with @DataJpaTest:

```
@RunWith(SpringRunner.class)
@DataJpaTest
public class YourRepositoryTest {
@Autowired
private YourRepository yourRepository;
@Test
public void testRepositoryMethod() {
// Test your repository method
}
}
```

**5** Service Layer Test with @MockBean:

```
@RunWith(SpringRunner.class)
@SpringBootTest
public class YourServiceTest {
@MockBean
private YourRepository yourRepository;
@Autowired
private YourService yourService;
@Test
public void testServiceMethod() {
// Mock repository
when(yourRepository.findById(anyLong())).thenReturn(Optional.of(new YourEntity()));
// Test service method
}
}
```

## 13.6 Deploying methods

These are the various deployment methods for Spring Boot applications, covering local, server, cloud, Docker, Kubernetes, and virtual machines. Each method provides different advantages based on the project and hosting requirements.

Here are the common deployment methods for Spring Boot applications:

**1.** Deploying on a Local Machine
- Build the Application: Use Maven or Gradle to build the Spring Boot application.
- For Maven:

```
mvn clean install
```

- For Gradle:

```
gradle build
```

**2.** Run the Application Locally: After building, you can run the application on your local machine.
- For Maven:

```
mvn spring-boot:run
```

- For Gradle:
- gradle bootRun

The application will run on the default port 8080. You can access it at:
http://localhost:8080

**2.** Deploying to a Server (e.g., Tomcat)
- Package the Application as a WAR File: Modify pom.xml (Maven) or build.gradle (Gradle) to package the app as a WAR.

- In Maven, add the following plugin to your pom.xml:
  <packaging>war</packaging>
- In Gradle, use this configuration:
  apply plugin: 'war'
- Deploy the WAR to Tomcat: Copy the generated .war file to the webapps/ directory in your Tomcat installation. Restart Tomcat to deploy your Spring Boot application.

**3.** Deploying to Cloud (e.g., AWS, Heroku)
- Prepare Application for Deployment: Use mvn clean package (or gradle build) to generate the executable JAR/WAR file.
- Push to AWS Elastic Beanstalk:

**1.** Install the AWS CLI and configure your AWS credentials.
**2.** Use the Elastic Beanstalk CLI (eb) to deploy:

```
eb init -p java <app-name>
eb create <environment-name>
eb deploy
```

For Heroku:
- Create a Procfile in your project directory:
  web: java -jar target/your-app.jar
- Push to Heroku using the Heroku CLI:

```
heroku create
git push heroku master
```

**4.** Deploying as a Docker Container
- Create a Dockerfile: In your project's root directory, create a Dockerfile:

```
FROM openjdk:11-jre-slim
COPY target/your-app.jar /app.jar
ENTRYPOINT ["java", "-jar", "/app.jar"]
```

- Build Docker Image: Build the Docker image using the following command:
  docker build -t your-app.
- Run the Docker Container: Run the Docker container:
  docker run -p 8080:8080 your-app

**5.** Deploying to Kubernetes
- Prepare Docker Image: Follow the Docker deployment steps to build your application as a Docker container.
- Create Kubernetes Deployment YAML: Example deployment.yaml:

```
apiVersion: apps/v1
kind: Deployment
metadata:
name: spring-boot-app
spec:
replicas: 3
```

selector:
matchLabels:
app: spring-boot-app
template:
metadata:
labels:
app: spring-boot-app
spec:
containers:
name: spring-boot-app
image: your-docker-repo/your-app:latest
ports:
containerPort: 8080
Deploy on Kubernetes: Use the following command to deploy the application to a Kubernetes cluster:
kubectl apply -f deployment.yaml

6. Deploying to a Virtual Machine (VM)
   - Package the Application: Package your Spring Boot application as a JAR using Maven or Gradle:
     mvn clean package
   - Transfer to the VM: Use SCP or any other file transfer method to copy the generated JAR file to the remote server:
     scp target/your-app.jar username@remote-server:/path/to/destination
   - Run the Application on the VM: SSH into the server and run the application:

   java -jar /path/to/your-app.jar

# Bibliography

Spring. (2024). Testing Docs. https://docs.spring.io/spring-boot/docs/current/reference/html/features.html.

JUnit. (2024). Documentation. https://junit.org.

Mockito. (2024). Docs. https://site.mockito.org.

GitHub. (2024). Deployment Docs. https://docs.github.com.

IBM. (2024). Testing Concepts. https://www.ibm.com/docs.

Spring. (2024). Auto-configured Tests. https://docs.spring.io.

# 14

# Monitoring and scaling Spring Boot applications

## 14.1 Monitoring in Spring Boot

Observation, tracking, and analysis of the performance, health, and behavior of a Spring Boot application is known as monitoring in Spring Boot. It entails gathering and visualizing metrics, logs, and alerts to verify the efficiency of the application being deployed and identify possible problems as well as expound problems in action in real time.

### 14.1.1 Types of monitoring in Spring Boot

Monitoring can be applied to a Spring Boot application in several different forms:

1. Health Monitoring:
   - Health checks are more than just monitoring whether an application is running smoothly. They are typically used to verify the health of system components such as database connections, caches, and third-party services.
   - Spring Boot Actuator: It has health endpoint and can be used through/actuator/health. It makes known the well-being of various aspects (e.g., database, disk space, services) within the system.
     Example:
   - By default, health monitoring is turned off: Add the following health monitoring to application.properties:
     management.endpoints.web.exposure.include=health
   - Access the health endpoint:
     curl http://localhost:8080/actuator/health
2. Metrics Monitoring:
   - Metrics monitoring is the act of gathering and examining some metrics associated with the application performance, for example, response time, memory consumption, CPU consumption, number of requests, etc.
   - To receive and provide our measurements, Spring Boot Actuator uses Spring Micrometer.
     Example:
     There is no need to monitor metrics, but one can do so by enabling it in the application.properties:

     management.endpoints.web.exposure.include=metrics
     Access metrics:
     curl http://localhost:8080/actuator/metrics

**Mastering Java Full Stack Development. DOI: https://doi.org/10.1016/B978-0-443-51683-2.00001-1**

3. Logging and Log Monitoring:
   - Logging will be important in monitoring application activities and debugging. Spring Boot builds on SLF4J and Logback, albeit they can also be configured to use other logging frameworks should this be necessary.
   - You are able to follow logs to verify mistakes, warnings, and other handy data. It also works with centralized logging solutions such as Elasticsearch, Logstash, Kibana (ELK) stack, Splunk, or Graylog.
     Example: Configure logging level in application.properties:

     ```
     logging.level.org.springframework=DEBUG
     logging.level.com.yourpackage=INFO
     ```

4. Tracing:
   - Distributed tracing helps trace requests as they flow across various microservices. Tools like Zipkin or Sleuth (both of which integrate seamlessly with Spring Boot) enable distributed tracing by adding trace IDs to logs and requests.
     Example:
   - Add Spring Cloud Sleuth to your dependencies for tracing:

     ```
     <dependency>
     <groupId>org.springframework.cloud</groupId>
     <artifactId>spring-cloud-starter-sleuth</artifactId>
     </dependency>
     ```

   - Enable Zipkin tracing:

     ```
     spring.zipkin.baseUrl=http://localhost:9411
     spring.sleuth.sampler.probability=1.0
     ```

5. Application Performance Management:
   - Application performance management (APM) tools (e.g., New Relic, Dynatrace, AppDynamics) help monitor and manage the application's performance. These tools offer deep insights into the performance of applications, including transaction tracing, resource utilization, and overall health.
     Example: Add New Relic to your Spring Boot app:
   - Download the New Relic agent.
   - Set the New Relic configuration in newrelic.yml.
   - Add the agent to the Java Virtual Machine (JVM) startup with the argument:
     -javaagent:/path/to/newrelic.jar
6. Audit Monitoring:
   - Audit monitoring entails recording the occurrences with regard to security. It assists in monitoring the actions of the users and changes of applications. Spring Security has audit event capabilities, such as access to resources or a failed attempt to log in.
     Example:

- Enable audit logging in application.properties:

spring.jpa.properties.hibernate.ejb.interceptor=org.springframework.security.web.authentication.preauth.PreAuthenticatedAuthenticationToken

## 14.1.2 Monitoring procedure

This process covers how to add the Spring Boot Actuator, enable endpoints, monitor health and metrics, configure logging, enable tracing, and integrate with external tools like Prometheus for application monitoring.

Step 1: Add Dependencies

1 Add Spring Boot Actuator Dependency:
   - Add the Spring Boot Actuator dependency in pom.xml for Maven or build.gradle for Gradle.

For Maven:

```
<dependency>
<groupId>org.springframework.boot</groupId>
<artifactId>spring-boot-starter-actuator</artifactId>
</dependency>
```

For Gradle:

```
dependencies {
implementation 'org.springframework.boot:spring-boot-starter-actuator'
}
```

Step 2: Enable Endpoints

1 Configure Exposed Actuator Endpoints:
   - By default, Spring Boot exposes a limited set of actuator endpoints. You can configure which endpoints to expose by adding the following in application.properties or application.yml.

application.properties:

```
management.endpoints.web.exposure.include=health,info,metrics
```

application.yml:

```
management:
endpoints:
web:
exposure:
include: health, info, metrics
```

Step 3: Health Monitoring

1 Access Health Endpoint:
   - To monitor the application's health, the /actuator/health endpoint can be accessed. It provides the health status of the application.

Example Request:
curl http://localhost:8080/actuator/health
Step 4: Metrics Monitoring

1 Access Metrics Endpoint:
- Spring Boot Actuator exposes a /actuator/metrics endpoint to monitor application metrics like memory usage, garbage collection, HTTP requests, etc.

Example Request:
curl http://localhost:8080/actuator/metrics
Step 5: Logging Configuration

1 Configure Logging Level:
- You can configure the logging level for various packages within the application using application.properties.

Example:
logging.level.org.springframework=DEBUG
logging.level.com.example=INFO

Step 6: Configure Health Indicators

1 Customize Health Indicators:
- You can configure custom health indicators (e.g., database, disk space) in your application.

Example (custom health check):

```
@Component
public class CustomHealthIndicator extends AbstractHealthIndicator {
@Override
protected void doHealthCheck(Health.Builder builder) throws Exception {
builder.up().withDetail("custom", "Custom Health Indicator is UP");
}
}
```

Step 7: Distributed Tracing with Sleuth

1 Enable Spring Cloud Sleuth for Tracing:
- Add Spring Cloud Sleuth to enable distributed tracing.

For Maven:

```
<dependency>
<groupId>org.springframework.cloud</groupId>
<artifactId>spring-cloud-starter-sleuth</artifactId>
</dependency>
```

For Gradle:

```
dependencies {
```

```
implementation 'org.springframework.cloud:spring-cloud-starter-sleuth'
}
```

Configuration:

```
spring.sleuth.sampler.probability=1.0
spring.zipkin.baseUrl=http://localhost:9411
```

Step 8: Enable Prometheus Metrics (Optional)

1 Add Prometheus Dependency:
   - To monitor with Prometheus, add the Prometheus starter dependency.

For Maven:

```
<dependency>
<groupId>io.micrometer</groupId>
<artifactId>micrometer-registry-prometheus</artifactId>
</dependency>
```

For Gradle:

```
dependencies {
implementation 'io.micrometer:micrometer-registry-prometheus'
}
```

Step 9: Set Up Prometheus and Grafana (Optional)

1 Expose Prometheus Metrics:
   - Expose the /actuator/prometheus endpoint for Prometheus to scrape the metrics.

Example Request:

```
curl http://localhost:8080/actuator/prometheus
```

Step 10: Monitoring with External Tools (Optional)

1 Integrate with External Monitoring Tools:
   - You can integrate Spring Boot with tools like New Relic, Datadog, or AppDynamics for advanced monitoring and APM features.
     Example for New Relic:
   - Add a New Relic agent and configure it in newrelic.yml.
   - Include the following JVM argument:

```
-javaagent:/path/to/newrelic.jar
```

## 14.1.3 Monitoring Spring Boot procedure

Monitoring a Spring Boot architecture involves tracking the application's performance, availability, and behavior in real time.

1 Monitoring Elements to Consider:
   - Application Layer: Monitors service-level metrics (request–response, error, resource), for example, request–response latency.

- Database Layer: Tracks query execution time, size of the connection pool, and health of the database.
- Infrastructure Layer: Focuses on server health (CPU, memory, disk usage), container metrics (if deployed in Docker or Kubernetes), and network latency.

2 Monitoring Strategies:
- Actuator Endpoints: Spring Boot provides built-in endpoints through the Spring Boot Actuator library for monitoring and managing the application. Examples:
- /actuator/health: Displays the health status of the application.
- /actuator/metrics: Provides application metrics like JVM memory, thread count, and custom metrics.
- /actuator/loggers: Shows and modifies log levels in real time.
- Custom Metrics: Use Micrometer (integrated with Spring Boot) to define and track custom metrics specific to your application.

3 Tools for Monitoring:
- APM Tools:
- Prometheus + Grafana: For scraping metrics and visualizing dashboards.
- New Relic/Dynatrace/AppDynamics: Full-stack monitoring solutions for applications, databases, and infrastructure.
- Log Aggregation:
  - ELK Stack: Centralizes and analyzes application logs.
- Splunk: For advanced log monitoring and analysis.
- Distributed Tracing:
  - Zipkin or Jaeger: Trace requests across services to identify bottlenecks.

4 Metrics to Monitor:
- Application Metrics:
  - Request count and success/failure rates.
  - Latency (e.g., average response time, 95th percentile response time).
  - Number of active sessions or threads.
  - HTTP status codes (e.g., 4xx, 5xx).
- JVM Metrics:
  - Heap and nonheap memory usage.
  - Garbage collection times.
  - Thread pool activity.
- Database Metrics:
  - Query execution times.
  - Active connections in the connection pool.
  - Cache hit/miss ratios (if applicable).
- Infrastructure Metrics:
  - CPU, memory, and disk usage of the server/container.
  - Network traffic (incoming and outgoing).

**5** Steps to Implement Monitoring:

**1** Enable Actuator:

- Add the dependency:

```
<dependency>
<groupId>org.springframework.boot</groupId>
<artifactId>spring-boot-starter-actuator</artifactId>
</dependency>
```

- Configure application.properties or application.yml:

```
management:
endpoints:
web:
exposure:
include: "*"
```

**2** Integrate Micrometer:

- Add Micrometer dependencies for tools like Prometheus or StatsD.

```
<dependency>
<groupId>io.micrometer</groupId>
<artifactId>micrometer-registry-prometheus</artifactId>
</dependency>
```

**3** Log Management:

- Use libraries like Logback or Log4j2 for structured logs.

Configure centralized log aggregation tools (e.g., ELK).

**4** Integrate Tracing:

- Add Zipkin or Jaeger dependencies for distributed tracing.
- Enable tracing in the application configuration.

**6** Deployment Considerations:

- Deploy monitoring tools alongside your application in the same environment for closer proximity.
- For containerized applications (e.g., Docker or Kubernetes):
  - Monitor container-specific metrics such as resource limits, pod health, and scaling events.
  - Use Kubernetes-native tools like Kubernetes Dashboard, Lens, or Prometheus Operator.

By combining Spring Boot Actuator, Micrometer, and external tools, you can build a robust monitoring framework for your Spring Boot architecture.

Spring Boot Monitoring Architecture Diagram:
Components in Spring Boot Monitoring

1. User Interface: Represents users interacting with the application via a browser or mobile app.
2. Spring Boot Application:
   - Contains REST Controllers for API handling.
   - Services for business logic.
   - Repositories for database access.
   - Exposes Actuator endpoints for metrics, health checks, and logs.
3. Database: Stores persistent application data (e.g., MySQL or MongoDB).
4. Monitoring Tools:
   - Prometheus and Grafana for metrics and dashboards.
   - Zipkin for distributed tracing.
   - ELK Stack for log aggregation and visualization.
5. Container Orchestration: Docker or Kubernetes to manage deployment, scaling, and monitoring of the application in a containerized environment.

## 14.1.4 Scaling

Scaling in Spring Boot applications refers to the process of adjusting the application's capacity to handle varying amounts of traffic or workload. It ensures that the application can serve an increasing number of requests efficiently or maintain performance during high load by adding or removing resources (Figs. 14-1 and 14-2).

Need for scaling in Spring Boot applications:

1. Increased Traffic:
   - As the number of users or requests grows, scaling ensures the application can handle the demand without degrading performance (Fig. 14-3).

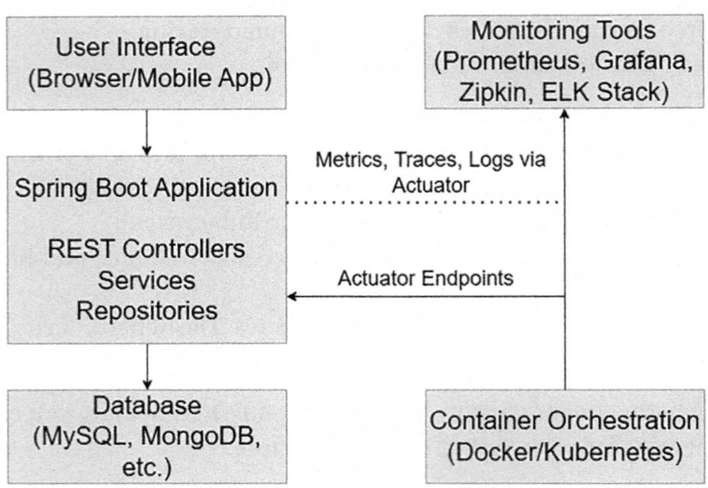


**FIGURE 14–1** Spring Boot monitoring architecture diagram.

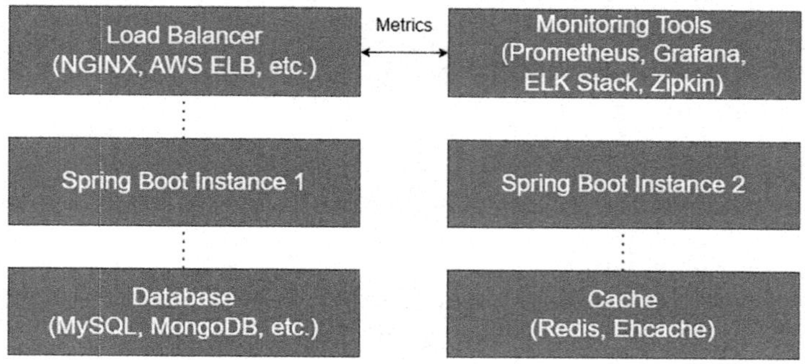


**FIGURE 14–2** Scaling architecture.

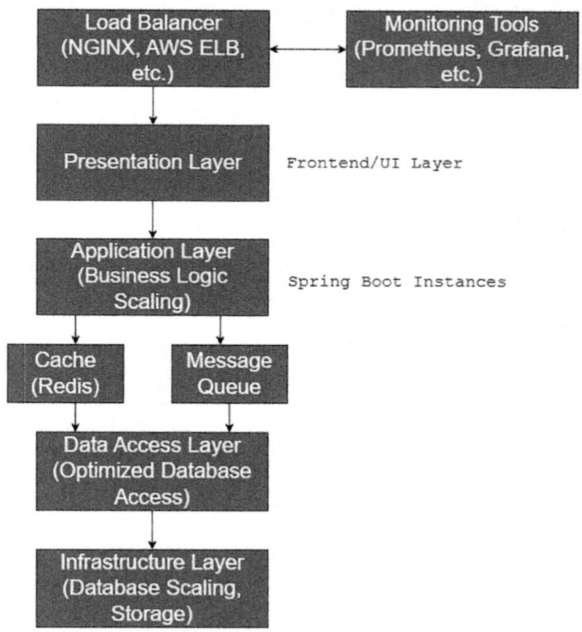


**FIGURE 14–3** Layered scaling architecture in Spring Boot.

**2** Improved Performance:
- Prevents slow response times and ensures the application remains responsive during peak usage.

**3** Fault Tolerance:
- Scaling helps maintain availability and reliability, even if some instances fail.

**4** Cost Efficiency:
- With the ability to scale down during low demand, resources can be optimized, saving infrastructure costs.

5 Support for Modern Architectures:
- Scaling is critical for microservice-based architectures where individual services may experience different levels of load.

Categories of scaling:
Scaling can be categorized into two main types:

1. Vertical Scaling (Scaling Up):
   - Involves adding more resources (CPU, memory, disk space) to a single machine or server where the application is running.
   - Suitable for monolithic applications where scaling is limited to the machine's capacity.
   Advantages:
   - Easier to implement.
   - No changes required in the application architecture.
   Disadvantages:
   - Has a physical limit (depends on the hardware).
   - Scaling downtime might be required for upgrades.
   Example:
   - Moving the application from a machine with 4 CPU cores and 16 GB RAM to one with 8 CPU cores and 32 GB RAM.
2. Horizontal Scaling (Scaling Out):
   - Involves adding more instances of the application to distribute the load across multiple machines or servers.
   - Suitable for microservices and cloud-native applications.
   Advantages:
   - Virtually unlimited scalability.
   - High availability and fault tolerance (if one instance fails, others continue to serve traffic).
   Disadvantages:
   - Requires a load balancer to distribute traffic across instances.
   - More complex to manage and monitor.
   Example:
   - Deploying the same Spring Boot application on five servers instead of one, with a load balancer like Nginx or AWS Elastic Load Balancer distributing requests.

When to use vertical versus horizontal scaling:
How scaling is achieved in Spring Boot applications:

Scaling a Spring Boot application entails making certain that the application is suitable for managing the rise or surge in workload, either by raising the capacity of an individual application (vertical scaling) or by placing numerous applications (horizontal scaling). The initial step is to define the performance indicators that require scaling, that is, high use of CPU, slowness in reaction time, or number of requests. To scale upward or downward on a vertical basis, you can scale the server that is holding the application by either configuration

**Table 14–1** Vertical scaling vs horizontal scaling.

| Aspect | Vertical scaling | Horizontal scaling |
|---|---|---|
| **Application type** | Monolithic | Microservices/Distributed |
| **Resource limit** | Hardware-dependent | No specific limit |
| **Implementation cost** | Lower | Higher (requires orchestration) |
| **Fault tolerance** | Limited | High |
| **Example use case** | Small-scale applications | Cloud-native or enterprise-level |

in a cloud platform or one of the physical hardware upgrades with CPU, memory, or disk space in an on-premise server (Table 14–1).

The process has been vital in making sure the Spring Boot application is scalable, robust, and able to give efficient loading of any dynamic workload.

The most common place of scaling in a Spring Boot application would be in the Application Layer and the Infrastructure Layer since these layers are what will carry the user request and resource utilization efficiency. The way in which scaling is done at the various layers and how all the layers interact in scaling has been given in detail below.

Layers and their role in scaling

1. Presentation Layer (User Interface/Frontend Layer):
   - The presentation interface is an interface, usually a web or mobile interface that communicates with the users.
   - Scaling does not take place directly here, but this layer enjoys the advantage of scaling on lower layers. Load balancers provide a seamless flow of response to the users in instances of heavy traffic.
2. Application Layer (Business Logic Layer):
   - The essence of business logic lies here and scaling aims at rolling out more than one instance of the Spring Boot application that is able to respond to requests effectively.
   - The architecture over stateless: The stateless architecture assures that every instance is independent of past states and can process any request.
3. Data Access Layer
   - This layer is the one that interacts with the database to retrieve and store data. Optimization of database queries and caching employed to minimize loads is a part of scaling at this layer.
   - Techniques include:
     - Connection pooling (e.g., HikariCP).
     - Scaling databases (reads or sharding).
     - OpenFire perimeter movable caches such as Redis or Memcached.
4. Infrastructure Layer
   - This layer comprises databases, caches, file storage, and messaging systems. Scaling here involves:

- Horizontally scaling databases (e.g., sharding, replicas).
- Installation of distributed caching of the most visited data.
- Decoupling services with the help of message queues (e.g., RabbitMQ, Kafka) and workload with high throughput.

How layers process during scaling

1. Load Balancer (Infrastructure Layer):
   - The user request is sent to the load balancer and is simply spread out over the available instances of Spring Boot (horizontal scaling).
   - Examples: NGINX, AWS ELB, or Spring Cloud Gateway.
2. Presentation Layer:
   - Request in the user interface layer is relayed to the load balancer and does not understand scaling in the rear. The scaling process would guarantee continuous service provision.
3. Application Layer:
   - Several examples of the Spring Boot application process the incoming requests. The requests are processed separately in each instance.
   - Stateless design: This design is such that requests can be sent anywhere, without keeping a session in the local state of one instance.
4. Data Access Layer:
   - Every instance communicates with the database or cache, when necessary.
   - In this layer, scaling of queries, read/write distribution of load, or caches can be optimized.
5. Database Layer: This layer has most of the information on board, including the database configuration and runtime environment.Database and Cache (Infrastructure Layer): This layer contains the majority of information on board such as the database setup and runtime.
   - The database can be scaled with read replicas or partitioning (sharding) in order to address the higher query volumes.
   - Distributed caches lower the load of the database by the frequent data.

Step-by-Step procedure for scaling in Spring Boot applications

Scaling of a Spring Boot application can be implemented by means of horizontal scaling (adding increased instances), as well as ensuring that both the application and the infrastructure are able to sustain distributed traffic. Here's the procedure with implementation steps and syntax:

1. Prepare the Spring Boot Application
   - a Build a Stateless Application
     - Ensure your Spring Boot application does not rely on local state (e.g., HTTP sessions).
     - Use external systems like Redis for session storage.
       Example: Configure session storage in application.properties:

```
spring.session.store-type=redis
spring.redis.host=localhost
spring.redis.port=6379
```

**b** Externalize Configuration

- Use environment variables or Spring Cloud Config for application configuration to make scaling easier.
  Example: Use environment variables in application.properties:

```
server.port=${PORT:8080}
```

**2.** Containerize the Application

**a** Create a Dockerfile

- Package the Spring Boot application into a Docker container.
  Dockerfile:

```
FROM openjdk:17-jdk-slim
VOLUME /tmp
ARG JAR_FILE=target/myapp-0.0.1-SNAPSHOT.jar
COPY ${JAR_FILE} app.jar
ENTRYPOINT ["java", "-jar", "/app.jar"]
```

**b** Build the Docker Image
docker build -t myapp:latest.

**c** Run Multiple Containers (Locally)
docker run -d -p 8080:8080 myapp:latest
docker run -d -p 8081:8080 myapp:latest

**3.** Set Up Load Balancing

**a** Use NGINX for Load Balancing

- Configure NGINX to distribute traffic across multiple instances.

NGINX Configuration (nginx.conf):

```
http {
upstream spring_boot_app {
server localhost:8080;
server localhost:8081;
}
server {
listen 80;
location / {
proxy_pass http://spring_boot_app;
}
}
}
```

**b** Run NGINX

```
nginx -c /path/to/nginx.conf
```

**4.** Deploy to a Container Orchestration Platform

**a** Deploy on Kubernetes

**1** Create a Kubernetes Deployment

```
apiVersion: apps/v1
kind: Deployment
metadata:
name: spring-boot-app
spec:
replicas: 3
selector:
matchLabels:
app: spring-boot-app
template:
metadata:
labels:
app: spring-boot-app
spec:
containers:
name: spring-boot-app
image: myapp:latest
ports:
-containerPort: 8080
```

*Create a Kubernetes Service*

```
apiVersion: v1
kind: Service
metadata:
name: spring-boot-service
spec:
selector:
app: spring-boot-app
ports:
-protocol: TCP
port: 80
targetPort: 8080
type: LoadBalancer
```

Apply the Configurations

```
kubectl apply -f deployment.yaml
kubectl apply -f service.yaml
```

5. Monitor and Scale Dynamically
   a Configure Horizontal Pod Autoscaling (HPA)
      - Scale instances dynamically based on CPU or memory usage.
        HPA Configuration:

```
apiVersion: autoscaling/v2
kind: HorizontalPodAutoscaler
metadata:
name: spring-boot-hpa
spec:
scaleTargetRef:
apiVersion: apps/v1
kind: Deployment
name: spring-boot-app
minReplicas: 2
maxReplicas: 10
metrics:
-type: Resource
resource:
name: cpu
target:
type: Utilization
averageUtilization: 70
```

Apply the Configuration:

```
kubectl apply -f hpa.yaml
```

6. Configure Distributed Caching
   a Use Redis as Cache
      - Add Redis dependencies to pom.xml:

```
<dependency>
<groupId>org.springframework.boot</groupId>
<artifactId>spring-boot-starter-data-redis</artifactId>
</dependency>
```

   b Enable Caching
      - Configure Redis in application.properties:

```
spring.cache.type=redis
spring.redis.host=localhost
spring.redis.port=6379
```

   c Enable Cache in Code

```
@SpringBootApplication
@EnableCaching
```

```
public class MyAppApplication {
public static void main(String[] args) {
SpringApplication.run(MyAppApplication.class, args);
}
}
@Service
public class MyService {
@Cacheable("data")
public String getData(String id) {
return "Data for ID: " + id;
}
}
```

7. Perform Load Testing
   Use tools like Apache JMeter or Gatling to simulate high traffic and test the scalability of the architecture.
   JMeter Setup:
   1 Add multiple HTTP request threads simulating concurrent users.
   2 Analyze response times, throughput, and error rates.
8. Monitor and Optimize
   a Use Spring Boot Actuator
   - Add the Actuator dependency to pom.xml:

```
<dependency>
<groupId>org.springframework.boot</groupId>
<artifactId>spring-boot-starter-actuator</artifactId>
</dependency>
```

   - Expose health and metrics endpoints in application.properties: management.endpoints.web.exposure.include=health,metrics

   b Integrate Monitoring Tools
   - Use Prometheus for metrics and Grafana for dashboards.
   - Export metrics using the Micrometer library:

```
<dependency>
<groupId>io.micrometer</groupId>
<artifactId>micrometer-registry-prometheus</artifactId>
</dependency>
```

# Bibliography

Spring Boot Actuator. (2024). Docs. https://docs.spring.io/spring-boot/docs/current/reference/html/actuator.html.

Micrometer. (2024). Docs. https://micrometer.io.

Prometheus. (2024). Docs. https://prometheus.io.

Grafana. (2024). Docs. https://grafana.com.

IBM. (2024). Monitoring Systems. https://www.ibm.com/docs.

AWS. (2024). Cloud Monitoring. https://aws.amazon.com/cloudwatch.

Microsoft. (2024). Azure Monitoring. https://learn.microsoft.com.

Red Hat. (2024). Monitoring Guide. https://www.redhat.com.

# 15 Node.js

## 15.1 What is Node.js?

Node.js is a cross-platform, open-source JavaScript runtime environment that enables developers to execute JavaScript on the server side. It is driven by Chrome's V8 JavaScript engine and is primarily used for the development of network applications that can scale.

Node.js is distinct from other web servers as it employs an event-driven, nonblocking I/O model, rendering it efficient and ideal for applications that are real-time in nature, such as chat applications, online games, and live streams.

Advantages of Node.js

1. Fast Execution
   - V8 engine-powered, which runs JavaScript directly to machine code and hence is extremely fast.
2. Asynchronous and Nonblocking
   - Follows event-driven architecture, that is, does not block to wait for one operation to finish before proceeding to the next, increasing performance and responsiveness.
3. Single Programming Language
   - Being able to run both on the frontend and backend using JavaScript enables full-stack development with just one language.
4. Scalability
   - Ideal for microservices and real-time applications due to its ability to handle many simultaneous connections efficiently.
5. Rich Package Ecosystem (npm)
   - Comes with Node Package Manager (npm), which provides thousands of reusable packages and modules.
6. Cross-Platform Development
   - Node.js can be used to develop applications that run on Windows, macOS, and Linux.

Key Characteristics of Node.js

Event-Driven Architecture

- An event loop functions along with callbacks to handle multiple requests simultaneously.

Nonblocking I/O Operations

- The difference between traditional servers and a Node.js server is that the latter does not prevent the execution process of the code when it is waiting in the file system or for database operations.

Single-Threaded but Highly Scalable

- Single-threaded event loop and can play thousands of connections asynchronously.

**Mastering Java Full Stack Development. DOI: https://doi.org/10.1016/B978-0-443-51683-2.00017-5**

Lightweight and Efficient

- Uses less resources than the traditional server-based technologies such as PHP or Java.

Supports WebSockets for Real-Time Apps

- Supports two-way communication between the client and the server, and is therefore suitable for chat applications, live notices, and games.

Common Use Cases of Node.js

- Web servers and APIs
- Real-time chat applications
- Streaming applications (Netflix, Spotify, etc.)
- IoT applications
- Single-page applications (SPAs)
- Microservices architecture

## 15.2 How Node.js can help in Spring applications

Java Spring is a widespread framework that is most commonly used to develop enterprise-level applications, whereas lightweight and scalable asynchronous applications are commonly created with Node.js. Even though they are dissimilar ecologies, Node.js can be used to complement Spring applications in multiple aspects, resulting in the creation of a more efficient and scalable system.

1. Using Node.js as a Frontend with a Spring Boot Backend
   - Many developers use Node.js (with frameworks like React, Angular, or Vue.js) for the frontend, while using Spring Boot as the backend.
   - Node.js efficiently handles client-side rendering, API requests, and WebSockets, while Spring Boot manages business logic and database transactions.
     Example Architecture
     Frontend (Node.js + React/Angular/Vue.js)
     Backend (Spring Boot REST APIs + Database)
     Communication: REST API or GraphQL
     Benefit: Improves performance by offloading UI rendering and API handling to a lightweight Node.js layer.
2. API Gateway Using Node.js
   - In microservices architectures, Node.js can act as an API Gateway to route requests to different Spring Boot microservices.
   - Libraries like Express.js and GraphQL in Node.js can help aggregate responses from multiple microservices.

     Example:
     Node.js API Gateway (Express.js)
     Multiple Spring Boot microservices
     Communication: REST API, WebSockets, or GraphQL
     Benefit: Enhances scalability and performance as there is less direct frontend to Spring Boot microservices dependency.

**3** Java Spring Boot and Node.js Features in Real Time

- Node.js supports WebSockets (e.g., using Socket.io), which can be used alongside Spring Boot applications to handle real-time messaging and notifications.
- Spring Boot handles core business logic and database transactions, while Node.js manages real-time updates.

Example Use Case:
Spring Boot for processing orders in an e-commerce app
Node.js + Socket.io for real-time order status updates to customers
Benefit: Improves user experience with instant notifications.

**4** Serverless or Lightweight Services with Node.js

- Some lightweight tasks in a Spring Boot app (e.g., image processing, file uploads, logging) can be offloaded to Node.js microservices.
- Node.js is well-suited for serverless computing (e.g., AWS Lambda, Firebase Functions) to handle async jobs.

Example:
Spring Boot: Handles complex business logic
Node.js Serverless Functions: Handles image resizing, notifications, or background tasks
Benefit: Reduces load on Spring Boot services, leading to better performance.

**5** Full-Stack Development with Node.js and Spring Boot

- Many teams use Spring Boot for backend APIs and Node.js for full-stack development (especially with Express.js for APIs).
- Developers can use both Node.js and Java Spring within a microservices architecture, leveraging the best of both worlds.

Example:
**Spring Boot for Core Backend Services**
Node.js for Lightweight Backend Services or Frontend
Communication: REST API, GraphQL, or Message Queues
Benefit: More flexibility, scalability, and use of the right tool for the right task.

**1** Calling a Spring Boot REST API from Node.js
Spring Boot exposes APIs, and Node.js (using axios or fetch) can consume them.
Spring Boot REST API (SpringBootApp.java)

```
@RestController
@RequestMapping("/api")
public class SpringBootApp {
@GetMapping("/message")
public ResponseEntity<String>getMessage() {
return ResponseEntity.ok("Hello from Spring Boot");
}
}
```

Node.js Code (Using axios to call the Spring Boot API)

```
constaxios = require('axios');
async function callSpringBootAPI() {
try {
const response = await axios.get('http://localhost:8080/api/message');
console.log("Response from Spring Boot:", response.data);
} catch (error) {
console.error("Error calling Spring Boot API:", error);
}
}
callSpringBootAPI();
```

This script calls the Spring Boot API and prints the response.

2 Using Node.js as an API Gateway for Spring Boot

Node.js can act as a proxy (middleware) API Gateway to route requests to Spring Boot.
Node.js API Gateway (Using Express.js)

```
const express = require('express');
constaxios = require('axios');
const app = express();
const PORT = 3000;
app.get('/api/message', async (req, res) => {
try {
// Forward request to Spring Boot API
const response = await axios.get('http://localhost:8080/api/message');
res.send(response.data);
} catch (error) {
res.status(500).send("Error connecting to Spring Boot");
}
});
app.listen(PORT, () => {
console.log(`Node.js API Gateway running on http://localhost:${PORT}`);
});
```

This script routes /api/message requests through Node.js to Spring Boot.

3 Real-time Communication with WebSockets (Node.js + Spring Boot)

Spring Boot handles backend logic, and Node.js manages real-time updates using WebSockets.
Spring Boot WebSocket Server (WebSocketConfig.java)

```
@Configuration
@EnableWebSocket
public class WebSocketConfig implements WebSocketHandler {
@Override
public void afterConnectionEstablished(WebSocketSession session) throws Exception {
session.sendMessage(new TextMessage("Connected to Spring Boot WebSocket"));
```

```
}
@Override
public void handleMessage(WebSocketSession session, WebSocketMessage<?> message)
throws Exception {
session.sendMessage(new TextMessage("Message received: " + message.getPayload()));
}
}
Node.js WebSocket Client (NodeWebSocket.js)
const WebSocket = require('ws');
constws = new WebSocket('ws://localhost:8080/ws');
ws.on('open', () => {
console.log("Connected to Spring Boot WebSocket");
ws.send("Hello from Node.js");
});
ws.on('message', (message) => {
console.log("Message from Spring Boot:", message.toString());
});
```

This allows real-time communication between Node.js and Spring Boot.

## 15.3 Node.js Modules

Elements of Node.js and their syntax:

Node.js is built on JavaScript and has several key elements that make it unique for server-side development. Below are the essential elements of Node.js along with their syntax and explanations (Tables 15–1 and 15–2).

**1** Modules (Importing and Exporting Code)
Modules help in organizing and reusing code.
Example: Creating and Importing a Module

**Table 15–1** Node.js elements.

| Node.js element | Description | Example |
|---|---|---|
| Modules | Organizes reusable code | require('./module') |
| HTTP server | Creates web servers | http.createServer() |
| File system (fs) | Reads/writes files | fs.readFile('file.txt', callback) |
| Events | Handles event-driven programming | eventEmitter.on('event', callback) |
| Express.js | Simplifies HTTP handling | app.get('/', callback) |
| Middleware | Processes requests | app.use(middleware) |
| Databases (MongoDB) | Stores and retrieves data | mongoose.connect() |
| JSON APIs | Handles JSON responses | res.json({}) |
| Async/Await | Manages asynchronous operations | await fs.readFile() |
| Environment Variables | Stores configuration securely | process.env.VARIABLE_NAME |

File: math.js (Creating a module)

```
function add(a, b) {
return a + b;
}
module.exports = add; // Export function
```

File: app.js (Importing the module)

```
const add = require('./math'); // Import module
console.log(add(5, 3)); // Output: 8
```

Explanation:
module.exports is used to export functions/variables from a module.
require('./math') imports the module in another file.

**2** HTTP Module (Creating a Server)
The http module helps create web servers.

Example: Basic HTTP Server

```
const http = require('http');
const server = http.createServer((req, res) => {
res.writeHead(200, { 'Content-Type': 'text/plain' });
res.end('Hello, Node.js!');
});
server.listen(3000, () => {
console.log('Server is running on http://localhost:3000');
});
```

Explanation:
http.createServer() creates a server.
res.writeHead(200, {.}) sets the response status and headers.
server.listen(3000,.) starts the server on port 3000.

**3** File System (fs Module)
The fs module allows reading/writing files.

Example: Writing to a File

```
const fs = require('fs');
fs.writeFile('example.txt', 'Hello, Node.js!', (err) => {
if (err) throw err;
console.log('File created successfully!');
});
```

Explanation:
fs.writeFile(filename, data, callback) writes data to a file.
The callback handles errors if any occur.

**4** Event Emitter (Handling Events)
The events module allows event-driven programming.

Example: Creating an Event

```
constEventEmitter = require('events');
consteventEmitter = new EventEmitter();
eventEmitter.on('greet', () => {
console.log('Hello, welcome to Node.js!');
});
eventEmitter.emit('greet'); // Triggers the event
```

Explanation:
.on('event', callback) listens for an event.
.emit('event') triggers an event.

**5** Express.js (Handling HTTP Requests Easily)
Express.js is a web app development framework that makes it easier to develop API and servers.

Example: Simple Express Server

```
const express = require('express');
const app = express();
app.get('/', (req, res) => {
res.send('Hello from Express.js');
});
app.listen(3000, () => {
console.log('Server running on http://localhost:3000');
});
```

**6** Middleware (Processing Requests in Express.js)
Middlewares are request-processing functions that are then sent to produce responses.

Example: Using Middleware

```
const express = require('express');
const app = express();
app.use((req, res, next) => {
console.log('Middleware executed!');
next();
});
app.get('/', (req, res) => {
res.send('Hello from Express.js with Middleware');
});
app.listen(3000);
```

**7** Working with Databases (MongoDB + Mongoose)
Databases can be connected to node.js through libraries such as Mongoose.

Example: Connecting to MongoDB

```
const mongoose = require('mongoose');
mongoose.connect('mongodb://localhost:27017/mydatabase', {
useNewUrlParser: true,
useUnifiedTopology: true
}).then(() => console.log("Connected to MongoDB"))
.catch(err =>console.error(err));
```

**8** Working with JSON Data (Handling APIs)
Node.js works with JSON to handle API responses.

Example: Serving JSON Data

```
const express = require('express');
const app = express();
app.get('/data', (req, res) => {
res.json({ name: 'Node.js', version: '18.x' });
});
app.listen(3000);
```

**9** Asynchronous Programming (Using Promises & Async/Await)
Node.js supports asynchronous operations using Promises or Async/Await.

Example: Using Async/Await with fs

```
const fs = require('fs').promises;
async function readFile() {
try {
const data = await fs.readFile('example.txt', 'utf8');
console.log(data);
} catch (error) {
console.error(error);
}
}
readFile();
```

**10** Handling Environment Variables (dotenv module)

Environment variables help manage configurations securely.
Example: Using Environment Variables

```
require('dotenv').config();
console.log(process.env.MY_SECRET_KEY);
```

## 15.4 Node.js events and their syntax

The events module in Node.js allows handling asynchronous events using an EventEmitter.

1 Importing the Events Module
constEventEmitter = require('events');
consteventEmitter = new EventEmitter();
**Creates an EventEmitter instance.
2 Creating and Emitting Events
eventEmitter.on('greet', () => {
console.log('Hello, welcome to Node.js!');
});
eventEmitter.emit('greet'); // Triggers the event
on('event', callback) listens for an event.
emit('event') triggers the event.
3 Passing Arguments with Events
eventEmitter.on('user', (name, age) => {
console.log(`User: ${name}, Age: ${age}`);
});
eventEmitter.emit('user', 'Alice', 25);
Arguments (name, age) are passed when emitting the event.
4 One-Time Event Listener (once method)
eventEmitter.once('greetOnce', () => {
console.log('This will only run once!');
});
eventEmitter.emit('greetOnce'); // Runs
eventEmitter.emit('greetOnce'); // Won't run again
once('event', callback) runs the event handler only once.
5 Removing an Event Listener
const greet = () =>console.log('Hello again!');
eventEmitter.on('greet', greet);
eventEmitter.removeListener('greet', greet);
eventEmitter.emit('greet'); // No output (listener removed)
removeListener('event', functionName) removes a specific event listener.
6 Removing All Listeners for an Event
eventEmitter.removeAllListeners('greet');
Removes all listeners attached to the 'greet' event.
7 Getting All Registered Event Names
console.log(eventEmitter.eventNames());
Returns an array of registered event names.

## 15.5 How Node.js works in a Spring Boot program

Node.js and Spring Boot are often used together in a microservices or full-stack architecture. The working procedure depends on how they interact. Below are the common ways Node.js and Spring Boot can work together, along with their working procedure.

1 Node.js as a Frontend, Spring Boot as a Backend
Use Case: A React.js or Angular frontend (running on Node.js) interacts with a Spring Boot backend via REST APIs.
Working Procedure:
Node.js (Frontend) makes an HTTP request to the Spring Boot server.
Spring Boot (Backend) processes the request, interacts with the database, and sends a response.
Node.js receives the response and updates the UI.

Example Flow:
React/Angular (Node.js server) calls http://localhost:8080/api/users
Spring Boot (Backend) responds with JSON data.
Node.js updates the frontend UI
Efficient for full-stack applications with a separate frontend.

2 Node.js as an API Gateway for Spring Boot Microservices
Use Case: Node.js serves as a middleware (API Gateway) to route requests to different Spring Boot microservices.
Working Procedure:
   1. Client sends a request to Node.js API Gateway.
   2. Node.js processes the request and forwards it to the appropriate Spring Boot microservice.
   3. Spring Boot microservice executes business logic and returns a response.
   4. Node.js sends the final response to the client.

   Example Flow:
   - Client calls: http://localhost:3000/users (Node.js API Gateway)
   - Node.js forwards the request to Spring Boot: http://localhost:8080/api/users
   - Spring Boot fetches data from the database and returns it.
   - Node.js sends the final response to the client.
     Useful in microservices architecture for better scalability.

3 Real-Time Communication (Node.js WebSockets + Spring Boot)
Use Case: Spring Boot handles backend logic, and Node.js manages real-time updates using WebSockets.
Working Procedure:
   1. Spring Boot processes requests and updates the database.
   2. WebSockets or event-driven architecture changes are listened to by Node.js.
   3. 3Node.js transmits real-time updates whenever data is changed to those clients who are connected.

   Example Flow:
   - User places an order (Spring Boot updates DB).
   - Node.js WebSocket detects the update.
   - Node.js provides the user with a real-time notification.
     Perfect in chat applications, notifications, and real-time updates.

4 Node.js for Background Tasks, Spring Boot for Main Business Logic
Use Case: Spring boot overcomes business capabilities at the expense of light background tasks by Node.js.

5 Working Procedure:
   1 Spring Boot is triggered by an event (i.e., registration of a new user).
   2 Node.js is an event listener (through a message queue such as RabbitMQ).
   3 Node.js does a background job (e.g., emailing).
   4 Spring Boot proceeds with processing the primary request.

   Example Flow:
   - Spring Boot saves a new user to the database.
   - Node.js (worker service) listens and sends a welcome email.

Useful for sending emails, notifications, and logging.

**Client request and response flow for Node.js and Spring Boot**

A standard request–response model of a client (browser or mobile application) and a backend system (Node.js and Spring Boot) has the following steps:

Client → Node.js → Spring Boot → Database (Standard API Flow)

Use Case: A request is sent to the React (or Angular or Vue or mobile application) client and then to the Node.js server, which passes it to Spring Boot.

Request Flow:

1 Client (Browser/ Mobile Application) makes an HTTP request (e.g., GET, POST) to Node.js API Gateway.
2 The request is processed using Node.js (authentication, logging, or load balancing).
3 The request is sent to Spring boot (Spring Boot deals with business logic) using Node.js.
4 The database is communicated with through Spring Boot, which retrieves or inserts data.
5 Spring Boot will be returning the answer to the Node.js.
6 The Node.js executes the response (when necessary) and routes it to the client.
7 The customer obtains and presents the information.

Example Flow:

- Client Calls: http://localhost:3000/users (Node.js)
- Node.js Calls: http://localhost:8080/api/users (Spring Boot)
- Spring Boot Queries Database (MySQL, MongoDB) and returns JSON.
- Node.js Sends Response to Client.

Best for API management, authentication, and microservices.

Client → Node.js (WebSockets) → Spring Boot (Real-Time Communication)

Use Case: Live applications (Chat, Notifications, Live Updates).

Request Flow:

1 Client connects to WebSocket on Node.js.
2 The node.js is waiting on real-time updates of Spring boot.
3 The database is updated (e.g., a new message is added) using Spring Boot.
4 Spring Boot informs the WebSocket or a queue of events in the Node.js.
5 The update is relayed to the client in real time by Node.js.

Example Flow:

- User sends a chat message (WebSocket to Node.js).
- Node.js forwards it to Spring Boot (Spring Boot saves it in DB).
- Spring Boot notifies Node.js (new message event).
- Node.js pushes the update to all connected clients.

Best for notifications, chat applications, and stock market updates.
Client → Node.js (Background Task) → Spring Boot (Main Logic)
Use Case: Background tasks such as email sending, logging, or image processing.
Request Flow:

1. The request is made to Spring Boot by the client (e.g., user registration).
2. The request is processed by Spring Boot to save the user in the database.
3. Spring Boot causes an event or message queue (RabbitMQ, Kafka).
4. Background tasks are processed, and the event is listened to by Node.js.
5. The task is accomplished with Node.js, which logs the response.

Example Flow:

- Client registers a user (Spring Boot saves the user).
- Spring Boot sends a message to RabbitMQ/Kafka.
- Node.js picks up the message and sends a welcome email.

Best for task scheduling, notifications, and logging.

**Table 15–2** Request flow.

| Flow type | Use case | Request flow |
|---|---|---|
| Client → Node.js → Spring Boot → DB | API Gateway, Microservices | Client → Node.js → Spring Boot → DB → Response |
| Client → Node.js (WebSockets) → Spring Boot | Real-time apps, Chat, Notifications | Client ↔ Node.js ↔ Spring Boot (Live updates) |
| Client → Node.js (Background Task) → Spring Boot | Task Scheduling, Emails, Logging | Client → Spring Boot → Event Queue → Node.js (Background processing) |

# Bibliography


Node.js. (2024). Documentation. https://nodejs.org.

MDN. (2024). Node.js Guide. https://developer.mozilla.org.

IBM. (2024). Node.js Overview. https://www.ibm.com/docs.

Microsoft. (2024). Node.js Docs. https://learn.microsoft.com.

Red Hat. (2024). Node.js Overview. https://www.redhat.com.

Express.js. (2024). Docs. https://expressjs.com.

# 16

# React.js

## 16.1 Introduction to React.js

React.js is a widespread JavaScript library created by Facebook to create interactive and dynamic user interfaces in general, and single-page applications (SPAs), in particular. It is a component-based architecture that allows the developer to develop reusable UI elements. React is based on a virtual Document Object Model(DOM) to render efficiently and has features like declarative programming and state management.

What is the need for React on Spring Applications?

Spring applications especially those built on Spring Boot are more of backend applications, which handle application programming interfaces (APIs), security, business logic, and database interfaces. Yet, web applications today demand interactive and dynamic frontends, and it is here where React.js fits in with Spring as it provides:

1. Separation of Concerns—Spring will deal with backend tasks, and React will deal with frontend, which will guarantee a clean architecture.
2. Enhanced UI/Ux—React allows building rich, dynamic, and interactive interfaces.
3. Effective Data Processing—React is an efficient state manager and dynamically renders components that rely on the backend data provided by Spring REST APIs.
4. Single-Page Application (SPA)—React favors and enables the use of smooth navigation and does not require a full page reload to enhance performance and user experiences.
5. Scalability and Maintainability—React is a component-based structure and thus can easily be scaled and maintained.

Pros of React.js and Spring application:

1. **Component-Based Architecture**
   - Encourages code reusability and modular development, reducing redundancy.
   - Improves maintainability and scalability of frontend applications.
2. **Effective Rendering through Virtual DOM**
   - Updates only the necessary parts of the UI, reducing rendering time and improving performance.
   - Enhances the responsiveness of applications interacting with Spring Boot APIs.
3. **Strong Ecosystem and Third-Party Integrations**
   - Supports Redux for state management, Material-UI for design components, and Axios for API calls to Spring Boot.
   - Easy integration with authentication services like OAuth and JWT.
4. **Asynchronous Data Fetching**
   - React efficiently handles asynchronous requests to Spring REST APIs using fetch() or Axios, ensuring a smooth user experience.

**Mastering Java Full Stack Development. DOI: https://doi.org/10.1016/B978-0-443-51683-2.00010-2**

- Enables real-time updates through WebSockets or server-sent events.

5. **SPA Development for Better User Experience**
   - Eliminates full-page reloads, providing a seamless and fast experience.
   - Enables client-side routing with React Router, reducing server load.
6. **Cross-Platform Compatibility**
   - React Native allows Spring applications to extend into mobile platforms easily.
   - React can be combined with Electron.js for desktop applications.

**Benefits for Spring applications**

1. Modern UI Framework—Supports modern, responsive, and dynamic interfaces.
2. RESTful API Consumption—This is suitable with RESTful APIs of Spring Boot to have a clean frontend-backend separation.
3. Quick Development and Deployment—React has reusable components, and Spring Boot has microservices, which make development quicker.
4. Improved Performance—Virtual DOM enables faster applications through client-side rendering.
5. Better Maintainability—Frontend and backend decoupling ease updates and debugging.

## 16.2 React.js Spring apps form elements

Forms are essential to web applications, and they are of particular importance to Spring-based applications, where the input by the user must be gathered and used in the backend. React.js offers a robust means of dealing with form controls and dynamically responding to user interaction with Spring Boot REST APIs.

### 16.2.1 The elements of form in React.js

React offers regular HTML form elements like:

React.js Spring Application Form Elements.

React.js form objects are needed to receive user input and transmit data to Spring Boot apps. Each form element is described and syntactically below.

1. Input field

   The <input> element is used to capture user input in text, email, password, or other formats. The value attribute is controlled by React state, and the onChange event updates the state.

   Syntax:
   ```
   <input type="text" value={stateVariable} onChange={handleChange} />
   <input type="email" value={stateVariable} onChange={handleChange} />
   <input type="password" value={stateVariable} onChange={handleChange} />
   ```

2. Textarea

   The <textarea> element allows multiline text input. In React, its value is controlled using state.

Syntax:
```
<textarea value={stateVariable} onChange={handleChange}></textarea>
```

3. Select dropdown
   The <select> element provides a dropdown menu for user selection. The selected value is controlled via state.

   Syntax:
   ```
   <select value={stateVariable} onChange={handleChange}>
   <option value="option1">Option 1</option>
   <option value="option2">Option 2</option>
   </select>
   ```

4. Checkbox
   Checkboxes allow users to toggle between checked and unchecked states. The checked attribute is controlled using state.

   Syntax:
   ```
   <input type="checkbox" checked={stateVariable} onChange={handleChange} />
   ```

5. Radio button
   Radio buttons allow users to select one option from multiple choices. The checked attribute ensures that only one radio button is selected at a time.

   Syntax:
   ```
   <input type="radio" value="option1" checked={stateVariable === "option1"} onChange=
   {handleChange} />
   <input type="radio" value="option2" checked={stateVariable === "option2"} onChange=
   {handleChange} />
   ```

6. Button
   Buttons trigger actions like form submission or other event handling.

   Syntax:
   ```
   <button type="button" onClick={handleClick}>Click Me</button>
   <button type="submit">Submit</button>
   ```

7. Form submission
   A <form> element groups input fields and handles submission events using onSubmit.

   Syntax:
   ```
   <form onSubmit={handleSubmit}>
   <input type="text" value={stateVariable} onChange={handleChange} />
   <button type="submit">Submit</button>
   </form>
   ```

**8.** File upload
The <input type="file"> element allows users to upload files. The onChange event handles file selection.

Syntax:
```
<input type="file" onChange={handleFileChange} />
```

**9.** Uncontrolled input with Refs
Instead of using state, an input field can be managed using ref to access its current value.

Syntax:
```
<input type="text" ref={inputRef} />
```

**10.** Sending form data to Spring Boot application programming interface
To send form data to a Spring Boot backend, we use the Fetch API or Axios.

Syntax (Using Fetch API):
```
fetch("http://localhost:8080/api", {
method: "POST",
headers: { "Content-Type": "application/json" },
body: JSON.stringify({ key: value }),
});
```

Syntax (Using Axios):
```
axios.post("http://localhost:8080/api", { key: value });
```

Such elements of the form enable a smooth acquisition of data in React.js, and it is easier to join with applications in Spring Boot.

These components are similar to regular HTML, but in React they need to be managed by the state.

## 16.3 Controlled versus uncontrolled components

Two ways of managing React forms exist as follows:

### 16.3.1 Controlled components

- The form elements are controlled by React state using useState or useReducer.
- Each input's value is updated based on state changes.

```
import { useState } from 'react';
function UserForm() {
const [name, setName] = useState('');
const handleSubmit = (event) => {
event.preventDefault();
console.log('Submitted:', name);
```

```
};
return (
<form onSubmit={handleSubmit}>
<label>Name:</label>
<input
type="text"
value={name}
onChange={(e) => setName(e.target.value)}
/>
<button type="submit">Submit</button>
</form>
);
}
export default UserForm;
```

### 16.3.2 Uncontrolled components

- Uses a ref to directly access the DOM element without managing state.
- Useful when integrating with third-party libraries.

```
import { useRef } from 'react';
function UserForm() {
const inputRef = useRef(null);
const handleSubmit = (event) => {
event.preventDefault();
console.log('Submitted:', inputRef.current.value);
};
return (
<form onSubmit={handleSubmit}>
<label>Name:</label>
<input type="text" ref={inputRef} />
<button type="submit">Submit</button>
</form>
);
}
export default UserForm;
```

## 16.4 Handling form submission in React.js with Spring Boot

Data may be sent to a Spring Boot backend using Fetch API or Axios with React forms.

Example: Sending Data to a Spring Boot API

Spring Boot Controller (UserController.java):

```
@RestController
@RequestMapping("/users")
public class UserController {
@PostMapping("/register")
public ResponseEntity<String> registerUser(@RequestBody User user) {
System.out.println("Received User: " + user.getName());
return ResponseEntity.ok("User registered successfully!");
}
}
```

React Form Component (UserForm.js):

```
import { useState } from 'react';
import axios from 'axios';
function UserForm() {
const [name, setName] = useState('');
const handleSubmit = async (event) => {
event.preventDefault();
try {
const response = await axios.post('http://localhost:8080/users/register', { name });
alert(response.data);
} catch (error) {
console.error('Error submitting form', error);
}
};
return (
<form onSubmit={handleSubmit}>
<label>Name:</label>
<input type="text" value={name} onChange={(e) => setName(e.target.value)} />
<button type="submit">Submit</button>
</form>
);
}
export default UserForm;
```

## 16.5 Form validation in React.js

Data prior to being sent to Spring Boot, form validation is important. React has event handlers or third-party libraries such as Formik and Yup to perform validation.

Example: Basic Form Validation

```
import { useState } from 'react';
function UserForm() {
```

```
const [name, setName] = useState('');
const [error, setError] = useState('');
const handleSubmit = (event) => {
event.preventDefault();
if (!name.trim()) {
setError('Name is required');
return;
}
setError('');
console.log('Submitted:', name);
};
return (
<form onSubmit={handleSubmit}>
<label>Name:</label>
<input type="text" value={name} onChange={(e) => setName(e.target.value)} />
{error && <p style={{ color: 'red' }}>{error}</p>}
<button type="submit">Submit</button>
</form>
);
}
export default UserForm;
```

## 16.6 Integrating React forms with Spring Security for authentication

React forms in a Spring Boot app with authentication can process the login credentials and send them to the backend server where they can be authenticated.

Spring Boot authentication application programming interface (AuthController.java)

```
@RestController
@RequestMapping("/auth")
public class AuthController {
@PostMapping("/login")
public ResponseEntity<String> login(@RequestBody LoginRequest request) {
if ("admin".equals(request.getUsername()) && "password".equals(request.getPassword
())) {
return ResponseEntity.ok("Login Successful");
} else {
return ResponseEntity.status(HttpStatus.UNAUTHORIZED).body("Invalid Credentials");
}
}
}
```

```
}
```

React login form (LoginForm.js)

```
import { useState } from 'react';
import axios from 'axios';
function LoginForm() {
const [username, setUsername] = useState('');
const [password, setPassword] = useState('');
const [message, setMessage] = useState('');
const handleSubmit = async (event) => {
event.preventDefault();
try {
const response = await axios.post('http://localhost:8080/auth/login', { username, pass-
word });
setMessage(response.data);
} catch (error) {
setMessage('Invalid credentials');
}
};
return (
<form onSubmit={handleSubmit}>
<label>Username:</label>
<input type="text" value={username} onChange={(e) => setUsername(e.target.value)} />
<label>Password:</label>
<input type="password" value={password} onChange={(e) => setPassword(e.target.-
value)} />
<button type="submit">Login</button>
<p>{message}</p>
</form>
);
}
export default LoginForm;
```

## 16.7 File upload form with Spring Boot

React can handle file uploads and send them to a Spring Boot backend.

Spring Boot Controller (FileController.java)

```
@RestController
@RequestMapping("/upload")
public class FileController {
```

```
@PostMapping
public ResponseEntity<String> uploadFile(@RequestParam("file") MultipartFile file) {
return ResponseEntity.ok("File uploaded: " + file.getOriginalFilename());
}
}
```

React file ppload form (FileUpload.js)

```
import { useState } from 'react';
import axios from 'axios';
function FileUpload() {
const [file, setFile] = useState(null);
const handleFileChange = (event) => {
setFile(event.target.files[0]);
};
const handleUpload = async () => {
const formData = new FormData();
formData.append('file', file);
try {
const response = await axios.post('http://localhost:8080/upload', formData, {
headers: { 'Content-Type': 'multipart/form-data' },
});
alert(response.data);
} catch (error) {
console.error('Upload failed', error);
}
};
return (
<div>
<input type="file" onChange={handleFileChange} />
<button onClick={handleUpload}>Upload</button>
</div>
);
}
export default FileUpload;
```

## 16.8 Properties

Properties of React.js for Spring applications with syntax are as follows:

React.js provides various properties that make it efficient when integrating with Spring Boot applications. Below are the key properties and their syntax:

1. state (Component state)
   State holds data that changes within a component. It is useful for managing form inputs before sending data to a Spring Boot backend.

   Syntax:
   ```
   const [inputValue, setInputValue] = useState("");
   <input type="text" value={inputValue} onChange={(e) => setInputValue(e.target.value)} />
   ```

2. props (Component properties)
   Props allow data to be passed from a parent component to a child component, making components reusable.

   Syntax:
   ```
   function ChildComponent({ name }) {
   return <p>Hello, {name}</p>;
   }
   <ChildComponent name="Spring Application" />
   ```

## 16.9 useEffect (Side effects)

The useEffect hook is used for lifecycle management, such as fetching data from a Spring Boot API when a component mounts.

Syntax:
```
useEffect(() => {
fetch("http://localhost:8080/api")
.then(response => response.json())
.then(data => setData(data));
}, []);
```

## 16.10 useContext (Context application programming interface)

useContext enables state to be exchanged on a global basis between components, which minimizes prop drilling.

Syntax:
```
const UserContext = React.createContext();
<UserContext.Provider value={user}>
<ChildComponent />
</UserContext.Provider>
```

## 16.11 useRef (Accessing Document Object Model elements)

useRef enables a mentor-editing of the elements more quickly (without rerendering the component).

```
Syntax:
const inputRef = useRef(null);
<input type="text" ref={inputRef} />
<button onClick={() => inputRef.current.focus()}>Focus Input</button>
```

6. useReducer (State Management Alternative)

A different variant of useState used to give complex state logic.

```
Syntax:
const reducer = (state, action) => {
switch (action.type) {
case "increment":
return { count: state.count + 1 };
default:
return state;
}
};
const [state, dispatch] = useReducer(reducer, { count: 0 });
<button onClick={() => dispatch({ type: "increment" })}>Increment</button>
```

## 16.12 fetch (Calling Spring Boot application programming interface)

Fetch API is applied to communicate with Spring Boot RESTs.

```
Syntax:
fetch("http://localhost:8080/api", {
method: "POST",
headers: { "Content-Type": "application/json" },
body: JSON.stringify({ key: value }),
})
.then(response => response.json())
.then(data => console.log(data));
```

## 16.13 axios (Simpler HTTP Requests)

Axios is a substitute for Fetch and has a more simple syntax of API requests.

```
Syntax:
axios.post("http://localhost:8080/api", { key: value })
.then(response => console.log(response.data));
```

## 16.14 Router (Navigation handling)

React-router-dom allows navigation among pages in a React application.

Syntax:
```
<BrowserRouter>
<Routes>
<Route path="/" element={<Home />} />
<Route path="/about" element={<About />} />
</Routes>
</BrowserRouter>
```

## 16.15 memo (Performance optimization)

React.memo prevents unnecessary re-rendering of components.

Syntax:
```
const MemoizedComponent = React.memo(({ name }) => {
return <p>Hello, {name}</p>;
});
```

The properties are used to complement React.js applications built on Spring Boot, which enhance the management of state, interactions between the API, and the performance of the application.

## 16.16 Form events in React.js for Spring applications

React.js allows working with a range of form events including user interaction through input change, submission, and focusing/blur. These events help capture user input and send data to a Spring Boot backend efficiently.

### 16.16.1 onChange (Handling input changes)

Triggers an event when the value of an input field changes. It is commonly used for controlled components.

Syntax:
```
<input type="text" value={stateVariable} onChange={(e) => setStateVariable(e.target.-
value)} />
```

### 16.16.2 onSubmit (Handling form submission)

Fires when a form is submitted, preventing the default browser behavior and handling data processing.

Syntax:
```
<form onSubmit={handleSubmit}>
<input type="text" value={stateVariable} onChange={handleChange} />
<button type="submit">Submit</button>
</form>
```

### 16.16.3 onFocus (Handling focus event)

Triggers when an input field gains focus. Useful for showing hints or validations.

Syntax:
```
<input type="text" onFocus={() => console.log("Input focused")} />
```

### 16.16.4 onBlur (Handling blur event)

Triggers when an input field loses focus. Useful for validation checks.

Syntax:
```
<input type="text" onBlur={() => console.log("Input lost focus")} />
```

### 16.16.5 onClick (Handling button clicks)

Fires when a button or any clickable element is clicked.

Syntax:
```
<button onClick={handleClick}>Click Me</button>
```

### 16.16.6 onKeyDown (Handling key presses—key down)

Triggers when a key is pressed down inside an input field.

Syntax:
```
<input type="text" onKeyDown={(e) => console.log(`Key pressed: ${e.key}`)} />
```

### 16.16.7 onKeyUp (Handling key presses—key release)

Fires when a key is released after pressing inside an input field.

Syntax:
```
<input type="text" onKeyUp={(e) => console.log(`Key released: ${e.key}`)} />
```

### 16.16.8 onKeyPress (Handling key press—deprecated in React 17+)

Previously used to detect key presses but is now replaced by onKeyDown and onKeyUp.

Syntax:
```
<input type="text" onKeyPress={(e) => console.log(`Key pressed: ${e.key}`)} />
```

### 16.16.9 onInput (Handling input changes in uncontrolled components)

Similar to onChange, but used in uncontrolled components to detect value changes.

Syntax:
```
<input type="text" onInput={(e) => console.log(e.target.value)} />
```

### 16.16.10 onReset (Handling form reset)

Fires when a form is reset, clearing all input fields.

Syntax:
```
<form onReset={handleReset}>
<input type="text" value={stateVariable} onChange={handleChange} />
<button type="reset">Reset</button>
</form>
```

Sending Form Data to Spring Boot API:
After handling form events, data can be sent to a Spring Boot backend using the Fetch API or Axios.
Using Fetch API:
```
fetch("http://localhost:8080/api", {
method: "POST",
headers: { "Content-Type": "application/json" },
body: JSON.stringify({ key: value }),
});
```
Using Axios:
```
axios.post("http://localhost:8080/api", { key: value });
```

These React form events ensure seamless user interactions and efficient data processing in Spring applications.

## 16.17 Class concept in React.js for Spring Applications

React.js supports class-based components, which use ES6 classes to manage state and lifecycle methods. They are helpful especially in large applications when it is necessary to integrate with a Spring Boot backend because of dealing with complex data and interactions with users.

### 16.17.1 Defining a class component

The React class component is an extension of React.Component and includes a render() method to provide UI elements.

Syntax:
```
class UserComponent extends React.Component {
```

```
render() {
return <h1>Welcome to React with Spring Boot</h1>;
}
}
```

### 16.17.2 Constructor and state management

The creator acts on the state of the component is set, and methods are bound.

```
Syntax:
class UserForm extends React.Component {
constructor(props) {
super(props);
this.state = { username: "" };
}
handleChange = (event) => {
this.setState({ username: event.target.value });
};
render() {
return (
<input type="text" value={this.state.username} onChange={this.handleChange} />
);
}
}
```

## 16.18 Handling events in class components

Components in the classes manage the events via custom methods.

```
Syntax:
class ButtonComponent extends React.Component {
handleClick = () => {
console.log("Button Clicked");
};
render() {
return <button onClick={this.handleClick}>Click Me</button>;
}
}
```

## 16.19 Lifecycle methods

Lifecycle approaches enable components of classes to do what they do at various phases.

```
Syntax:
class LifecycleExample extends React.Component {
componentDidMount() {
console.log("Component Mounted");
}
render() {
return <h1>Lifecycle in React</h1>;
}
}
```

## 16.20 Fetching data from Spring Boot application programming interface

Components of the classes can communicate with a Spring Boot backend through Fetch or Axios.

```
Syntax:
class DataFetcher extends React.Component {
constructor(props) {
super(props);
this.state = { data: [] };
}
componentDidMount() {
fetch("http://localhost:8080/api/data")
.then(response => response.json())
.then(data => this.setState({ data }));
}
render() {
return <ul>{this.state.data.map(item => <li key={item.id}>{item.name}</li>)}</ul>;
}
}
```

React applications can effectively handle state, react to on-screen events, and communicate with the Spring Boot APIs in an organized and scalable way through the use of class-based components.

## Bibliography

React. (2024). Documentation. https://react.dev.

MDN. (2024). React Guide. https://developer.mozilla.org.

IBM. (2024). React Overview. https://www.ibm.com/docs.

Microsoft. (2024). React Docs. https://learn.microsoft.com.

# Index

*Note*: Page numbers followed by "*f*" and "*t*" refer to figures and tables, respectively.

## N



## O



## P



## R

## T



## U



## V



## W

Printed and bound by CPI Group (UK) Ltd, Croydon, CR0 4YY
14/09/2026
02216396-0004